Computer Monographs

GENERAL EDITOR: Stanley Gill, M.A., Ph.D.

ASSOCIATE EDITOR: J. J. Florentin, Ph.D. Birkbeck College, London

An Introduction to Compiler Writing

An Introduction to Compiler Writing

J. S. Rohl
University of Manchester Institute of Science and Technology

Macdonald and Jane's · London and
American Elsevier Inc. · New York

Sole distributors for the United States and Dependencies and Canada:
American Elsevier Publishing Co. Inc., 52 Vanderbilt Avenue, New York, N.Y. 10017

Sole distributors for the Continent of Europe excluding the British Isles and Commonwealth and the Republic of Ireland:
Elsevier Publishing Company, P.O. Box 211, Jan Van Galenstraat 335, Amsterdam, The Netherlands

Sole distributors for all remaining areas:
Macdonald and Jane's, Macdonald & Co. (Publishers) Ltd.,
Paulton House, 8 Shepherdess Walk, London, NI7LW

Macdonald ISBN 0 356 08173 7
American Elsevier ISBN 0 444 19523 8
Library of Congress Catalog Card No. 74 16914

Text set in 10/12 pt. Monotype Times New Roman, printed by letterpress and bound in Great Britain at The Pitman Press, Bath

To Mary

who cheerfully accepted the intrusion of the book into our life, and who kept me going through those periods in which I felt like abandoning the task.

Preface

This is, as its title suggests, an introduction to compiler writing. It is written in a narrative style. We start with a basic language and show how to compile it; and then expand the language by degrees showing how the compiler can be modified to accommodate these expansions. Thus, the description of a technique might be enhanced from chapter to chapter. Since the information is not collated (except through the index) the book's use as a work of reference is, to that extent, limited.

Since it is an introductory book, the number of language facilities that we consider is restricted. The basic language expands to about the full power of Algol, but not to, say, Algol 68. We assume a working knowledge of Algol and, in so far as Fortran is the classical representative of the class of languages which can be implemented with a static storage allocation scheme, we assume a knowledge of it, too.

We are concerned with the broad principles rather than detailed representation. Accordingly, language facilities described have sometimes been modified to avoid some of the well-known minor problems of implementation. We do not consider jumping out of blocks, for example, or own arrays. The order code of the target machine has been carefully chosen to reflect the structure of the source language. It is, in fact, the order code of MU5 (see ref. 0.1) and this book might serve to illuminate the philosophy on which the order code of that machine is based. Since the order code of ICL's New Range, the 2900 Series, derives from that of MU5 it will apply to that series as well, except that some concepts (in particular the Boolean facilities) are not relevant.

All books reflect their author's views on his subject. Three views have shaped this book.

First, that computer science has become of age to the extent that its structure as a discipline is now clearer.

There are areas such as program design, data structures and so on in which a coherent body of knowledge now exists. I have assumed that readers of this book will be well versed in the program structures of Algol (in particular the recursive calls of procedures and the while clause) and in data structures (particularly binary and general trees).

Second, and almost as a corollary, that the theory of grammars is a subject in its own right rather than a part of compiler writing. The compiler writer will see it as a tool, of course, in the same way as he sees data structure techniques, and will use it as such. Most other books on compiler writing treat the theory of grammars as central to the whole subject. This is, perhaps, the major difference between this book and those: here the subject is introduced at the point at which it is relevant, views from both ends of the spectrum (the source-driven precedence technique and the syntax-driven, top-down analysis technique) are given, and references made to the theory for those wishing to refine the techniques. If I had to put in one sentence what I feel compiler writing is about, I would say that it is about the structures which have to be maintained by the compiler and the procedures by which they are created and transformed.

Third, that the compiler writer has an important role in the design of computer systems as an interpreter, both of the users' needs to the machine designer, and of the machine's capabilities to the language designer. Consequently, throughout the book, I make references to the curious constructions still existing in the languages in use today and to the lines along which hardware might develop to make it more amenable to the requirements of high-level languages.

There are a restricted set of references in this book. I have tried to be selective, referring only to those papers and books that a student might be expected to read. Such a choice is, of necessity, a personal one. For those students who are fired with enthusiasm the references themselves contain the further references.

This book has had a long gestation period. It started with some post-graduate lectures I gave in 1967 in the University of Queensland and I am grateful to Professor S. A. Prentice for giving me the opportunity of developing my ideas of teaching the subject along these lines. Since then, of course, they have been refined many times in the course of presenting them to many sets of students, and I should like to thank all those who, wittingly or unwittingly, have helped me comb out a number of errors. In its draft form this book has been read by a number of people and I should like to record my appreciation of all the comments, corrections and suggestions I have received. I would particularly single out my research students, Graham White and Alan Brook, and Professor Gordon Rose.

Finally, I should like to record my indebtedness to Hilary Mayor, who, as Hilary Shaw, typed and retyped my many attempts to get the early chapters to say what I wanted to say and who drew all the diagrams in those chapters; and to Susan Green who typed subsequent chapters, drew the diagrams they contained and undertook the quite substantial revisions of the whole book.

Contents

1 Introduction

What is a compiler? Conceptually at least, a compiler is a program just like any other program. If we consider Fig. 1.1 (i), a program is something which reads in some data and produces some results.

A compiler is a program which takes as data the program being compiled (called the *source program*), and produces as its results, an equivalent program in binary machine code (called the *object program*), as shown in Fig. 1.1 (ii). This object program is of course

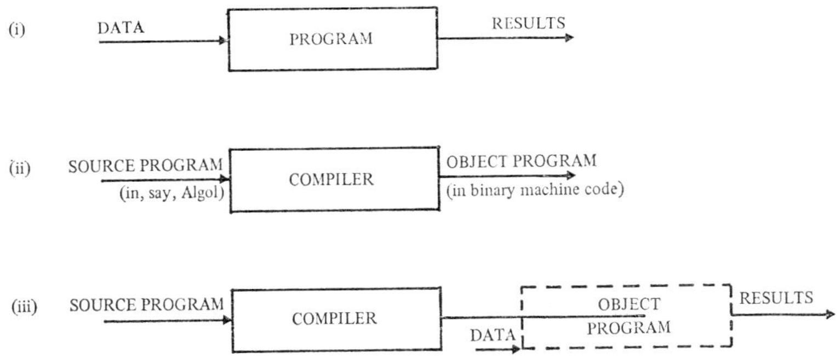

Fig. 1.1. The structure of (i) a program; (ii) a compiler; (iii) a compiler and its compiled program.

a program, so it then usually reads in some conventional data and prints out some results, as shown in Fig. 1.1 (iii).

We have said that this is conceptually what happens, and in many cases it is precisely what happens. This is the simplest form of compiling system, called a *compile-and-go* system, and we will assume it throughout the main part of this book. In Chapter 15, however, we will consider other systems.

Most programs these days are written in a high-level language such as Fortran, Algol, Cobol, PL/1 and so on. (Hence the need for compilers.) The same is becoming true of compilers: sometimes Fortran, Algol or PL/1, sometimes in languages specially designed for the purpose. When we wish to illustrate some point we will use Algol, augmented if necessary; in Chapter 16 we will discuss the problem in more detail.

2 A compiler for a basic language

Let us approach the basic problems of compiler writing by considering a very *basic language* and a compiler for it.

2.1 The basic language

Consider a very small sub-set of Algol which results from the following restrictions:

(i) There are no blocks, compound statements or procedures.
(ii) Only one 'instruction' is permitted per line.
(iii) Identifiers (including those for labels) consist of single letters.
(iv) All real constants contain a decimal point; no integer constants do.
(v) Arrays are real, and of one dimension only (they are vectors); the lower bound is always 0, and the upper bound is always a constant, as shown by the declaration:

array $p[0:10]$

Further, the bounds of each individual array must be given explicitly.
(vi) Expressions are very simple in that they contain only one or two operands, that the operators available are +, −, *, / (where + and − are always binary, never unary) and that both operands (where there are two) must be of the same type. For example:

$h * i$
0
$j + 1$

(vii) In an assignment statement the left-hand side variable must be of the same type as the right-hand side expression.

(viii) The go to statement can refer only to a simple label as in:

go to *l*

There are no switches.

(ix) The only statement that can be made conditional is the go to statement. For example:

if $j \neq n$ **then go to** *l*

(x) The only form of Boolean expression is the relation between two operands of the same type.

(xi) There are no built-in functions.

(xii) All programs end with a dummy statement.

These restrictions are designed to make the language as simple as possible while still retaining the essential characteristics of a high-level language.

To fix ideas, let us consider a program to calculate n integrals using Simpson's Rule:

$$\int_a^b f(x)\,\mathrm{d}x \approx \frac{h}{3}\,[f0 + 4f1 + f2]$$

where $h = (b - a)/2, f0 = f(a), f1 = f\left(\frac{a+b}{2}\right), f2 = f(\mathrm{b})$.

The values of $h, f0, f1$ and $f2$ are given as data for each integral. If we add some rudimentary input and output statements for completeness we arrive at a program such as:

```
   begin
   real h, e, f, g, i;
   integer j, n;
   j := 0;
   read n;
l: read h, e, f, g;
   i := 4·0*f;
   i := e + i;
   i := i + g;
   i := h*i;
   i := i/3·0;
   print i;
   j := j + 1;
   if j ≠ n then go to l;
   end
```

We will continually refer to this program, which we shall call the *integration program*, throughout this chapter. At the appropriate places we need to discuss arrays and then we will assume that this declaration:

array $p[0:10]$, $q[0:7]$

has been added to the program after the existing declarations.

It is important to note that the language is perfectly viable if rather tedious.

2.2 A compiler for this language

The restrictions on the language are such that we can compile *statement-by-statement*, that is, we can compile the statements independently of each other. *Statement-by-statement* compilers are included within the class of *one-pass* compilers, so called because only one pass is made through the text. Although more than one pass may be made over a line (here there are two) during its processing, once a line has been processed, the compiler does not return to it. In Chapter 15 we will discuss *multi-pass* compilers. Since each statement occupies one line, the compiler is also described as *line-by-line*. A flow diagram of the compiler is quite simple as shown in Fig. 2.1.

Most programs have an initialisation phase in which pointers and counters are zeroed and areas of store are cleared. Compilers are no exception: the details of the *initialise* procedure will emerge as we progress. The heart of the compiler lies in the loop of two procedures to *read the next line* and then *process it.* We return to these in the next two sections. When all the lines have been read and processed, the *finalise* procedure performs various tidying up tasks. The details will also emerge as we progress. If, during the reading, processing or finalisation, faults are found, it is usually not worthwhile obeying the compiled object program and so we stop. Let us now return to the heart of the compiler, considering the two procedures in turn.

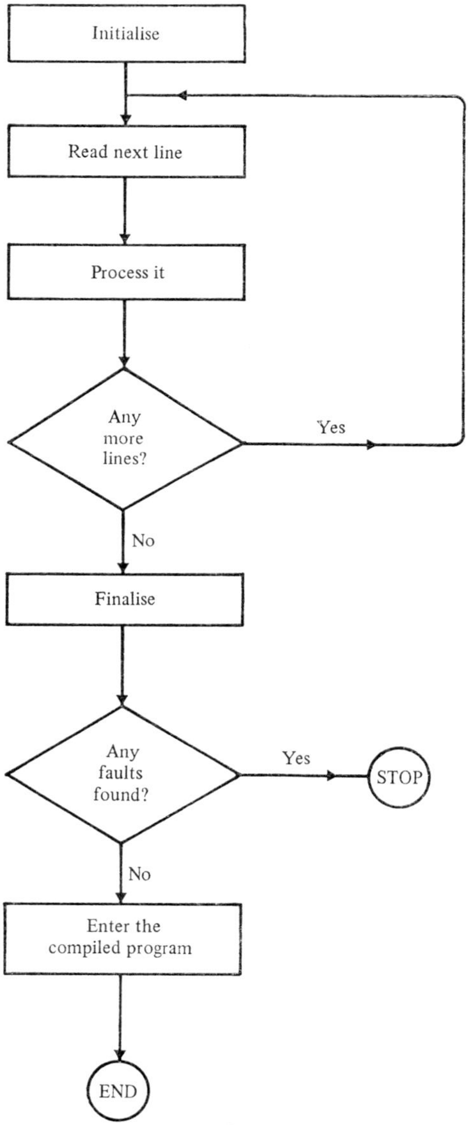

Fig. 2.1. Over-all flow diagram of a compiler.

2.3 Read a line

First, *read a line*. This reads a line of source text into the store, one character to a word. We will assume an unusual character set which includes, as well as upper- and lower-case letters, underlined versions of the lower-case ones. In practice, cards are much more restrictive than this and we would adopt punching conventions to overcome the problem. For example, **begin*** might be punched as 'BEGIN'. We will pursue this further in section 3.6. Paper tape does allow this full character set, since the tape editing equipment is provided with a backspace facility. The procedure for reading a line punched on paper tape is quite complicated since **begin** can be punched an infinite number of ways (for example, by punching the letters b, e, g, i and n, followed by five backspaces, followed by five underlines, or the letter b followed by a backspace, followed by an underline, followed by the letter e, and so on), and all alternatives should be accepted. A procedure to do this (*line reconstruction* it is called) is described in Appendix 3. For the rest of the book we will assume a sufficiently powerful set of characters, and a correspondingly simple input procedure.

One of the reasons for reading the characters into the store a line at a time can be found in line reconstruction. The component parts of a character such as **b** in the first alternative described above, might be spread out along the tape intermixed with parts of other characters.

Even if we assume that we have a sufficiently powerful character set available, it is still convenient to read them in, as it is then possible to scan the characters more than once, as we will do in subsequent sections.

It is also convenient in this procedure to delete what are called *noise symbols*, that is, symbols that are redundant. These are blanks on cards; and the space, underlined space and erase characters on paper tape. In most of our examples we will leave them in for readability reasons.

* style note: the use of bold face throughout the text represents underlining.

2.4 Process a line

The heart of the heart of the compiler is the procedure to *process a line*. If we refer back to the integration program given earlier, we notice that with only one exception, the first one or two characters determine the type of the statement (unless it turns out to be a meaningless statement such as **begun**). For example, if it begins with the character **g**, it is a go to statement; if it begins with a letter followed by the becomes symbol, := (which is regarded as a single character), it is an assignment statement. Thus, we can construct a flow diagram as shown in Fig. 2.2.

2.5 Modular hierarchical structure

The line-processing procedure performs a number of simple tests and accordingly calls one of a number of lower-level procedures. Thus, we find that the compiler has a *hierarchical structure* of procedures. We define operations in terms of simpler ones, which are in turn defined in terms of simpler ones, until at the bottom-most level they are explicitly described. The hierarchical structure has advantages both in the design of a compiler and in the control of its implementation.

The hierarchical structure is, of course, one form of a *modular structure*.

2.6 Faults

One of the major problems in writing compilers is dealing with incorrect programs. It is comparatively easy to compile correctly programs that are correct, as this monograph attempts to show; it is a little more difficult to process faulty programs, finding all the errors, without the compiler's producing irrational effects.

One example can be seen here. If a line starts with a digit, say, then the line is faulty. The compiler must clearly monitor it as such. The problem is: what should happen next? Should the compiler abandon the line and carry on to the next one? Or should it look to see whether

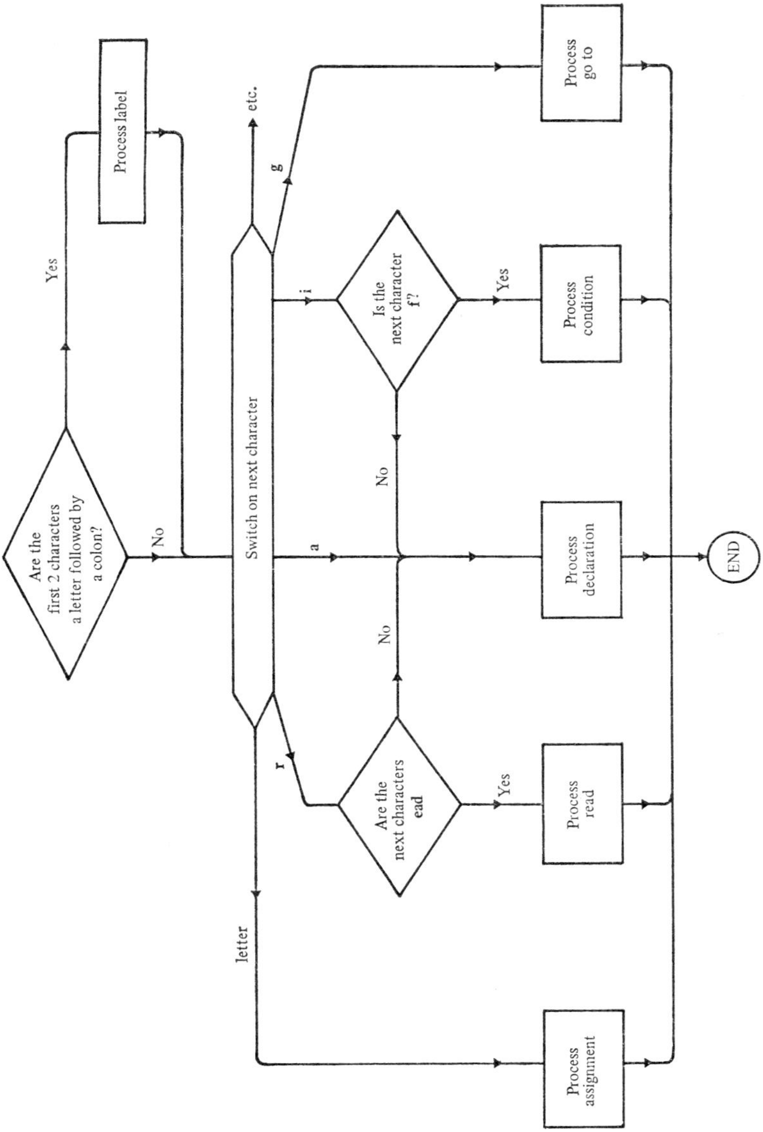

Fig. 2.2 Process a line

the next character is a colon? If it is a colon, it might assume that the line was a (faultily) labelled statement, and go on to process the statement. In this chapter we will ignore these problems and merely indicate those places at which errors might be recognised. We return to this problem in Chapter 14.

2.7 Information needed by the compiler

The processing procedures of Fig. 2.2 perform two functions:

(i) Each must check that the source line is in fact a statement of the appropriate type, and if not, monitor it.

(ii) Each must either compile the correct object code (as in processing an assignment) or else store some relevant information for use in later translation (as in processing a declaration). This implies that there are two types of statement:

(a) A *declarative* statement such as:

real h, e, f, g, i

which gives the compiler some information about the interpretation of the rest of the program.

(*b*) An *imperative* statement such as:

$i := i + g$

which causes the compiler to compile some object code, the precise coding being determined by the previous declarations of i and g.

Before we look at these procedures in turn we must consider the information which we will need during compiling and running and determine how storage might be allocated to it.

During compilation we require:

(i) The compiler itself.
(ii) The current line of source text.
(iii) The object program being built up.
(iv) The list of constants appearing in the program for use at run time.
(v) A list of the properties (or characteristics) of the quantities involved.

At run time we require:

(i) The object program.
(ii) The list of constants.
(iii) The object program's variables.

Note that object program and constants list are required at both times and to avoid unnecessary movement at the end of compilation should coincide. Further some items are of fixed size (for example, the line of source might be 80 characters long if the program were on cards); others are of an unknown size (for example, the size of the constants list will vary from program to program). We need pointers in all of these lists. We will use a simple mnemonic scheme: for example, cp will be the *c*onstants list *p*ointer and cp0 the pointer to its start. These values will all be set in the initialisation procedure.

A possible storage layout is shown in Fig. 2.3.

There is a problem in choosing the sizes and, if necessary, adjusting them to ensure that they are large enough. This is a well-known problem in computer science, with well-known solutions. We will ignore it in what follows, assuming the size always to be adequate.

Let us now consider the processing procedures in more detail.

2.8 Declarations

First the declarations. As we have noted previously, declarations provide information for the compiler about the quantities involved. We shall call the individual pieces of information *properties*. For variables there are two important properties:

(i) The *mode* of the quantity: **integer, real** or **array**. This is required to ensure that the correct arithmetic unit is used and to check subscripting. We will simply use the codes 1, 2 and 3 for **integer, real** and **array,** respectively.

(ii) The *address* to be allocated at run time to the variable (or, if it is an array, the address of the zeroth element of the array, called the *base address*). This is allocated by the compiler using the variables pointer, vp. It allocates the word at vp to the variable (or words from vp onwards in the case of array elements) and advances vp over it (or them).

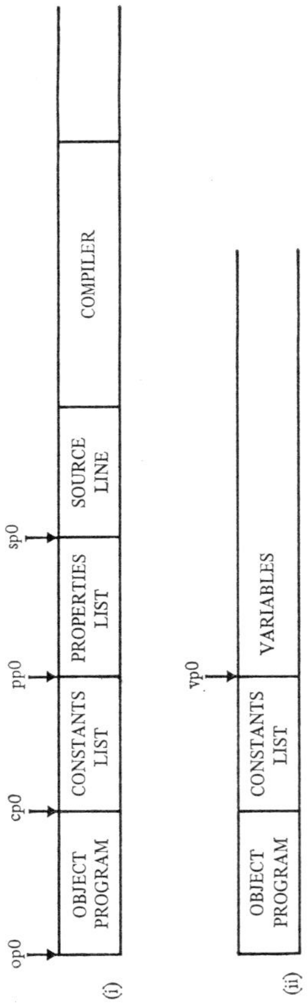

Fig. 2.3. Storage layout: (i) at compile time; (ii) at run time

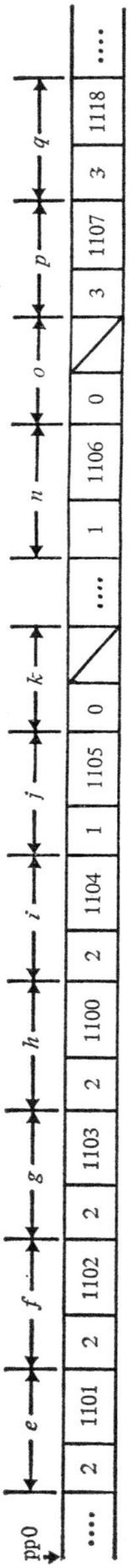

Fig. 2.4. Properties list after the declarations:

real *h*, *e*, *f*, *g*, *i*;
integer *j*, *n*;
array *p*[0:10], *q*[0:7];

[There are other properties which might be stored. For example, we might have a *reference count* which counts the number of references to the quantity in the program. If at the end of the program the count is still zero, the variable is unreferenced and its declaration redundant. We might then print out this fact for the programmer to act on.]

Thus, we need two words to store the properties of a quantity. There are 52 possible quantities (there are only 52 possible identifiers) and so we require 104 words for the properties list. (We shall see later that this is consistent with the requirements of labels.) We will store the properties in alphabetical order of the identifiers. The properties are initially set in the initialise procedure, the mode to 0, the address to some 'undefined' value. We will represent this undefined value in our diagrams by an oblique slash.

To illustrate we assume vp initially = 1100. Then the declarations of the integration program supplemented by the array declaration given earlier:

> **real** *h*, *e*, *f*, *g*, *i;*
> **integer** *j*, *n;*
> **array** *p*[0:10], *q*[0:7];

would cause the properties list to be set up as shown in Fig. 2.4, assuming, as we do for the sake of simplicity, that both integer and real variables occupy one word.

So the procedure which processes declarations must:

(i) Check that the statement is indeed a declaration.
(ii) Check that none of the identifiers has been previously declared.
(iii) Fill in the appropriate pair of words in the properties list.

A flow diagram to do this is given in Fig. 2.5.

2.9 Assignments

Before we consider the details of how we process assignments let us first of all consider what we would compile for a couple of statements. To do this we need the definition of the language of the machine that we are compiling for. The language we shall use is for a machine

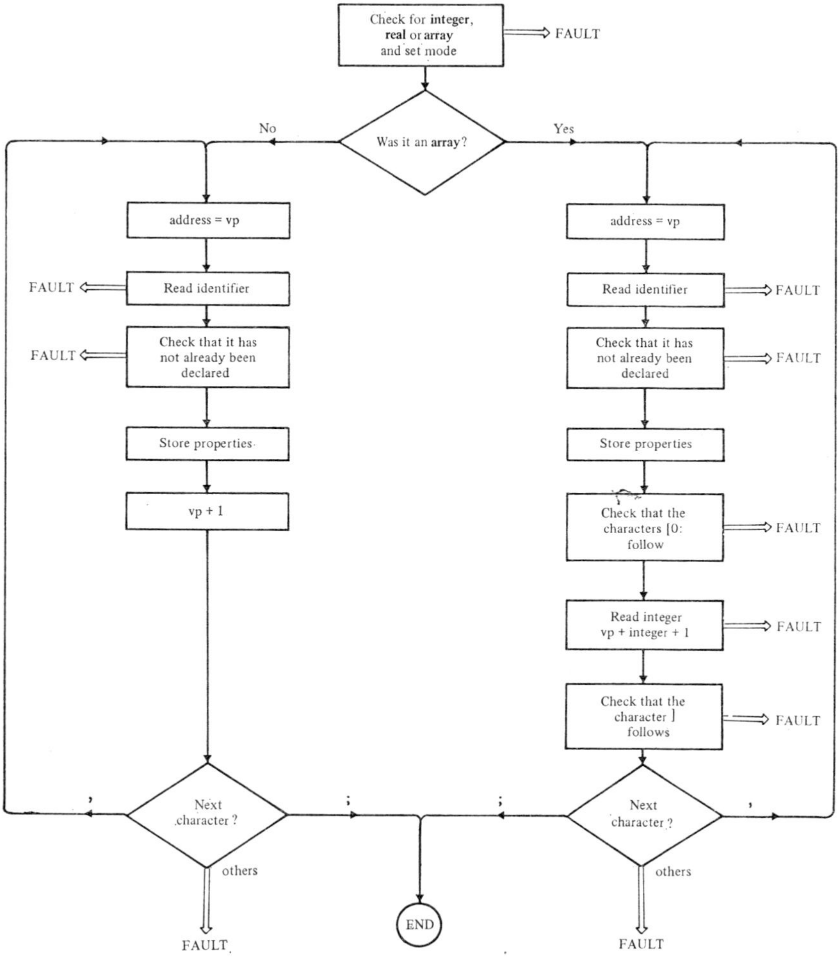

Fig. 2.5. Process declaration

that has been designed with the requirements of high-level languages in mind. We will describe this language as we proceed, a full definition being given in Appendix 2.

There are no general-purpose registers, only registers that are

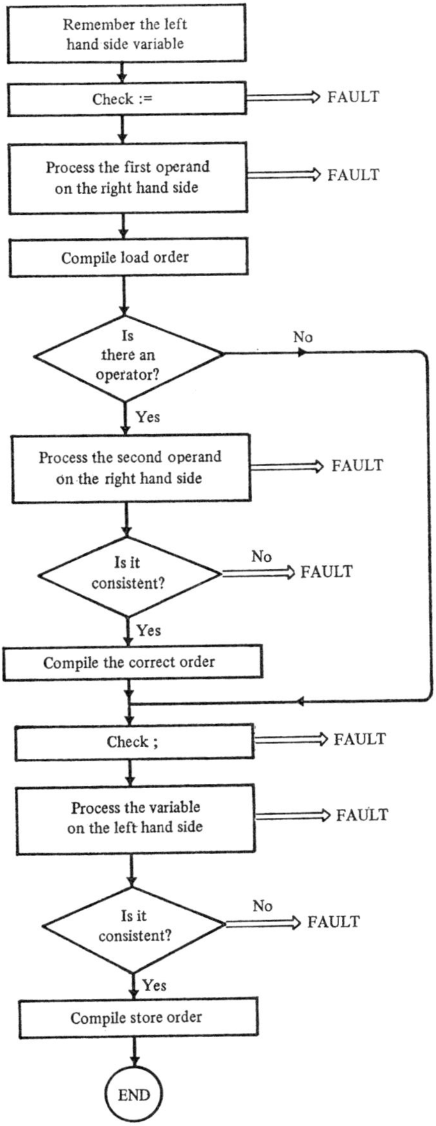

Fig. 2.6. Process assignment

dedicated to a specific purpose. Assuming the declarations of the example program (see Fig. 2.4), the statement:

$$i := i + g$$

would compile into:

AFL = {1104}
AFL + {1103}
AFL ⇒ {1104}

The form is rather different from that of more conventional assembly languages. In functional orders like these the function part is divided into two parts. The first (here AFL) describes the register being used (the *fl*oating point *a*ccumulator); the second (here =, +, and ⇒) define the operation (loading, adding and storing, respectively). The braces { and } mean 'the contents of'.
The procedure for processing assignments then must:

(i) Check that the statement is, indeed, an assignment.
(ii) Check that all the identifiers have been declared.
(iii) Check that the identifiers are consistent (i.e. that they have been declared either all integer or all real).
(iv) Compile the correct sequence of orders.

Fig. 2.6 shows a flow diagram for processing the assignment.

The procedure for processing an operand may compile code, as we shall see soon. In any event, it will return three quantities to the procedure processing the expression. They are:

Firstly, the *type* of the operand, say 1 for integer or 2 for real (either a real scalar or an array element). This quantity is trivially found from the mode stored in the property list and is used:
(i) For checking the consistency of operands.
(ii) For deciding the orders to be planted.
For example, still using the declarations of Fig. 2.4:

$$j := j - n$$

would compile into:

AFX = {1105}
AFX − {1106}
AFX ⇒ {1105}

where AFX refers to a *f*i*x*ed point *a*ccumulator. [The reason for restricting types in our language (restrictions (vi) and (vii)) is to avoid the complication of converting from fixed to floating point and vice versa. We return to this problem in Chapter 8.]

The second quantity returned is the *address* of the operand. For scalar variables this is simply extracted from the properties list.

However, the operand can, as well, be a constant, or an array element. If the operand is a constant, its value is calculated from the digits (and perhaps decimal point) from which it is made up and stored in the constants list at cp, which is then advanced. Suppose cp is initially 1000. If we use the symbol ⇛ to stand for 'is compiled into' then, from the integration program:

$$\begin{array}{rl} & \text{AFL} = \{1001\} \\ i := 4{\cdot}0 * f \Rrightarrow & \text{AFL} \ * \ \{1102\} \\ & \text{AFL} \Rrightarrow \{1104\} \end{array}$$

$$\begin{array}{rl} & \text{AFX} = \{1105\} \\ j := j + 1 \Rrightarrow & \text{AFX} + \{1003\} \\ & \text{AFX} \Rrightarrow \{1105\} \end{array}$$

After compiling the integration program, the constants list would appear as in Fig. 2.7:

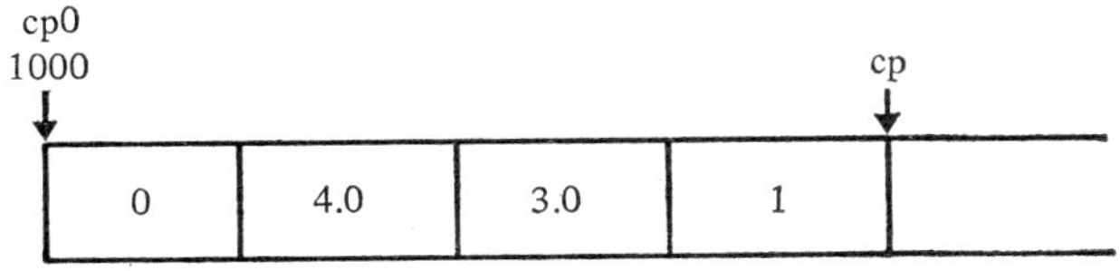

Fig. 2.7. Constants list after compiling the integration program.

The operand can also be an array element. This is the case which requires the operand-processing procedure to compile code.

Let us first of all consider the orders we would compile. The machine has a modifier register called (for historical reasons) BM. The accessing of an array element involves, firstly, loading the modifier register and secondly, modifying the base address of the array by this subscript in the subsequent accessing order. There are no arrays in the integration program, so we assume the addition of the arrays mentioned earlier and create some assignments.

Thus:

$$p[n] := q[j] \Rightarrow \begin{array}{l} \text{BM} \;\; = \{1105\} \\ \text{AFL} = \{\text{BM} + 1118\} \\ \text{BM} \;\; = \{1106\} \\ \text{AFL} \Rightarrow \{\text{BM} + 1107\} \end{array}$$

It is convenient to compile the order to load the modifier register in the procedure which processes the operand. This procedure needs to inform the procedure which calls it (process assignment) that the accessing order that it is going to compile must be modified. This is the third quantity returned.
These three quantities returned then are:

(i) The type of the operand.
(ii) Its address.
(iii) Whether or not modification is to take place.

A flow diagram for this might be that of Fig. 2.8, in which the third quantity above is represented by 'modified?'.

2.10 Efficiency

A brief perusal of the above technique shows some inefficiencies. For example:

$$p[2] := q[3] \Rightarrow \begin{array}{l} \text{BM} \;\; = \{1008\} \\ \text{AFL} = \{\text{BM} + 1118\} \\ \text{BM} \;\; = \{1009\} \\ \text{AFL} \Rightarrow \{\text{BM} + 1107\} \end{array}$$

(assuming arbitrary addresses for 2 and 3 in the constants list), when, in fact, only two orders are required:

$$\begin{array}{l} \text{AFL} = \{1121\} \\ \text{AFL} \Rightarrow \{1109\} \end{array}$$

Similarly:

$$p[j] := q[j] \Rightarrow \begin{array}{l} \text{BM} \;\; = \{1105\} \\ \text{AFL} = \{\text{BM} + 1118\} \\ \text{BM} \;\; = \{1105\} \\ \text{AFL} \Rightarrow \{\text{BM} + 1107\} \end{array}$$

where the third order is redundant.

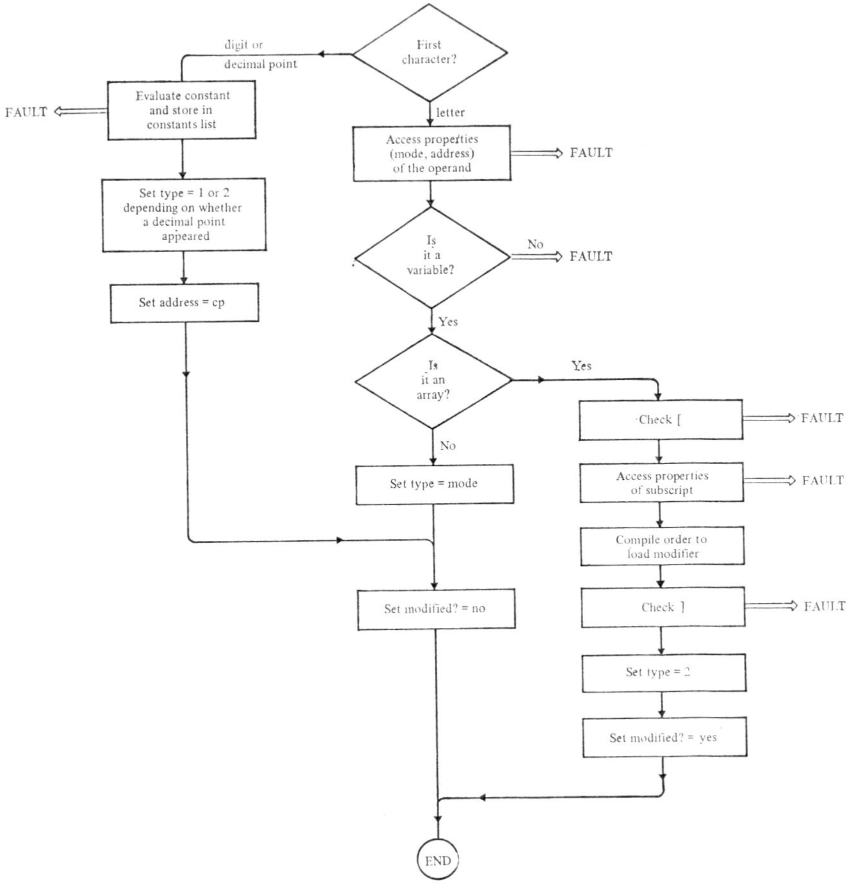

Fig. 2.8. Process operand

To deal with the first instance of inefficiency is simple. The process-operand procedure is expanded to recognise the case where the subscript is a constant. It then adds the subscript to the base address and returns this as the address; it also indicates that no modification is required.

The second instance of inefficiency given above is less simple.

One of the consequences of modularity is that it is easy to produce inefficiencies: not inevitable, but very easy. To overcome the inefficiencies, the *interface between modules* must be extended. We define the interface between a procedure and its subprocedure to be the set of quantities used or generated by the subprocedure on performing its task. The interface between the process-assignment procedure and the process-operand procedure consists of five quantities:

(i) The type of the operand.
(ii) Its run time address.
(iii) Whether the address is to be modified.
(iv) The source line pointer (sp).
(v) The constants list pointer (cp).

The first three are produced by the process-operand procedure; the rest are updated by it.

We need to expand the interface so that the process-operand procedure knows, if it can be uniquely determined, what will be in BM when the instruction it is about to compile is obeyed. If the order it is about to compile would load the same quantity then that order is redundant and can be omitted. It must also update the 'what will be in BM' quantity for future reference.

This optimisation is within a statement. A similar situation occurs across statements. Consider the two statements from the integration program below, and their translation:

$$
\begin{array}{rl}
 & \text{AFL} = \{1101\} \\
i := e + i \Rightarrow & \text{AFL} + \{1104\} \\
 & \text{AFL} \Rightarrow \{1104\}
\end{array}
$$

$$
\begin{array}{rl}
 & \text{AFL} = \{1104\} \\
i := i + g \Rightarrow & \text{AFL} + \{1103\} \\
 & \text{AFL} \Rightarrow \{1104\}
\end{array}
$$

The fourth order is clearly redundant and so can be omitted. We use a 'what will be in AFL' quantity in the same way as 'what will be in BM'. [The third order is redundant, too, since *i* is used only in the fourth order, which we have just decided to omit, before being reset in the sixth. It requires a more sophisticated optimisation process to deal with this, however.]

In fact, we need a series of 'what will be in . . .' quantities, one for each register, and their effect can be felt across statements.

Consider though the case where the second order above is labelled:

$$i := e + i$$
$$l: i := i + g$$

then, for the second statement, what will be in AFL at run time depends on what was loaded into it before any **go to** *l* statement as well as by the first statement. In a one-pass compiler such as the one we are describing, it is, in general, impossible to determine whether this is unique, so that in practice the procedure which processes the label (see next section) must set all the 'what will be in' quantities to indicate that it is unknown. The order to load AFL must then be compiled.

The subject of optimisation is a fascinating one which will reappear throughout this book. For the moment we content ourselves with the observation that achieving efficiency often implies complicating the interface between procedures.

In what follows we will assume that the properties list and constants list mechanisms just described are well understood in order to avoid using the actual address of an operand in an instruction: instead, we will simply use the identifier of the operand. For example we will use the notation:

$$i := e + i \Rightarrow \begin{array}{l} \text{AFL} = e \\ \text{AFL} + i \\ \text{AFL} \Rightarrow i \end{array}$$

$$p[n] := q[j] \Rightarrow \begin{array}{l} \text{BM} = j \\ \text{AFL} = q[\text{BM}] \\ \text{BM} = n \\ \text{AFL} \Rightarrow p[\text{BM}] \end{array}$$

We will also use examples unrelated to the integration program.

2.11 Labels and go to statements

Labels and go to statements are two sides of a single problem. Let us suppose that our object code contains an unconditional control transfer order such as:

JUMP 712

which jumps to location 712. A go to statement such as:

go to *l*

clearly compiles into one such order. The problem is to associate *l* with the correct address—the address of the order labelled—and to use this as the address part of the JUMP order.

Consider first the easy case in which each label appears before any go to statement referring to it, as in the following sequence:

$k\!:\!e := f;$

.

.

.

go to k;

A label, like the **integer**s, **real**s and **array**s has two properties:

(i) The mode of the quantity: label. Suppose we use the code 4 for this.

(ii) The address associated with the label.

Thus, the **properties** list structure we've defined is adequate.

When a label appears, the code 4 and the address of the next location in the object program are stored in the appropriate place in the properties list. A check is made first to ensure that the appropriate entries are not already set. If they are, then either:

(i) The label has already been used; or

(ii) The identifier has previously been used for a variable or an array.

Fig. 2.9 (i) shows the situation. Instead of creating artificial addresses in the object program, we use the convention that if a location holds an address we draw a pointer from the location to the address it holds.

When a go to occurs, then the address part of the JUMP order to be compiled can be found quite simply from the properties list. Fig. 2.9 (ii) illustrates the details.

In practice, of course, go to statements often appear before the label and so we need a more sophisticated scheme. One solution is as follows:

For the first go to statement that refers to a label that has not appeared we compile the statement:

JUMP 0

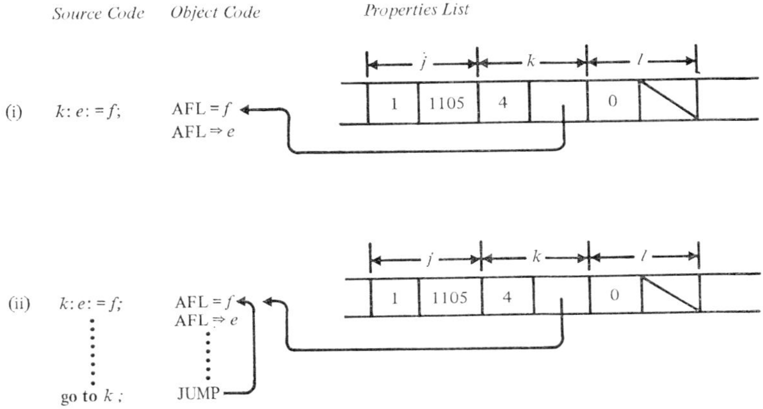

Fig. 2.9. Object code and properties list structures for backward label references: (i) at the appearance of the label; (ii) at a go to statement

and store the address of this order in the properties list. We use code 5 for this case as shown in Fig. 2.10 (i).

When a second such go to statement appears we compile a JUMP order whose address part contains the address of the JUMP 0 order, and change the entry in the properties list to point to this new order, as shown in Fig. 2.10 (ii). And so on, so that we build up for each label which has not yet appeared, a chain of JUMP orders each pointing to the previous.

When the label *l* subsequently appears, the properties list contains the address of the last order which references label *l*. This instruction can be modified to jump to the correct place. It also contains a reference to the next order in the chain which can now be corrected and so on until the last reference which points to location 0. We can plant the correct address in the properties list too, as shown in Fig. 2.10 (iii). Thereafter, all references are backward references and so the mode is changed to 4.

Let us now consider the implementation of this scheme. First the labels. When a label appears there are three cases depending on the mode:

(i) The mode is zero. This implies that the identifier has not previously appeared. The properties can be stored.

(ii) The mode is 1, 2, 3 or 4. The identifier has already been used either as a label (code 4) or a variable, and so a fault must be monitored.

(iii) The mode is 5. The label has not already appeared but there are references to it. The references can all be updated and the properties stored as in case (i).

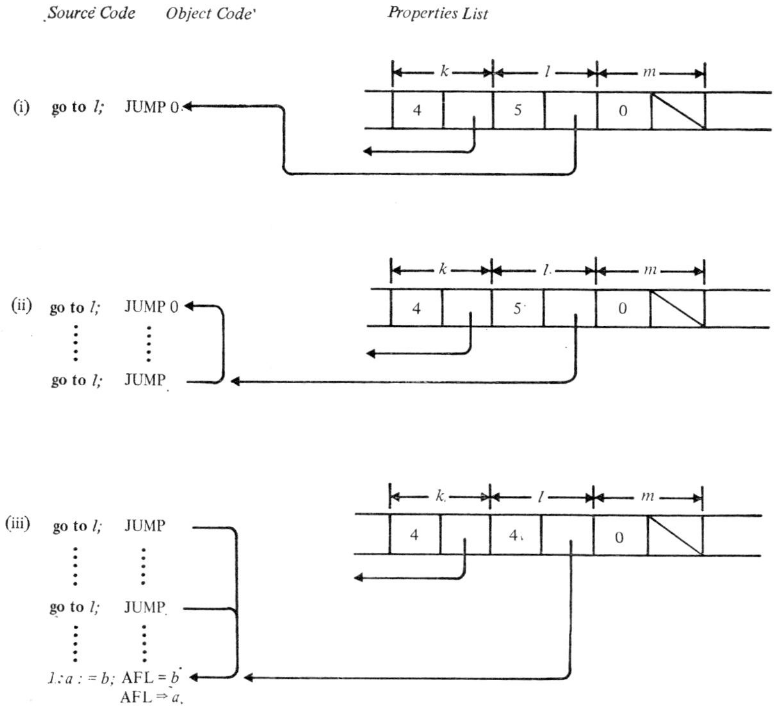

Fig. 2. 10. Object code and properties list structures for forward label references: (i) at first reference; (ii) at second and subsequent references; (iii) at the label

Fig. 2.11 shows the technique.

There are four cases to consider with a go to statement, depending once again on the mode.

(i) The mode is zero. The identifier has not yet appeared and this is the first reference to the label. We initiate the chain of references

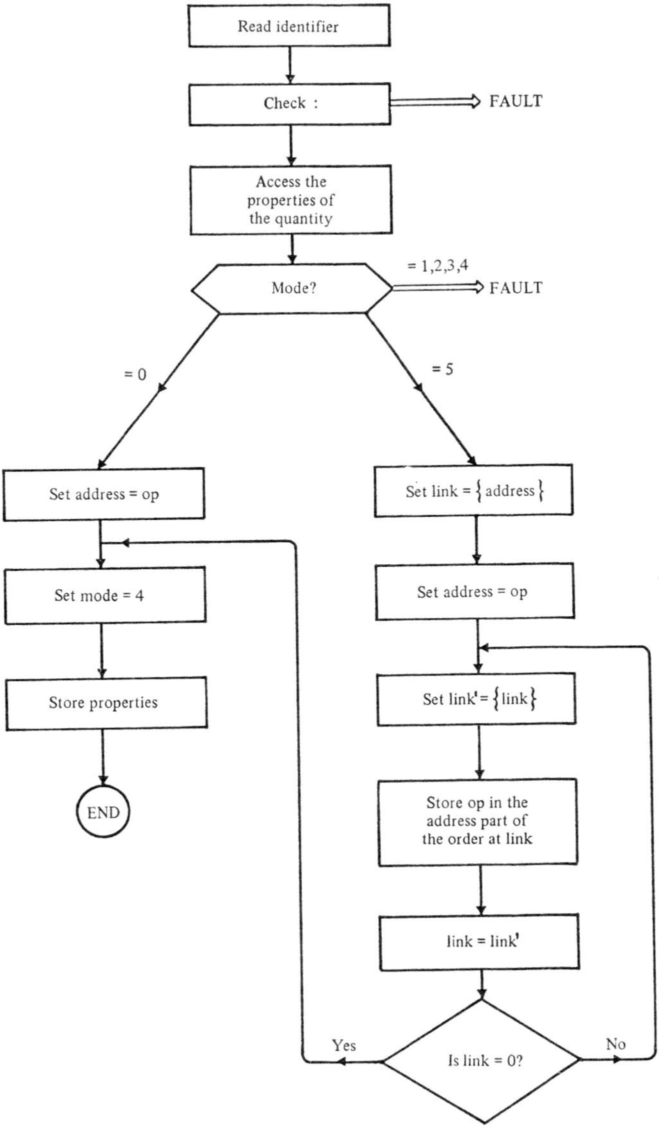

Fig. 2.11. Flow diagram for processing a label

by compiling JUMP 0, and storing the address of this order in the properties list.

(ii) The mode is 1, 2 or 3. The identifier has been used as a variable—a fault.

(iii) The mode is 4. The label has already appeared and so the correct jump order can be compiled.

(iv) The mode is 5. The label has not yet appeared but there have been previous references to it. We add a JUMP order to the chain, and update the address word in the properties list.

Fig. 2.12 gives a flow diagram to implement this.

Note that at the end of compilation (the procedure finalise) the properties list must be scanned to ensure that no identifier has mode 5 since this indicates that a label which is referred to has not appeared.

In what follows we will further assume that the technique of dealing with labels is well understood and so we will simply use the label as the address part of the JUMP order. All assembly languages in fact cater for this.

2.12 Conditional go to statements

In our basic language the conditional go to statement is of the form:

if $j \neq n$ **then go to** l
if $a \geqslant b$ **then go to** m

Let us first of all see what they might be compiled into. We need to introduce two further groups of orders for our object machine. First:

AFL COMPARE *b*

This compares the floating point accumulator with *b* and sets a register accordingly. We need not specify the details of the register except to say that it must be possible to test the register for all six possible relations ($=$, $\neq$, $>$, $\geqslant$, $<$, $\leqslant$).

The order:

AFX COMPARE *n*

performs a very similar operation on the fixed point accumulator and *n*.

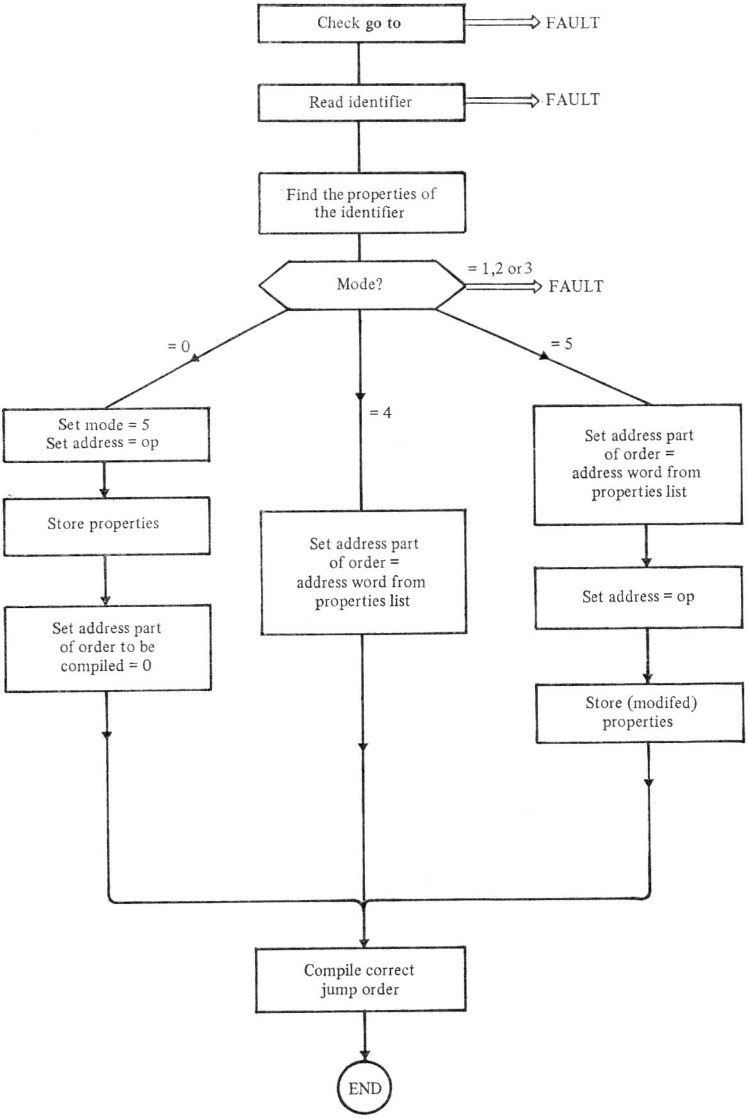

Fig. 2.12 Process ***go to***

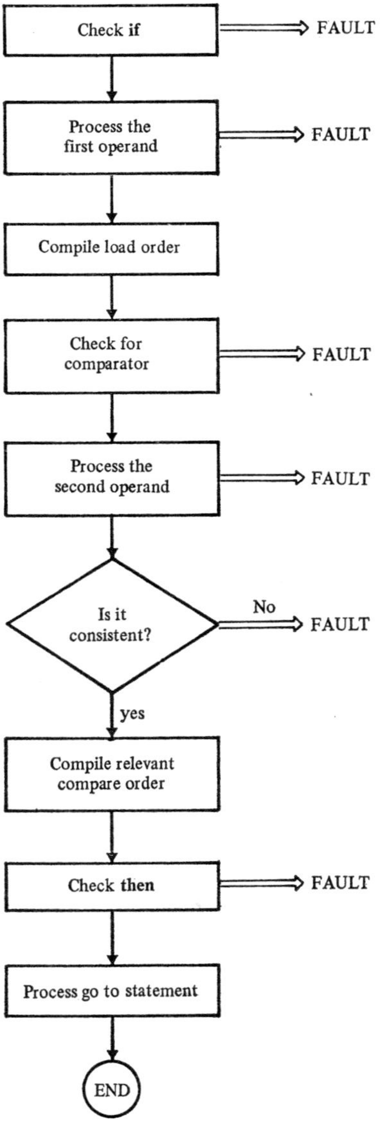

Fig. 2.13. Process condition

The second group consists of a series of six orders which test this register and jump according to whether the specified relation is true. Examples are:

IF $\neq$ JUMP l
IF $\geqslant$ JUMP m

Given these orders, then the compilation of the two statements referred to earlier is quite straightforward.

		AFX $= j$
if $j \neq n$ **then go to** l	$\Rightarrow$	AFX COMPARE n
		IF $\neq$ JUMP l
		AFL $= a$
if $a \geqslant b$ **then go to** m	$\Rightarrow$	AFL COMPARE b
		IF $\geqslant$ JUMP m

The procedure for processing conditional go to statements can clearly use the procedure for processing go to statements. Fig. 2.13 illustrates how, and explains why the final box of Fig. 2.12 refers to the 'correct jump order'.

2.13 Input and output

The remaining statements are read and print. They differ from the other statements in that they require a large number of orders to be obeyed at run time: to perform the conversion between the decimal digits read or printed on the one hand, and the binary number held internally. Of course the sequence is not compiled for each statement. A subroutine is used. Each print and read statement is compiled into a call sequence for the appropriate subroutine, and the subroutines are added at the end of the compiled program.

We will consider the problem in more detail in Chapter 15.

3 Multi-character identifiers and lexical analysis

In this chapter and the next we will expand the basic language in two ways, first by allowing multi-character identifiers, later by allowing a more general form of expression, and show how these features affect the structure of the compiler. First, *multi-character identifiers.*

3.1 Multi-character identifiers

Let us suppose that instead of restricting ourselves to single-character identifiers, we expand to include identifiers of virtually unrestricted length. We assume that, as in Algol, they are composed of letters and digits, the first character being a letter.

The integration program might now be written:

```
      begin
      real h, f0, f1, f2, integral;
      integer j, no;
      j := 0;
      read no;
loop: read h, f0, f1, f2;
      integral := 4·0 * f1;
      integral := f0 + integral;
      integral := integral + f2;
      integral := h * integral;
      integral := integral/3·0;
      print integral;
      j := j + 1;
      if j ≠ no then go to loop;
      end
```

For single-letter identifiers, since there were only 52 of them, we were able to reserve a pair of words for each conceivable quantity whether or not it was actually used. This made both the storing and the accessing of the properties of a given quantity very fast: they were both direct processes.

With multi-character identifiers we cannot reserve a pair of words for each conceivable quantity since there are an infinite number of them. Instead we store for each quantity declared, its identifier together with its other properties.

We can do this in one of, at least, three ways:

(i) We can store the identifier with the other properties in the properties list. The term *symbol table* is then often used for this joint list.

(ii) We can store the identifiers in a separate list (the *identifiers list*), associating with each identifier a word which in some way refers to the other properties in the properties lists. This could be done by making the word point to the associated properties in the properties list.

(iii) We may associate with each identifier in turn the numbers 0, 1, 2 . . ., storing the number in the extra word. To make diagrams and examples a little more readable we will precede this number by ≠. If we assume that not all quantities require just two other properties (see arrays, for example, in Chapter 10), then the properties list now requires an index to point to the start of each set of properties.

The three structures which would result from the first declaration of the integration program:

real $h, f0, f1, f2,$ integral

are shown in the three parts of Fig. 3.1, in which we use the notation that @1, @2, etc., stand for the run time addresses of the variables.

The lists are now becoming structures: they contain pointers within themselves and to each other: for example, the identifiers are preceded by a word which points to the start of the next identifier. We use an arrow from the word pointing to the appropriate word for this. The structures will become more complicated yet. It is indeed one of the main characteristics of a compiler that it has to maintain structures.

We will choose the third solution (separate identifiers list) for reasons which will be explained partly in section 3.3, and partly in Chapter 14.

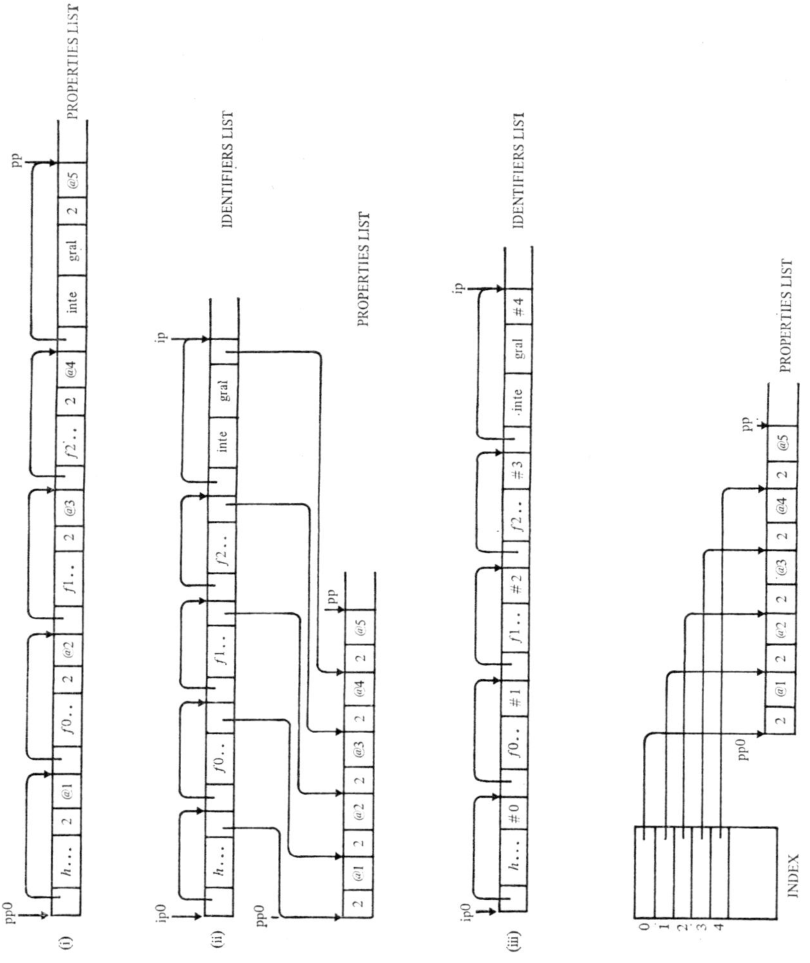

Fig. 3.1. Alternative structures for dealing with multi-character identifiers: (i) identifiers within properties list; (ii) identifiers list linked to properties list; (iii) separate identifiers list

To access the properties of a quantity now we must first of all *look-up* its identifier in the identifiers list. Then we can directly access the other properties. This look-up is associative. We must compare the identifier with all the others in the identifiers list, until a match is found. Fig. 3.2 illustrates how.

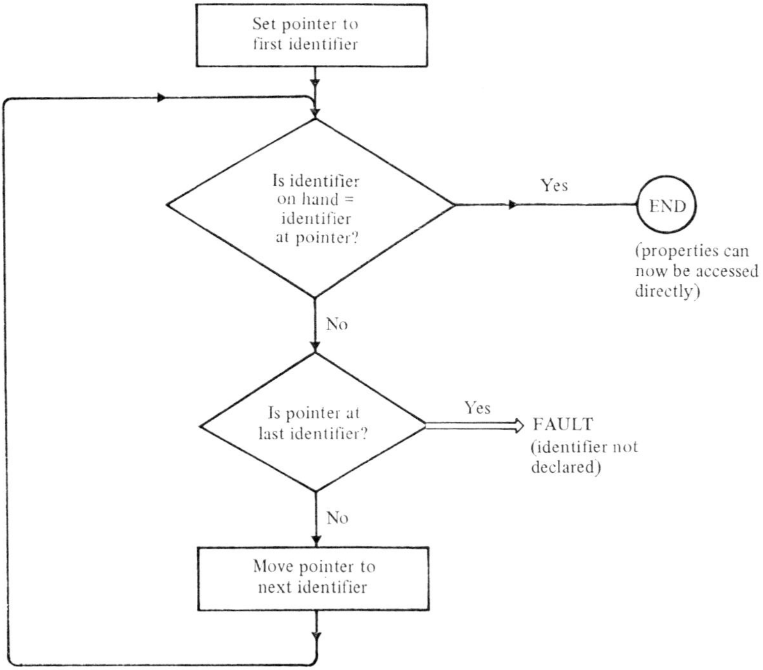

Fig. 3.2. Look-up of a multi-character identifier

This is a slow process since if we have *n* identifiers in the list, then on average we must do $n/2$ comparisons and this tends to dominate compiling time.

To look ahead for a moment to Chapter 11, block structure exaggerates this effect. Consider the skeleton of an Algol program shown in Fig. 3.3.

Suppose for the purposes of this discussion we number the blocks from 1 to 4, the number being assigned as a block is started.

When trying to find the properties of a quantity in block 4 we must be prepared to search the identifiers declared in blocks 4, 3 and 1. Further if the identifier is not found there we must search the

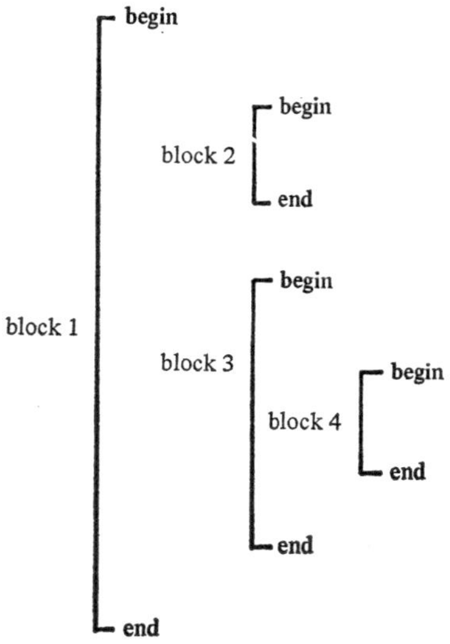

Fig. 3.3. Skeleton of an Algol program

identifiers of the run time package (the input-output procedures, the basic mathematical functions and so on). We search backwards through the structure shown in Fig. 3.4.

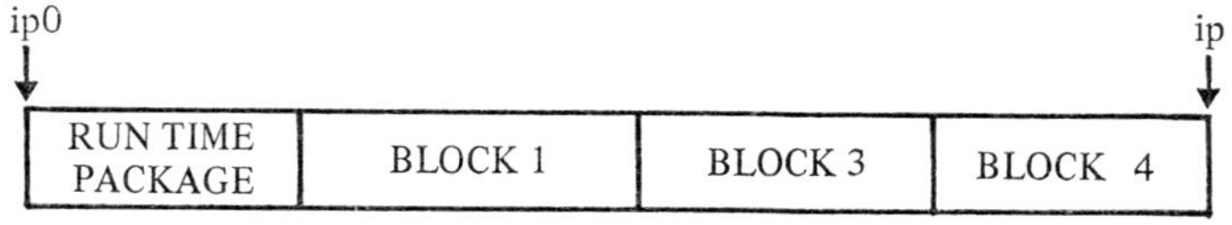

Fig. 3.4. Outline structure of the identifiers list in the program of Fig. 3.3

Since the run time package by definition contains material that is frequently accessed, the fact that their identifiers are searched last compounds the problem.

3.2 Hashing

The problem of slow search remains even in a language without block structure and we seek a method of speeding up this process. One solution is called *hashing*. We group identifiers together by some convenient means and then look-up an identifier by comparing it only with identifiers in the same group.

One *hashing algorithm* might be to group according to the first letter of the identifier. This suffers from the disadvantage that in many programs identifiers fall into closely related groups. For example:

$$f0, f1, f2$$

and so on.

A better algorithm will allow all characters of an identifier to influence the grouping (to hash up all characters). For example, if we refer to the integer corresponding to the ith character of an n character identifier as C_i, we can calculate:

$$[C_1{*}2^{n-1} + C_2{*}2^{n-2} + \ldots C_i{*}2^{n-i} + \ldots C_n] \text{ modulo } 64$$
$$= [(\ldots(\ldots((C_1{*}2 + C_2){*}2 + \ldots + C_i){*}2 + \ldots C_n] \text{ modulo } 64$$

We call this number the *hash number*. We can calculate this hash number by shifting and adding, as we read the characters of the identifier.

Assuming, for ease of arithmetic, that the letters a to z have the straight-forward values 1 to 26 and the digits 0 to 9 have the values 30 to 39, the hash numbers of the identifiers of the integration program are given in Table 3.1.

In order to limit comparison to those identifiers with the same hash number we need to link together all the appropriate identifiers. The heads of these links we store in a *hash number index*. Fig. 3.5 shows the identifiers list structure at the end of compiling the integration program.

Each identifier has associated with it an extra word which points to the next identifier with the same hash number. If there is no further identifier the link is undefined. (We indicate this in the diagram by an oblique slash.)

Exactly the same flow diagram (Fig. 3.2) holds as before for looking up an identifier except that the coding of 'move pointer to next identifier' will involve this new 'same hash number link' rather than the 'next identifier link' as before.

Identifier	*Hash number*
h	8
*f*0	42
*f*1	43
*f*2	44
integral	30
j	10
no	43
loop	10

Table 3.1. Identifiers of the sample program and their hash numbers.

So far we have concentrated on looking up an identifier. This process is required when processing assignment statements and go to statements. When processing declarations and labels the converse problem arises: that of storing the properties of a quantity. A similar technique is required. The identifiers list is searched to ensure that the identifier is not there. (If it is, then the identifier has already been declared.) Fig. 3.6 shows the algorithm. The identifier is then added to the identifiers list and the other properties of the quantity to the properties list.

The term hashing has been used in the past to describe a whole family of techniques for looking up identifiers in a table. The subject has been more thoroughly studied in recent times and theoretical investigations carried out. (See, for example, Chapter 4 of Hopgood [ref. 3.1].) The modern description of hashing techniques such as Hopgood's are quite different from that given here, but, nevertheless, their common characteristics are clear enough.

3.3 Lexical analysis

Comparison of Figs. 3.2 and 3.6 shows them to be exactly the same except in the interpretation of the two exit paths. So the question

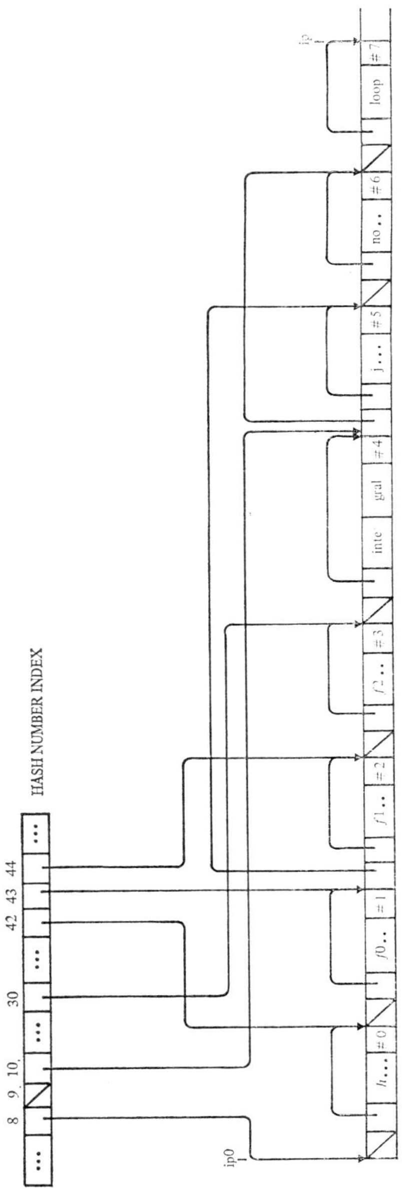

Fig. 3.5. Identifiers list structure with hashing

naturally arises: can we coalesce them into one? The answer is, of course, yes. (Any competent programmer might well have done so.) Further this procedure is called in almost all the processing procedures and a supplementary question arises: can we do a separate processing

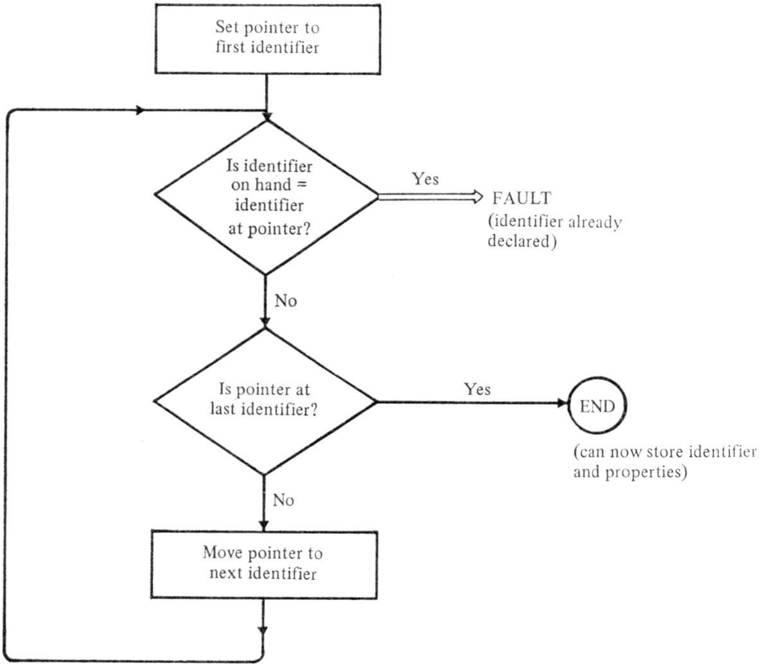

Fig. 3.6. Storing the properties of a quantity

scan on the source line which causes each identifier to be looked up in the identifiers list (being added if necessary) and which produces a modified version of the source line in which the identifiers have been replaced by a single symbol? Again the answer is yes. The process is called *lexical analysis*. It would have been more accurate to call it lexical processing, but we will use the conventional term. We will call the symbol in the *lexical analysed line* which replaces an identifier, a *pseudo-identifier*. Clearly there must be some relation between the pseudo-identifier and the real identifier. We will use the number associated with the identifier in the identifiers list as the pseudo-identifier.

Thus, from the integration program:

real *h*, *f*0, *f*1, *f*2, integral;

would be converted to:

real #0, #1, #2, #3, #4;

and:

integral := *f*0 + integral;

would be converted to:

#4 := #1 + #4;

In Fig. 3.7 we revise the over-all flow diagram of the compiler (Fig. 2.1) to include lexical analysis.

It is important to note that lexical analysis operates without any knowledge of the structure of the statement being analysed. Thus, in lexical analysis, no properties are stored or accessed. This is done by the following stage of processing which does establish the type of statement involved. Further, all identifiers are added to the identifiers list, even those which have not been declared. In this case no properties are ever stored.

An alternative way of approaching lexical analysis is to consider it as a procedure which reduces a program with multi-character identifiers to an equivalent program with single-character (pseudo-) identifiers, using the identifiers list to do so. The point of this is that the compiler discussed in Chapter 2 can process this lexically analysed line. It is a universal device, to transform a new problem into one whose solution is already known. One of the reasons for separating the identifiers list from the properties list is that the lists are required at different times by different processes: the identifiers list by the lexical analysis procedure, the properties list by subsequent processing procedures. [But see Chapter 14.]

In the processing stage we need to be able to distinguish a pseudo-identifier from a normal character. One solution would be to use two words for each character or pseudo-identifier, the first word saying whether it is a character or pseudo-identifier or whatever (see later); the second being the actual character, pseudo-identifier or whatever. In the case of characters, the first word could also contain coded

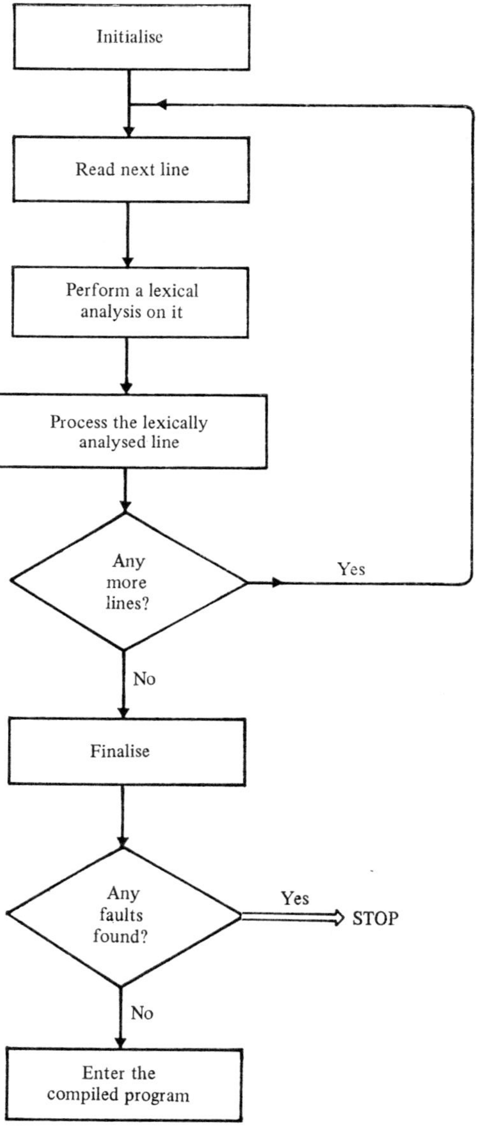

Fig. 3.7. Revised over-all flow diagram to allow for lexical analysis

information such as the priority of the operator, whether it is arithmetic, Boolean or relational and so on. Alternatively, since characters have values in the range 0–127 (and, see later, delimiters can be given values in the range 128–255), we could add, say, 256 to the numerical value associated with the identifier. In the text we will continue to use the ≠ convention introduced earlier to distinguish a pseudo-identifier.

3.4 Lexical analysis of constants

Are there any other groups of characters which could be condensed in lexical analysis? In our basic language there are two.

(i) Constants. The lexical analysis procedure processes the digits of the constant (and decimal point and exponent) to produce the binary constant itself which it looks up in the constants list (adding it if necessary). It replaces the symbols in the source string by a *pseudo-constant* (its index in the constants list).

(ii) Delimiter words. The underlined words such as **begin** and **end** are called delimiter words. Strings of underlined symbols could also be replaced by some single symbol. We will not do this during lexical analysis, for reasons given in section 3.6.

Fig. 3.8 is a flow diagram for lexical analysis.

3.5 Backtracking

There is a further very practical reason for lexical analysis. Consider the processing of:

temperature := temperature0

according to the algorithm of Fig. 2.2, without lexical analysis. We would initially look for a label. In doing this we would recognise 'temperature' as an identifier; but because we couldn't find a colon we would conclude there was no label. We'd then proceed to recognise 'temperature' *again* as an identifier when processing the assignment statement. This backtracking, this recognising correctly an identifier as part of an unsuccessful look for a label, is quite inefficient. Unfortunately it is more or less inevitable. Lexical analysis alleviates the problem to the extent that the identifiers are recognised only once in lexical analysis; and in the subsequent processing only the one-word pseudo-identifier is involved in backtracking instead of the 11-character identifier proper.

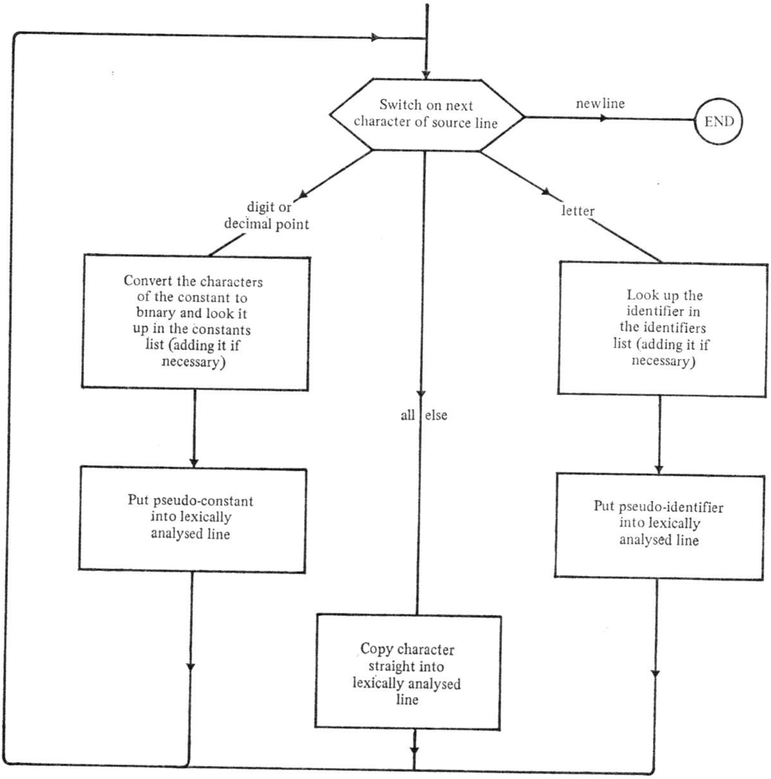

Fig. 3.8. Lexical analysis

In this example the back-tracking could be avoided by redesigning the processing algorithm of Fig. 2.2. The principle, however, remains valid as can be seen by considering Algol 60 which allows multiple labels and multiple left-hand sides in assignment statements. Consider, for example, the following:

start: restart: pointer1 := pointer2 := pointer

3.6 Punching conventions

In practice a program is likely to be presented to a machine in different ways, due to different punching conventions. These conventions generally affect the delimiters. On paper tape we might punch a delimiter exactly as given. Since this underlining is time-consuming we might have an option which allows us to use upper case letters for delimiters (without underlining), while restricting identifiers to lower-case letters. On punching devices with a restricted character set we may have to surround our delimiters with quotes instead of underlining them. With cards we have the further (minor) complication that only upper case letters are available.

Thus **begin** might be punched:

begin
BEGIN
'begin'
'BEGIN'

Small character set devices like cards tend not to have all the delimiter symbols such as '≠' available. Extra delimiter words such as **ne** must generally be used instead. These words are then punched as the normal delimiter words.

So the statement:

if *j* ≠ no **then goto** loop;

might be punched:

if *j* ≠ no **then goto** loop;
IF *j* ≠ no THEN GOTO loop;
'if' *j* 'ne' no 'then' 'goto' loop;
'IF' *J* 'NE' NO 'THEN' 'GOTO' LOOP;

Clearly it would be advantageous if all forms were converted to a *standard form* before any processing at all takes place—that is, before lexical analysis. The rest of the compiler then is invariant to punching conventions. New conventions can be catered for by modifying only the procedure which performs the conversion to standard form; or by providing separate procedures for each set of punching conventions. For example, a procedure could be added to

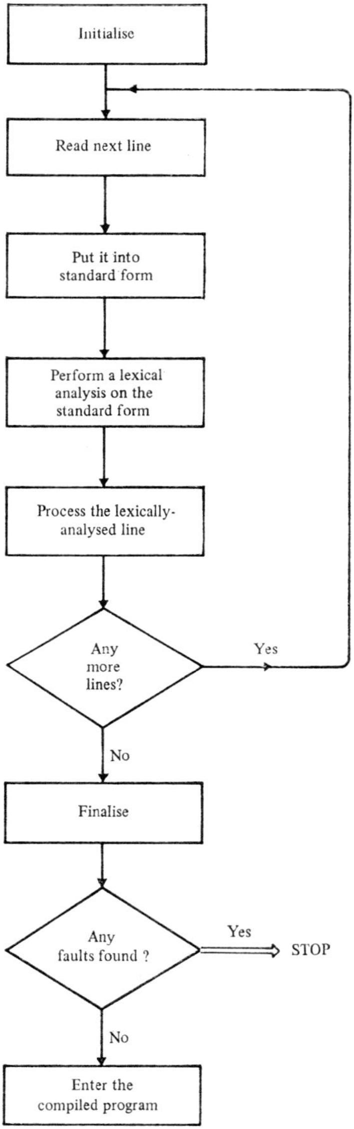

Fig. 3.9. Re-revised over-all flow diagram to allow for a standard form

allow French delimiters, so that the statement above could be punched:

si $j \neq$ no **alors allera** loop;

Fig. 3.9 is the over-all flow diagram remodified to allow for conversion to standard form.

The choice of standard form can be made along one of two lines.

(i) We can choose the most general form of input (the one with underlining and all the available delimiter symbols) and convert input punched according to all other conversions into this form. With this solution, delimiter words would not be converted into single symbols until lexical analysis. (This would involve the appropriate additions to Fig. 3.8.) This solution has the disadvantage that each delimiter word has to be processed twice, once during conversion to standard form, once during lexical analysis.

(ii) We can choose as standard, a form in which all delimiters (including delimiter words) are converted to single symbols. As indicated earlier the delimiter words might be converted into symbols in the range 128–255. The procedure to do this is concerned with minor programming problems rather than broad general principles and so will not describe it further except in one detail. Converting a delimiter word into its corresponding symbol is very similar to converting an identifier into its corresponding pseudo-identifier, and so the technique of hash addressing is relevant. Since the number of delimiter words is fixed, however, it is possible by experimentation to produce a perfect hashing algorithm so that only one comparison is required.

In practice though, the problems of fault detection (Chapter 14) often lead to a different technique.

We will assume the method (ii). Fig. 3.10 summarises the actions of the three stages of processing, and Fig. 3.11 illustrates them with respect to the statements:

real $h, f0, f1, f2$, integral;
integral: $= f0 +$ integral;

In practice the distinction between converting to standard form and lexical analysis is not often made. If the only form of input to be considered is cards then clearly it is sensible to make the standard the same as that used for input. Delimiter conversion then is done in the lexical analysis phase. We have separated them because we seek in this book to identify the essentially different processes that go to make up a compiler. The delimiter conversion is a process related to the nature of

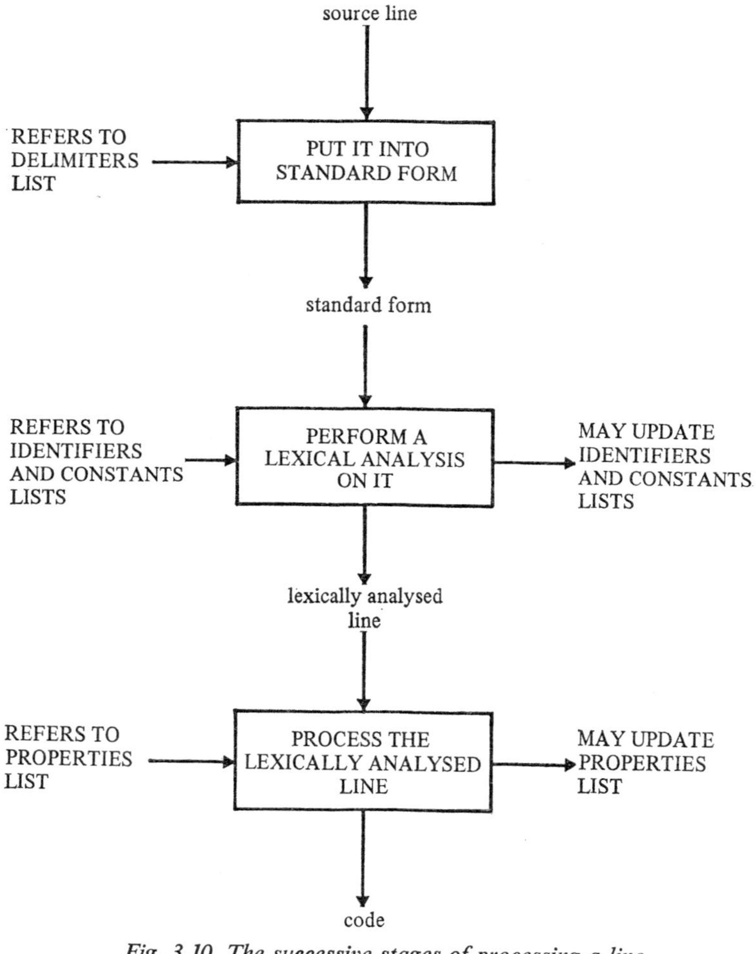

Fig. 3.10. The successive stages of processing a line

the available editing devices (and could be done by the operating system); lexical analysis is concerned with a programmer's choice of identifiers. In practice, of course, a compiler writer might well decide that the similarities of the two processes are more significant than their differences.

3.7 Comments and strings

The fundamental characteristics of the lexical analysis phase is that it proceeds from left to right processing a symbol at a time. While proceeding through the line, it can tell from the next character whether an

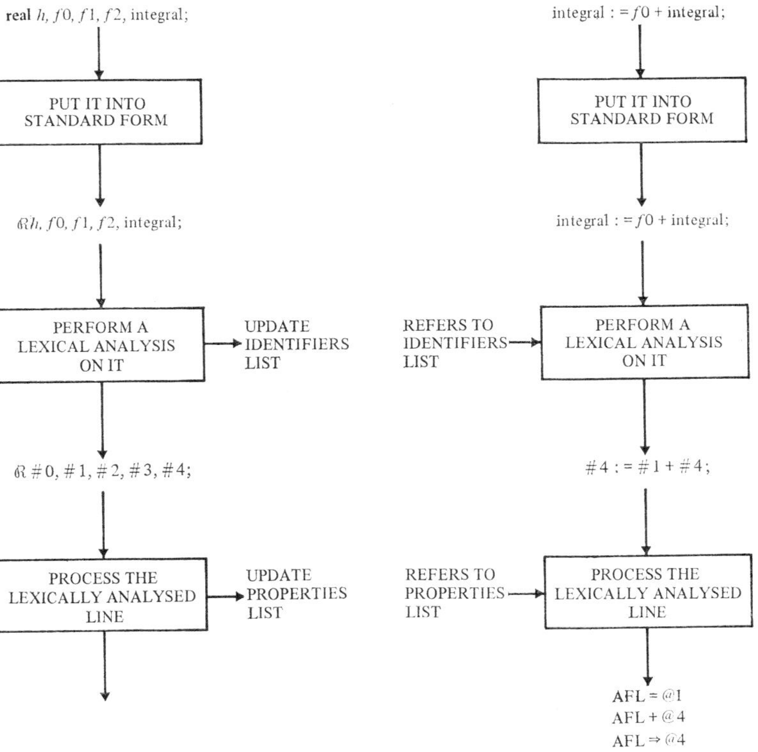

Fig. 3.11. The successive stages of processing
real *h*, *f* 0, *f* 1, *f* 2, integral;
integral: = *f* 0 + integral;

identifier has been encountered; while proceeding through the identifier, it can tell from the next character when the identifier has terminated. [In terms of the theory of grammars, identifiers and constants are described by Chomsky Type 3 grammars.] Consequently any other operation which is of this nature can be performed during lexical analysis. In Algol 60, comments and strings are classical examples.

Suppose we allow any line of our basic (but expanding) language to be followed by a **comment** of the form:

comment ⟨any string of characters except semi-colon⟩;

In the standard form **comment** appears as one symbol which indicates that, during lexical analysis, it and everything else up to and including the following semi-colon can be deleted. The comment allowed after an **end** can similarly be deleted.

There is no call in our basic language to add strings and string variables as yet. Nevertheless we will consider, for a moment, a string of the form:

'⟨any string of characters except string quotes⟩'

Clearly during lexical analysis the string of characters can be added to a strings list, being replaced in the lexically analysed line by a pseudo-string.

Strings and constants are both *literals*, and, in general, all literals can be processed during lexical analysis.

3.8 Other actions

The basic justification for the lexical analysis phase is one of efficiency: it makes the subsequent processing phase easier. Its scope has often been expanded in this area, though always at the cost of making it a more *ad hoc* procedure. For example, in the next chapter we find it convenient to have expressions surrounded by the special brackets $\vdash$ and $\dashv$ when we process them. These brackets can always be added in the lexical analysis phase. In our basic language, expressions appear only within assignments so that we simply insert a $\vdash$ after each := and the corresponding $\dashv$ before the next semicolon.

3.9 The relevance to Fortran

Because Fortran was designed for use with a very restricted character set (48-character cards), there is no notion of punching conventions. [Except, that is, for some minor deviations in some compilers.] Consequently there is no need for a procedure for converting to standard form: the input is the standard form.

We will, however, find it convenient to regard the logical and relational operators (.AND., .OR., .NOT., .LT., .LE., .GT., .GE., .EQ., .NE.) as if they were punching conventions (for, say, $\wedge$, $\vee$, $\neg$, $<$, $\leqslant$, $>$, $\geqslant$, $=$, $\neq$), and to have a procedure for processing them. Consider:

P = I .LE. 3 .AND. 3 .LE. J

If there were no pass to process these operators then subsequent procedures would have to be non-trivially modified to decide whether the constants were '3' or '3.'.

So the conversion to standard form produces:

$$P = I \leqslant 3 \wedge 3 \leqslant J$$

There is, however, very little formal lexical analysis that can be done. It is not possible to process the identifiers (or symbolic names, as Fortran calls them) or constants. The reason is simply that it is not possible to determine where an identifier or a constant starts. Consider these two statements:

```
DO 1 I = 1, 10
DO 1 I = 1
```

The first is a DO-statement, the second an (unlikely) arithmetic assignment statement. In the first DO is a keyword, 1 is an integer (a statement label) and I is an identifier. In the second DO 1 I is the identifier.

Lexical analysis, though, can process Hollerith constants, Fortran's equivalent of strings.

Further, in the spirit of section 3.8 it is possible to expand the lexical analysis procedure so that it determines by *ad hoc* rules what statement it is processing. That is, it passes on not only the lexically analysed line but also a parameter specifying what statement it is (unless it turns out to be faulty).

For example, if we define a zero-level '=' to be an '=' not enclosed within brackets and a zero-level comma to be a comma not enclosed in brackets, then any statement with no zero-level commas to the right of a zero-level '=' is an assignment statement. [Or a statement function which is syntactically similar.]

Sale (see ref. 3.2) lists all the rules.

4 Expressions and syntactical analysis

In this chapter we make our second major expansion of the language, to encompass full arithmetic expressions and show how this, too, leads to a change in the over-all structure of a compiler.

It has to be remembered that by the time the processing procedure starts to work, lexical analysis will have replaced all identifiers by pseudo-identifiers, and constants by pseudo-constants. In what follows we will use the identifiers in place of the pseudo-identifiers for readability purposes.

4.1 Expressions

So let us expand our expressions up to the power of the Algol simple arithmetic expression or the Fortran arithmetic expression, in that the number of operands is unlimited, and that brackets are allowed. The integration program can now be written:

```
      begin
      real h, f0, f1, f2, integral;
      integer j, no;
      j := 0;
      read no;
loop: read h, f0, f1, f2;
      integral := h*(f0 + 4.0*f1 + f2)/3·0;
      print integral;
      j := j + 1;
      if j ≠ no then go to loop;
      end
```

In this chapter and the next two we consider how to process the expression, but restrict ourselves to scalar operands, which, in all our examples, will be real.

Consider for the moment this well-known expression for calculating the velocity after time t, of an object whose initial velocity is u, and whose acceleration is f:

$$u + f * t$$

If we process this from left to right as we did with the basic language of Chapter 2 then we would produce this code:

AFL $= u$
AFL $\Rightarrow \delta 0$
AFL $= f$
AFL * t
AFL + $\delta 0$

where $\delta 0$ is the name of some location allocated by the compiler for temporary storage.

The more optimal form is, of course:

AFL $= f$
AFL * t
AFL + u

We could modify the algorithm to deal with this particular case but the general point is valid. The problem lies in discovering the structure of the expression only as the production of code progresses. Clearly some advantage would be gained in finding the structure first and then producing code from the representation of the structure. This process is called *syntactical analysis*.

4.2 A revised over-all flow diagram

If we introduce a syntactical analysis pass over the line before the ultimate processing we arrive at the revised version of the over-all flow diagram given in Fig. 4.1.

Syntactical analysis encompasses rather more than finding the structure of an expression; it finds the structure of all statements. [Though in our (expanded) basic language, the assignment statement is the only one with any real structure.] More precisely its function is to analyse the lexically analysed line to determine what statement

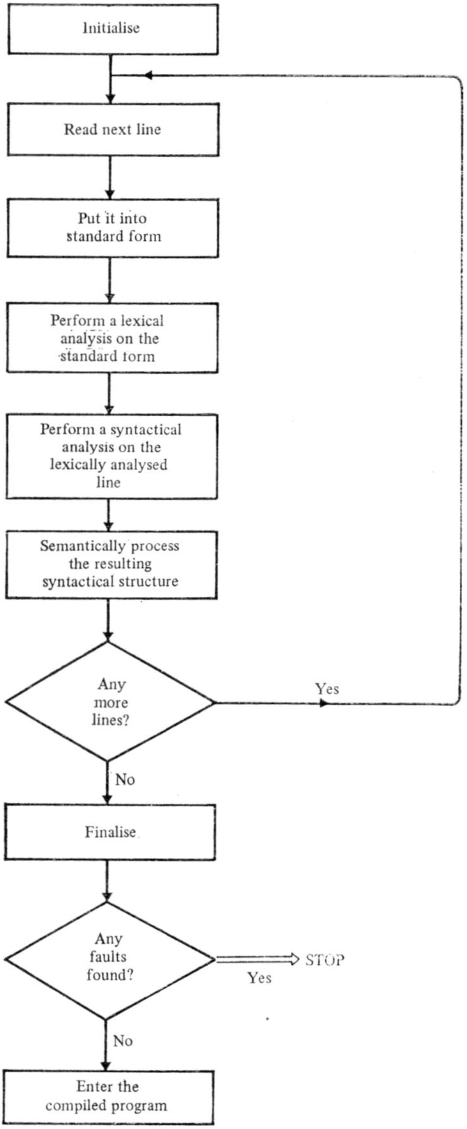

Fig. 4.1. Revised over-all flow diagram

it is and to produce some description of its structure. We call this description the *syntactical structure* or the *internal structure.*

We will return to this more general aspect in Chapter 13. For the next few chapters we will concern ourselves with expressions, which are the dominant problem.

We will consider throughout this chapter the expression:

$$h*(f0 + 4{\cdot}0*f1 + f2)/3{\cdot}0$$

taken from the integration program, which we shall refer to as the *integration expression.* If we were to encode this in a simple left-to-right algorithm (which is similar to the one in section 2.9 but which will not be described) we would produce the code of Table 4.1.

AFL = h
AFL ⇒ $\delta 0$
AFL = $f0$
AFL ⇒ $\delta 1$
AFL = 4·0
AFL * $f1$
AFL + $\delta 1$
AFL + $f2$
AFL * $\delta 0$
AFL / 3·0

Table 4.1. Left to right encoding of $h*(f0 + 4{\cdot}0*f1 + f2)/3{\cdot}0$ (10 orders)

4.3 Equivalent simple assignments

Finding the structure of an expression really means finding out what operations have to be done in what order. The following description of a technique based on the precedence of the arithmetic operators is largely due to Graham (see ref. 4.1).

Suppose initially that the expression is fully parenthesised: that is the priority of the operators is indicated by brackets. When the priorities are equal we assume that they are bracketed to the left.

Thus our integration expression would appear:

$$((h*((f0 + (4{\cdot}0*f1)) + f2))/3{\cdot}0)$$

The technique can be described as follows:

(i) Set a counter = 0.
(ii) Move from the left to the right through the string until a right bracket is met. It will be preceded by a left bracket and two operands separated by an operator.
(iii) These define a simple assignment of the form:

$$\delta\text{counter} := \text{operand1 operator operand2}$$

which is generated.
(iv) Replace the five symbols (brackets, operator and operands) in the string by δcounter.
(v) Add 1 to the counter.
(vi) If the expression is not exhausted return to (ii) above.

The operation of this technique on the integration expression is shown step by step in Table 4.2.

(Reduced) string	*Assignment created*
$((h*((f0 + (4{\cdot}0*f1)) + f2))/3{\cdot}0)$	
$((h*((f0 + \quad \delta 0 \quad) + f2))/3{\cdot}0)$	$\delta 0 := 4{\cdot}0 * f1$
$((h*(\quad \delta 1 \quad + f2))/3{\cdot}0)$	$\delta 1 := f0 + \delta 0$
$((h* \quad \delta 2 \quad)/3{\cdot}0)$	$\delta 2 := \delta 1 + f2$
$(\quad \delta 3 \quad /3{\cdot}0)$	$\delta 3 := h * \delta 2$
$\delta 4$	$\delta 4 := \delta 3 / 3{\cdot}0$

Table 4.2. Generation of simple assignments from the fully parenthesised form of $h*(f0 + 4{\cdot}0*f1 + f2)/3{\cdot}0$

These simple assignments are very easy to deal with. For a three-address machine (such as the CDC 6000, 7000 and CYBER ranges) they reflect exactly the structure of the machine code and can be simply encoded. Since there is one assignment per operator no better code could be produced. (Not, at least, from this point of view.)

For our one-address machine the coding is quite simple too. The simple assignments are exactly the assignment statements of the basic language of Chapter 2. The typical assignment:

$$\delta\text{counter} := \text{operand1 operator operand2}$$

is encoded:

AFL = operand1
AFL operator operand2
AFL ⇒ δ counter

Thus the translation of the simple assignments for our integration expression is given in Table 4.3.

Assignments	*Code*
	AFL = 4·0
δ0 := 4·0 * *f*1	AFL * *f*1
	AFL ⇒ δ0
	AFL = *f*0
δ1 : = *f*0 + δ0	AFL + δ0
	AFL ⇒ δ1
	AFL = δ1
δ2 := δ1 + *f*2	AFL + *f*2
	AFL ⇒ δ2
	AFL = *h*
δ3 := *h* * δ2	AFL * δ2
	AFL ⇒ δ3
	AFL = δ3
δ4 := δ3 / 3·0	AFL / 3·0
	AFL ⇒ δ4 (ignore in comparisons)

Table 4.3. Direct encoding of the simple assignments produced from *h**(*f*0 + 4·0**f*1 + *f*2)/3·0 (14 orders)

In our comparisons we will ignore the final order, comparing sequences which leave their result in the accumulator. The comparison 14 against 10 for the simple left-to-right scan is not favourable.

If we consider orders 6 and 7 of Table 4.3:

AFL ⇒ δ1
AFL = δ1

they are both redundant, the second because AFL already contains the correct quantity, the first because δ1 is used only in the following (now redundant) order. Although the orders came from the translation of different simple assignments, the situation is easily recognised and the orders can be omitted.

Orders 12 and 13 may be similarly omitted. Table 4.4 shows the results:

Assignments	*Code*
	AFL = 4·0
δ0 := 4·0 * *f*1	AFL * *f*1
	AFL ⇒ δ0
δ1 := *f*0 + δ0	AFL = *f*0
	AFL + δ0
δ2 := δ1 + *f*2	AFL + *f*2
	AFL ⇒ δ2
δ3 := *h* * δ2	AFL = *h*
	AFL * δ2
δ4 := δ3 / 3·0	AFL / 3·0
	AFL ⇒ δ4 (ignore in comparisons)

Table 4.4. A more subtle encoding of the simple assignments produced for h(f0 + 4·0*f1 + f2)/3·0* (10 orders)

This comparison 10 orders, as against 10 for the simple left-to-right scan, still does not justify the use of an internal structure.

4.4 Re-ordering simple assignments

The code produced in this way from the simple assignments may even contain more orders; it will never contain fewer. [This is because the left-to-right algorithm is not quite as simple as all that.]

However, the operands within a simple assignment can be re-ordered to advantage. For example, the second assignment:

$$\delta 1 := f0 + \delta 0 \text{ is equivalent to } \delta 1 := \delta 0 + f0$$

and, if this reordering is performed, the code generated would replace:

AFL $= f0$		[AFL $= \delta 0$]
AFL $+ \delta 0$	by	AFL $+ f0$
[AFL $\Rightarrow \delta 1$]		[AFL $\Rightarrow \delta 1$]

where the square brackets enclose orders which will be deleted.

Table 4.5 illustrates the effect when the second and fourth assignment have been reordered.

Re-ordered assignments	*Code*
$\delta 0 := 4{\cdot}0 * f1$	AFL $= 4{\cdot}0$ AFL $* f1$
$\delta 1 := \delta 0 + f0$	AFL $+ f0$
$\delta 2 := \delta 1 + f2$	AFL $+ f2$
$\delta 3 := \delta 2 * h$	AFL $* h$
$\delta 4 := \delta 3 / 3{\cdot}0$	AFL $/ 3{\cdot}0$ AFL $\Rightarrow \delta 4$ (ignore in comparisons)

Table 4.5. Encoding of the re-ordered simple assignments produced from $h*(f0 + 4{\cdot}0*f1 + f2)/3{\cdot}0$ (6 *orders*)

The code produced (6 orders) is optimal.

Note that this code would have been produced directly (i.e. without any re-ordering) from the expression:

$$(4{\cdot}0*f1 + f0 + f2)*h/3{\cdot}0$$

Thus the re-ordering has effectively *transformed*:

$$h*(f0 + 4{\cdot}0*f1 + f2)/3{\cdot}0$$

into:

$$(4{\cdot}0*f1 + f0 + f2)*h/3{\cdot}0$$

It is often convenient when discussing the re-ordering (or to use a more general term, the *transformation*) to regard it as having taken place on the source string rather than the internal structure.

The re-ordering algorithm is simple and is invoked only if one or both of the operands is a temporary variable (e.g. $\delta 0$). If there is one such operand it will be the same as that appearing on the left-hand side of the previous assignment; if there are two such operands, one of them will also appear on the left-hand side of the previous assignment. The assignment should be re-ordered, so that this operand comes first.

Consider, however, the expression for the reactance of a serial *L-C* circuit:

$$\omega L - \frac{1}{\omega C}$$

An expression for calculating this might be:

$$w*L - 1{\cdot}0/(w*C)$$

which, when fully parenthesised, appears:

$$((w*L) - (1{\cdot}0/(w*C)))$$

The assignments are shown in Table 4.6:

Assignments	*Re-ordered assignments*
$\delta 0 := w * L$	$\delta 0 := w * L$
$\delta 1 := w * C$	$\delta 1 := w * C$
$\delta 2 := 1{\cdot}0 \,/\, \delta 1$	$\delta 2 := \delta 1 \,\phi\, 1{\cdot}0$
$\delta 3 := \delta 0 - \delta 2$	$\delta 3 := \delta 2 \,\theta\, \delta 0$

Table 4.6. Assignments and re-ordered assignments for $w*L - 1{\cdot}0/(w*C)$

The last two assignments have non-commutative operators, / and –, and we must introduce the 'reverse operators', ϕ and θ, for the re-ordering.

These are defined by the relations:

$$a \,\phi\, b \equiv b \,/\, a$$
$$a \,\theta\, b \equiv b - a$$

[Of course reverse add is just the same as add; and reverse multiply is the same as multiply.]

We have effectively transformed:

$$w*L - 1{\cdot}0/(w*C)$$

into:

$$w*L - w*C\phi 1{\cdot}0$$

This example also illustrates the fact that the optimal code may require temporary storage. Here $w*L$ must necessarily be stored while $1{\cdot}0/(w*C)$ is calculated.

It is mainly because we can transform it that we go through this intermediate form. The transformation is in theory unnecessary in that we could always write an encoding algorithm which produced the same code by sophisticated programming. In practice, though, it is always much easier to separate the two phases of transforming the syntactical structure, and the processing of it. We will not seek to justify the statement here. An example is, however, given in Chapter 5.

4.5 A finally revised flow diagram

If we concede this separation then the over-all flow diagram appears as shown in Fig. 4.2.

It will be noticed that it is quite unnecessary to store the only internal structure we have considered so far, the simple assignments. As each was created it could have been transformed, encoded and then deleted. In the subsequent sections we shall show reasons why the complete internal structure should be created, then transformed, then encoded.

4.6 Re-ordering in Algol

One of the characteristics of the code produced from the simple assignments is that the operands will be accessed in an order which, in general, will not be a left-to-right one. This is how it achieves its efficiency. For example, the operands of the integration expression:

$$h*(f0 + 4{\cdot}0*f1 + f2)/3{\cdot}0$$

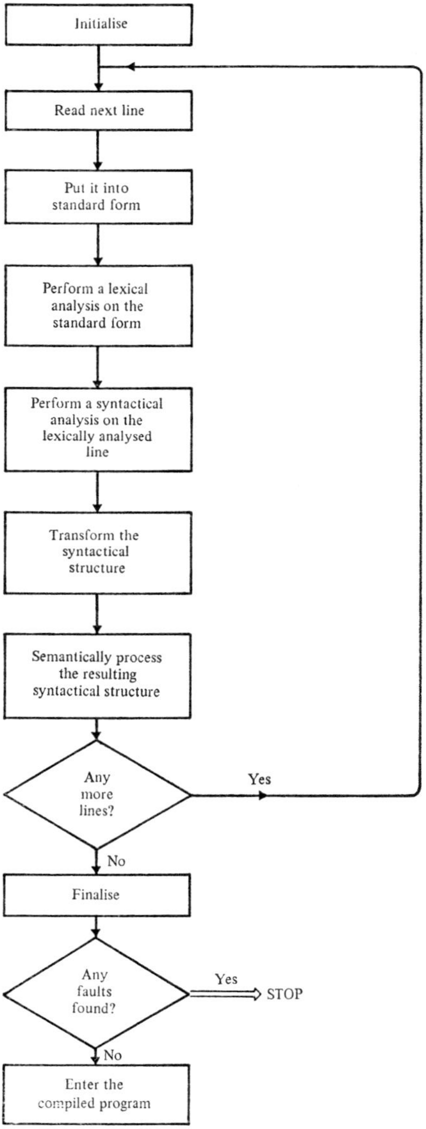

Fig. 4.2. Final revised over-all flow diagram

are processed in the order 4·0, *f*1, *f*0, *f*2, *h*, 3·0. In some languages, such as Fortran, this is quite acceptable since they are defined in such a way that re-ordering of operands is allowed. Indeed the re-ordering is encouraged since it is one of the devices for improving efficiency.

In Algol, however, the evaluation of operands is specified to be left-to-right. Of course, if re-ordering produces exactly the same effect as would be produced without it, then clearly the re-ordering is acceptable.

Consider the expression:

$$u + f*t$$

which could be re-ordered to:

$$f*t + u$$

and suppose that one operand (or indeed all of them) is not a scalar but a function call which alters the value of the others. Clearly when this operand is evaluated is of the utmost significance. The classical example is:

read + read*read

where 'read' is a function whose value is the next data number (as in ICL 1900 Algol). Re-ordering this to:

read*read + read

would produce drastically different results. However, if u, f and t were scalars then:

$u + f*t$ and $f*t + u$

would produce the same results.

Let us define the *environment* of an operand to be the set of variables which can be accessed during the evaluation of the operand together with the state of all the peripheral devices. Then in Algol two operands may be re-ordered provided that neither of them alters the environment of the other. The environment can be altered in this way only by function calls, the alteration being called a *side-effect*.

An Algol compiler can be written to achieve efficiency by re-ordering in one of two ways:

(i) The user can be given the option of saying that he does not capitalise on side-effects and so the compiler can re-order the simple assignment if it sees fit. If the user does not exercise this option then no re-ordering is performed.

(ii) The compiler can discover those expressions which are not sensitive to side-effects, and re-order the assignments. It is difficult to find all such expressions and so compilers will usually settle for a subset, such as all expressions which have no function calls in them. Those which might be sensitive are not re-ordered.

However, it must be remembered that an Algol compiler *must* be able to process the operands of an expression from left to right. This technique of producing simple assignments is, therefore, deficient.

4.7 Binary trees

An alternative internal structure for representing expressions, and one which overcomes this deficiency, is the *binary tree* such as those given in Fig. 4.3.

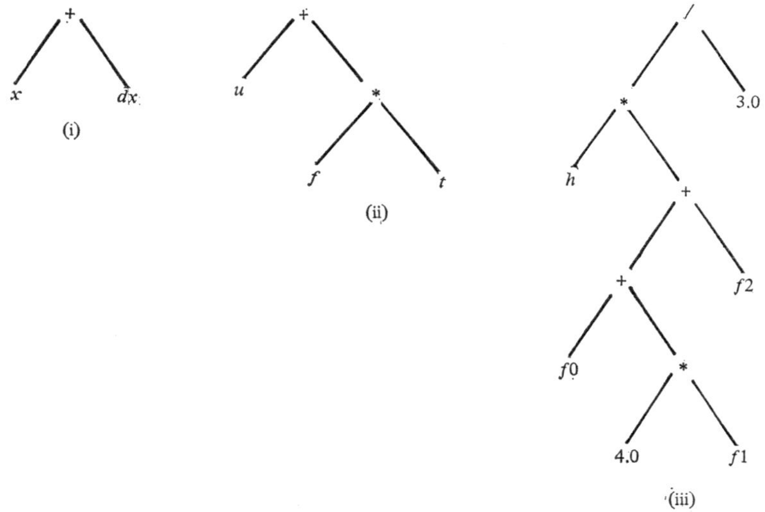

Fig. 4. 3. Binary trees for: (i) $x + dx$; (ii) $u + f*t$; (iii) $h*(f0 + 4{\cdot}0*f1 + f2)/3{\cdot}0$

We assume that the idea of a tree structure is well understood. We will, however, give a brief description in order to introduce our terminology. A binary tree is a set of *nodes*, each node comprising a *datum* (which, in our case, is the operator), a *left branch* and a *right branch* (which refer to other nodes). Since the tree is finite, some nodes, called *leaves*, do not refer to further nodes. In this case the datum is the operand. Each node, with one exception, has exactly one branch referring to it. The exception, called the *root*, has no incident branches. For an expression which consists merely of a single operand (an important case) the tree consists of just one node, a leaf.

The significance of this tree representation is threefold.

(i) Tree are easy to visualise.
(ii) Because it is one structure it is easier to process than a series of smaller structures such as the simple assignments.
(iii) A left-to-right encoding is possible.

The tree is, of course, very closely related to the equivalent simple assignments and the procedure for producing these assignments as given in section 4.3, can be simply modified to produce the tree.

Instead of producing an assignment at each stage we produce a node of the tree, inserting in the reduced string a reference to the node instead of the name of a temporary variable.

The algorithm becomes:

(i) Move from left to right through the string until a right bracket is met. It will be preceded by a left bracket and two quantities (each being either an operand or a reference to a node already created) separated by an operator.
(ii) Output the node formed by the operator and the two quantities.
(iii) Replace the five symbols in the string by a reference to the node.
(iv) If the expression is not exhausted return to (i) above.

For the integration expression:

$$h*(f0 + 4{\cdot}0*f1 + f2)/3{\cdot}0$$

this produces the tree of Fig. 4.3 (iii).

4.8 Code generation from a binary tree

There are a number of ways of generating code from a binary tree. We will give an algorithm which processes the tree from left to right. It will produce code which evaluates, in the specified register, the expression represented by the tree. This is the simplest way. In section 4.10 we will show how the tree can be transformed, so that this simple left-to-right algorithm produces optimised code.

The algorithm is best described by an Algol procedure. We will expand the capabilities of Algol in an informal (but obvious) way to deal with structures such as a tree. [In Algol 68 there would be no problem.] We introduce a new 'type', *tree*, which consists of three elements: left branch, datum, right branch. The branches refer to further trees which may be leaves. In this and subsequent procedures we sometimes include redundant if-clauses for readability reasons.

```
procedure encode (register, operation, expr, n);
string register, operation; tree expr; integer n;
    if datum is an operand then compile (register, operation,
                                                        datum)
    else if datum is an operator then
        begin
        if operation is '=' then
            begin
            encode (register, '=', left branch, n);
            encode (register, datum, right branch, n)
            end
        else begin
            compile (register, '⇒', δn);
            encode (register, '=', left branch, n + 1);
            encode (register, datum, right branch, n + 1);
            compile (register, reverse (operation), δn)
            end
        end
```

The **integer** n is concerned with the allocation of temporary variables. Fig. 4.4 illustrates the application of the algorithm to the tree of Fig. 4.3 (iii) (the integration expression), assuming the call:

encode ('AFL', '=', tree, 0)

At each node are placed, in braces, the values of the other three parameters, when a call is made with that node as the root. Code produced at a node is indicated by an arrow, ⇒, and is underlined. The distortion of this particular tree enables the code to be read

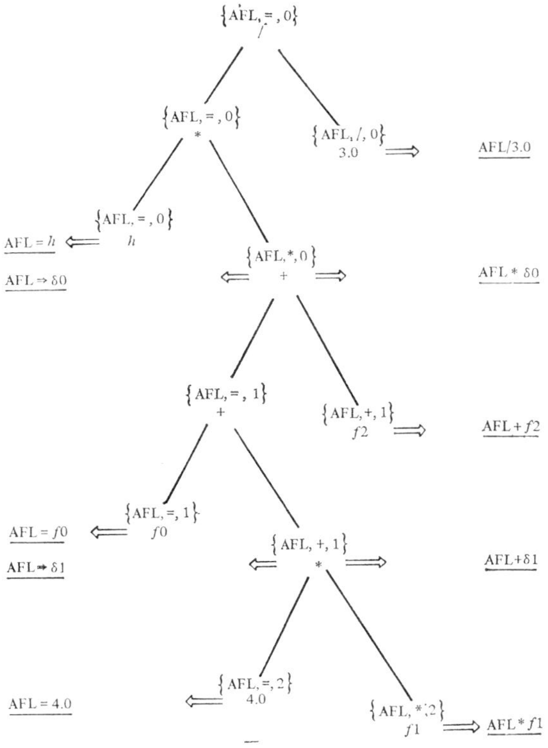

Fig. 4.4. Encoding from the tree for $h*(f0 + 4{\cdot}0*f1 + f2)/3{\cdot}0$

from top-to-bottom down the left-hand side, followed by bottom-to top up the right-hand side.

The compile procedure would include checks on the operand, both for its being declared and for consistency of type, as well as actually compiling the appropriate order.

Note that the tree is processed in a different order from that in which it is produced and so the separation of the two phases is natural.

4.9 Allocation of temporary variables

It is interesting to note the way in which this algorithm allocates the temporary variables. Fig. 4.5 shows a skeleton of a general tree in

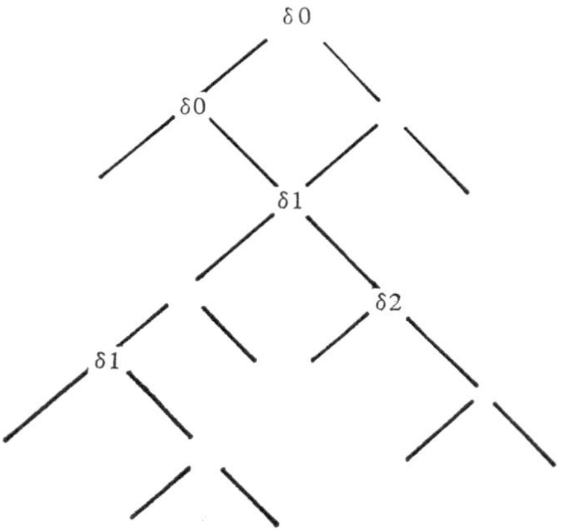

Fig. 4.5. Allocation of temporary variables

which the leaves have been omitted and the operator at the node has been replaced by the temporary variable to be used to store the value calculated by the orders planted for its left branch.

Within the object code the δs will appear in a nested structure. Because of this the temporary variables can be stored at run time in a stack if such a structure is maintained either by software or hardware. [We discuss this further in section 11.4.]

4.10 Transformation of a binary tree

Perusal of the algorithm of section 4.8 shows that it is the right branch of a node which is important in determining the resultant code. If all right-hand branches refer to leaves then there will be no store orders compiled. Thus if any node has a left branch which refers to a leaf, and a right branch which does not, then the two should be inter-changed (i.e. they should be rotated about the node) and the operator at the node reversed. Fig. 4.6 shows the tree for the integration expression:

$$h*(f0 + 4{\cdot}0*f1 + f2)/3{\cdot}0$$

before and after transformation.

The encoding algorithm now produces the optimum code: the same code as produced by the simple assignments (Table 4.5).

The algorithm is again recursive:

```
procedure transform (expr);
tree expr;
     if datum is an operator then
               begin
               transform (left branch);
               transform (right branch);
               if left branch refers to a leaf ∧ right branch
                                         does not refer to a leaf then
                         begin
                         tree dummy;
                         datum := reverse (datum);
                         dummy := left branch;
                         left branch := right branch;
                         right branch := dummy
                         end
               end
```

We have encoded the tree in this algorithm from top to bottom, exploring the left-hand branch first. There are, of course, other ways of encoding it. The algorithm for encoding the simple assignments essentially encoded the tree in the order in which it was generated; Hopgood (see ref. 4.3) gives an algorithm which at some stages explores the right-hand branch first. As we have noted earlier we will always consider algorithms which operate from left-to-right. If re-ordering is allowed, we first transform the tree and then the left-to-right procedure produces an optimised coding.

This means that we write two simple procedures, one of which is always called (encode) and one of which may be omitted (transform). The alternative is to produce two encode procedures, one simple, one more complicated and call only one of them. We will illustrate this alternative in the next chapter.

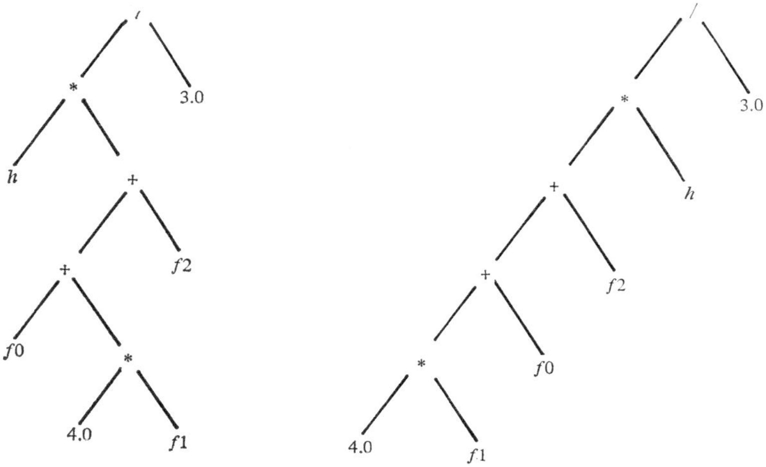

(i) (ii)

Fig. 4.6. The binary trees for $h*(f0 + 4{\cdot}0*f1 + f2)/3{\cdot}0$: (i) before transformation; (ii) after transformation

4.11 A precedence algorithm

We introduced the notion of precedence techniques by considering a fully parenthesised expression. Of course, expressions are not, in practice, fully parenthesised. However, it is relatively easy to decide where the extra parenthesis would go if inserted. To take the integration expression:

$$h*(f0 + 4{\cdot}0*f1 \ + f2)/3{\cdot}0$$

The operator * has higher precedence than + so that there would be brackets around $4.0*f1$. On the other hand, + has the same priority as +, and so the operator on the left takes priority. Hence, there would be brackets around $f0 + (4{\cdot}0*f1)$. And so on. The algorithm is quite easily modified to operate on these implicit brackets. It is convenient to assume that the expression is surrounded by the special brackets ⊢ and ⊣ which could be put there during lexical analysis as we have observed before. It is convenient but not essential: the algorithm could be easily modified to work without them. The classical way of implementing a procedure which processes its data 'from the inside out' is to use a stack. The symbols of the string are stacked one-by-one. When the algorithm determines that the three preceding symbols form a node of the tree, they are unstacked and added to the tree being constructed. The algorithm can be implemented using a number of different techniques. Fig. 4.7 gives, in flow diagram form, one using a *transition matrix*. Gries (see ref. 4.2) considers the alternatives in some detail.

This is a fundamental algorithm, and we will have cause to refer to it from time to time, updating it to deal with extra facilities.

Because the 'top-most operator of the stack' might be either at the top (if it is a left bracket of either sort) or next to the top (if it is a true operator), implementations often use two stacks, one for operators and one for operands.

As the matrix of Fig. 4.7 indicates the algorithm detects an expression which contains unmatched brackets. (The appropriate action takes place at label ERROR.) This is one of the strengths of the algorithm. It must be pointed out, however, that the algorithm as described performs no other checks. For example, an expression which contains consecutive operators or consecutive operands would be processed with curious (perhaps disastrous) results. The algorithm would, in practice, be modified to perform all the necessary tests. This is left here as an exercise for the reader. (This is not to say that it is unimportant. We have already stressed the problems of faulty programs.)

4.12 Unary operators

Real expressions contain unary as well as binary operators. For example, $-$ and $+$ can be used as unary operators; in Algol (and Fortran) the operator $\neg$ (.NOT.) appears in Boolean (logical) expressions; in Algol 68 it would be possible to define **sin** and **cos** as unary operators (instead of as functions as is more usually done). Within a binary tree, a node corresponding to a unary operator has no right branch.

For example, the tree structure for:

$$\mathbf{sin}\ x + \mathbf{log}\ \mathbf{cos}\ (x + y)$$

is given in Fig. 4.8.

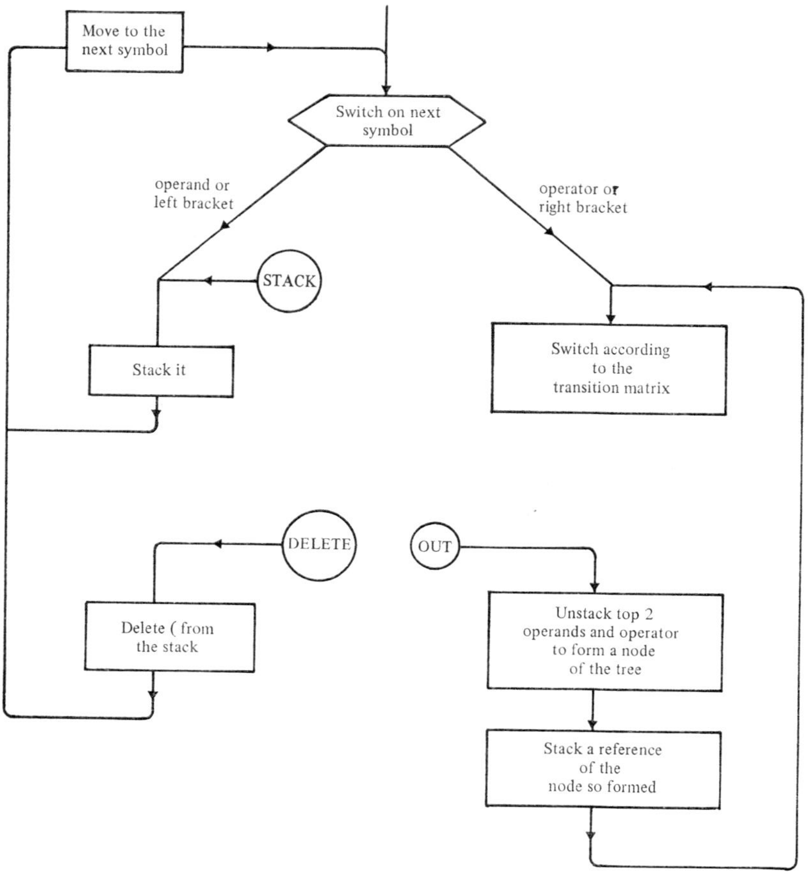

Operator on hand

Operator at top of stack	+	−	*	/	↑	)	⊣
+	OUT	OUT	STACK	STACK	STACK	OUT	OUT
−	OUT	OUT	STACK	STACK	STACK	OUT	OUT
*	OUT	OUT	OUT	OUT	STACK	OUT	OUT
/	OUT	OUT	OUT	OUT	STACK	OUT	OUT
↑	OUT	OUT	OUT	OUT	OUT	OUT	OUT
(	STACK	STACK	STACK	STACK	STACK	DELETE	ERROR
⊢	STACK	STACK	STACK	STACK	STACK	ERROR	END

Fig. 4.7. A precedence algorithm

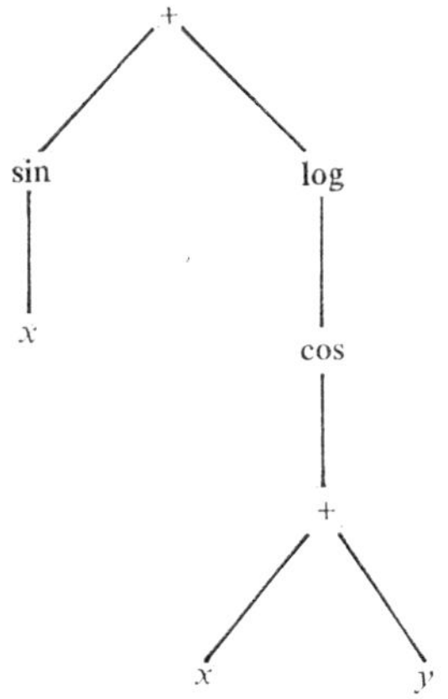

Fig. 4.8. Binary tree for **sin** x + **log cos** $(x+y)$

The algorithm can be modified to deal with unary operators relatively easily. We allow ourselves the liberty of calling the compile procedure with a variable number of parameters.

procedure encode (register, operation, expr, n);
string register, operation; **tree** expr; **integer** n;
    if datum **is an operand then** compile (register, operation, datum)
    else if datum **is a unary operator then**
        begin
        if operation **is** '=' **then**
            begin
            encode (register, '=', left branch, n);
            compile (register, datum)
            end
        else begin
            compile (register, '⇒', δn);
            encode (register, '=', left branch, n + 1);
            compile (register, datum);
            compile (register, reverse (operation), δn)
            end
        end

```
else if datum is a binary operator then
    begin
    if operation is '=' then
        begin
        encode (register, '=', left branch, n);
        encode (register, datum, right branch, n)
        end
    else begin
        compile (register, '⇒', δn);
        encode (register, '=', left branch, n + 1);
        encode (register, datum, right branch, n + 1);
        compile (register, reverse (operation), δn)
        end
    end
```

This is a fundamental procedure which we will continually refer to, expanding it, or indicating how it might be expanded to include further facilities.

It is convenient when producing the tree to be able to distinguish easily unary + and − from the binary + and −; and in practice the lexical analysis procedure could convert the unary operators to special symbols such as ꝏ and ∾ (or even delete the unary +). These unary operators can be easily recognised as they appear only in a restricted set of positions.

5 Reverse Polish notation

In this chapter we are going to consider a different form of internal structure—*Reverse Polish*. It is called Polish because it was first employed by a Pole, J. Lukasiewicz; Reverse Polish to contrast with a similar notation—Forward Polish. While we are going to consider Reverse Polish essentially as an internal form, it could well be used as an external form. Popplestone's POP-1 language was Reverse Polish though with POP-2 he reverted to the more normal infix notation. It is interesting to note that some modern pocket calculators such as Hewlett-Packard's HP35 use Reverse Polish.

Reverse Polish has lead to fairly significant changes in computer hardware. In the early 1960s, the English Electric KDF9 and the Burroughs B5000 were provided with hardware stacks. That is, instead of one accumulator, they have a *stack* of accumulators. Orders then are of two types:

(i) Store-access. These orders have a single address part (referring to the appropriate operand). On loading, the operand is put on the top of the stack, pushing down all the others. On storing, the value at the top of the stack is sent to the store, and the other quantities in the stack popped up.

(ii) Operation. These have no address (and so the machines came to be called *zero-address*). Unary operators operate on the top element of the stack, replacing it with the result. Binary operators operate on the top two elements of the stack, leaving the result at the top and popping everything else up.

Many of the more recent machines are provided with this hardware stacking either fully or partially. For example, DEC's PDP-11 can be used as if it were a stacking machine.

In a classic paper, Dijkstra (see ref. 5.2) has provided an interesting insight into the basic philosophy.

5.1 Reverse Polish

Reverse Polish notation is one in which the operator comes after its operands instead of between them.

Table 5.1 gives some examples.

Infix	Reverse Polish
$x + dx$	$x\ dx\ +$
$u + f*t$	$u\ f\ t\ *\ +$
$b \uparrow 2 - 4{\cdot}0*a*c$	$b\ 2 \uparrow\ 4{\cdot}0\ a*c*\ -$
$h*(f0 + 4{\cdot}0*f1 + f2)/3{\cdot}0$	$h\ f0\ 4{\cdot}0\ f1*\ + f2\ +\ *\ 3{\cdot}0\ /$
$w*L - 1{\cdot}0/(w*C)$	$w\ L\ *\ 1{\cdot}0\ w\ C\ *\ /\ -$

Table 5.1. Reverse Polish Notation

We sometimes talk of a *Reverse Polish String*. One characteristic of Reverse Polish is that it is parenthesis-free as Table 5.1 shows. Another characteristic which is more important for us is that the operands appear in the original order and this may be the order in which they have to be evaluated.

Because the operator appears after its operand this notation is also called *post-fix notation* or *suffix notation;* by contrast the usual notation is called *infix notation.*

5.2 Conversion to Polish notation

As we did in the last chapter when producing a tree structure, we will surround the expression with the special brackets ⊢ and ⊣. We will restrict ourselves to binary operators: unary operators are catered for in a straight-forward way. It is traditional to explain the conversion to Reverse Polish by the shunting-yard diagram of Fig. 5.1.

The principles are simple. The symbols of the source string move in from the right towards the junction. The brackets ⊢ and (go immediately to the siding. When an operand arrives it passes straight through the junction. When an operator arrives it pauses at the junction and looks at the operator which is at the top of the siding (i.e. nearest it). If the incoming operator is of the same or lower priority, the operator in the siding moves up to the junction and out to the left; the incoming operator looks at the operator now

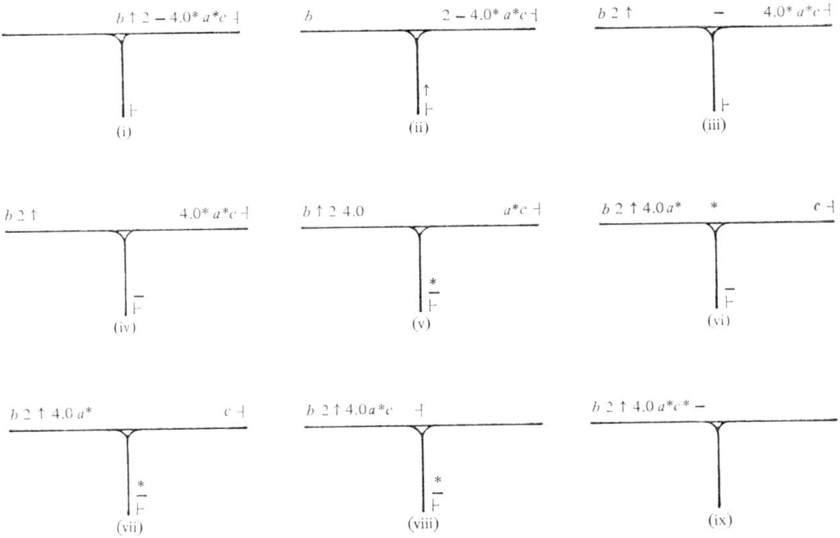

*Fig. 5.1. Conversion of b↑2−4·0*a*c to Reverse Polish*

at the top of the siding, and the step described in this sentence repeated. When the incoming operator is of higher priority than the top of the siding, it too is shunted into the siding. Since ⊢ and (appear in the siding, they must be given a low priority. Thus, the priorities are:

↑
* /
\+ −
(
⊢

When a) reaches the junction it causes all the operators in the siding back as far as a (to be shunted out and then both brackets disappear.

Clearly the siding can be simulated by a stack.

The algorithm is expressed in flow diagram form in Fig. 5.2.

As with the algorithm for deriving a binary tree, no checks are performed here to ensure that the expression is legitimate. Nor does it deal with unary operators. Both of these are left as exercises for the reader.

For the rest of the chapter we will continue to restrict ourselves to binary operators.

5.3 Code generation for a zero-address machine from Reverse Polish

As the preamble to this chapter suggested this is trivial. Consider the integration expression once again:

$$h*(f0 + 4{\cdot}0*f1 + f2)/3{\cdot}0$$

which in Reverse Polish is:

$$h\,f0\;4{\cdot}0\,f1* + f2 + *3{\cdot}0/$$

The reader who is unfamiliar with Reverse Polish is encouraged to verify this using the shunting yard and the algorithm of Fig. 5.2. If we assume a function LOAD which loads its operand onto the top of the stack, pushing down the current contents of the stack, the zero-address machine code is simply that of Table 5.2.

LOAD *h*
LOAD *f*0
LOAD 4·0
LOAD *f*1
*
+
LOAD *f*2
+
*
LOAD 3.0
/

Table 5.2. Zero-address code for $h\,f0\;4{\cdot}0\;f1* + f2 + *3{\cdot}0/$

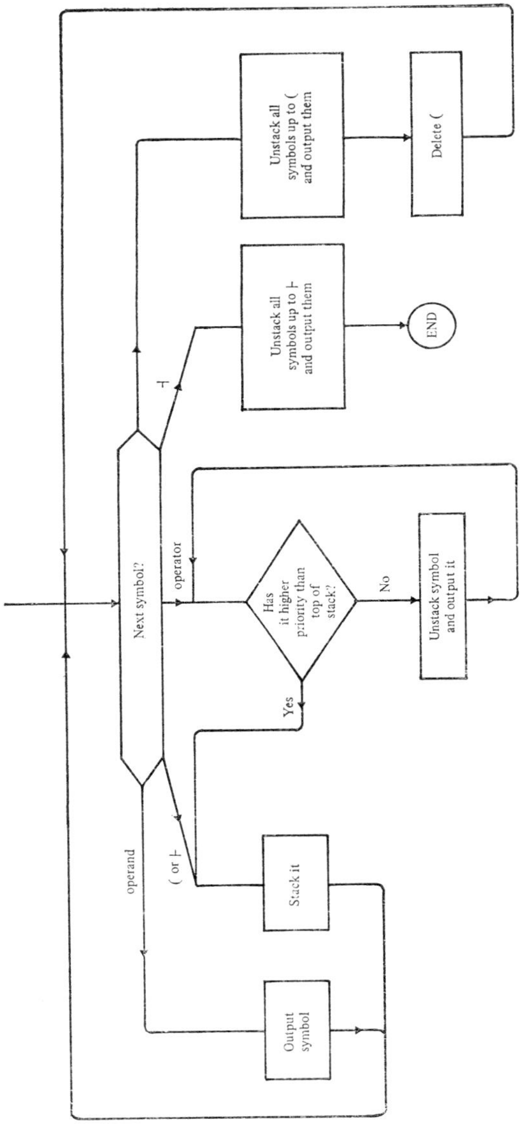

Fig. 5.2. Flow diagram for conversion to Reverse Polish

Clearly there is a one-to-one correspondence between the object code and the Reverse Polish. Indeed to all intents and purposes the Reverse Polish form is the object code. The operands are evaluated from left to right (as required if re-ordering is not allowed). Further (ignoring sub-expressions) the code is bound to be optimal since there is always one order per operand and one order per operator. Optimisation is an irrelevant concept except that for hardware reasons it might be preferable to limit the maximum depth of stack. (Here it is 4 because at one point we have $h, f0$, 4·0 and $f1$ all in the stack.)

5.4 Code generation for a one-address machine from Reverse Polish

We first consider the case where re-ordering is not allowed. The algorithm is a little more complicated than that for a zero-address machine. We first compile:

AFL = first operand

set a counter = 0 and move over the first operand. We then proceed along the string. At each stage one of three situations arises:

(i) The symbol is one operand followed by another. We compile:

AFL ⇒ δcounter
AFL = operand

add 1 to counter and move over the (first) operand.

(ii) The symbol is an operand followed by an operator. We compile:

AFL operator operand

and move over both operand and operator.

(iii) The symbol is an operator. We subtract 1 from counter, compile:

AFL reverse (operator) δ counter

and move over the operator.

The action of the algorithm is illustrated in Table 5.3 with respect to the integration expression.

h	AFL $= h$
$f0$	AFL $\Rightarrow \delta 0$ AFL $= f0$
4·0	AFL $\Rightarrow \delta 1$ AFL = 4·0
$f1$ *	AFL * $f1$
+	AFL + $\delta 1$
$f2$ +	AFL + $f2$
*	AFL * $\delta 0$
3·0 /	AFL / 3·0

Table 5.3. One address code for
*h f*0 4·0 *f* 1* + *f* 2 + *3·0/

It produces the same code as the other left-to-right algorithms.

5.5 Code generation for a one-address machine from Reverse Polish allowing re-ordering

We now consider an algorithm which re-orders the operands. It achieves efficiency without transforming the internal structure, and, therefore, it is rather more complicated. It scans through the Reverse Polish string seeking each operator in turn, since once it finds an operator it can find its operands. (They will immediately precede it.) It then reduces the string by extracting the operator and its operands and replacing them by a temporary variable. The algorithm is described below. First we set the counter = 0 and move to the first operator. It will be preceded by (at least) two operands.

We compile:

AFL = first operand
AFL operator second operand

and replace the operator and both operands in the (reducing) string by δcounter. The counter is incremented and we then proceed along the string in steps moving to each operator in turn. If at any step we pass more than one operand then we compile:

AFL ⇒ δcounter

and add 1 to counter.
Four cases arise at the operator depending on the operands that precede it.

(i) The three symbols are operand1 operand2 operator. We compile:

AFL = operand1
AFL operator operand2

replace the three symbols in the reduced string by δcounter and add 1 to counter.

(ii) The three symbols are operand δcounter-1 operator. We compile:

AFL reverse (operator) operand

and replace the three symbols in the reduced string by δcounter-1.

(iii) The three symbols are δcounter-2 δcounter-1 operator. We subtract 1 from counter and compile:

AFL reverse (operator) δcounter-1

(iv) The three symbols are δcounter-1 operand operator. We compile:

AFL operator operand

and replace the three symbols in the reduced string by δcounter-1.

The action of the algorithm is illustrated in Table 5.4 with respect to the integration expression.

The code produced is the same as that produced in Table 4·5 from the re-ordered equivalent simple assignments; and is equivalent to

Observation	*Case*	*Code*	*Reduced String*
Move to 1st operator		AFL = 4·0 AFL * $f1$	$hf0\ \delta0 + f2 + *3{\cdot}0/$
Move to +	(ii)	AFL + $f0$	$h\ \ \delta0\ \ f2 + *3{\cdot}0/$
Move to +	(iv)	AFL + $f2$	$h\ \ \delta0\ \ *3{\cdot}0/$
Move to *	(ii)	AFL * h	$\delta0\ \ 3{\cdot}0/$
Move to /	(iv)	AFL / 3·0	$\delta0$

Table 5.4. One address code for $hf0\ 4{\cdot}0\ f1* + f2 + *3{\cdot}0\ /$ *(with re-ordering)*

that which would be produced by the simple left-to-right algorithm for:

$$4{\cdot}0\,f1 * f0 + f2 + h * 3{\cdot}0/$$

which is, of course, the Reverse Polish of:

$$(4{\cdot}0*f1 + f0 + f2)*h/3{\cdot}0$$

5.6 Re-ordering a Reverse Polish string

The equivalence just noted suggests an algorithm for transforming the Reverse Polish string so that it can be optimally encoded using the simple left-to-right algorithm of section 5.4. This transformation has been investigated by Colin (see ref. 5.1) to whose paper the reader is referred if he wants further clarification. The transformation can be simply expressed: if an operator has an operand which is simply a variable, and one that is itself an expression, then they should be interchanged if necessary (reversing the operator) so that the expression becomes the first of the two. Thus in the integration expression:

$$hf0\ 4{\cdot}0\,f1 * + f2 + * \ 3{\cdot}0\ /$$

the operands of the first + are:

$$f0 \quad \text{and} \quad 4{\cdot}0\,f1\ *$$

They should be re-ordered so that the expression $4{\cdot}0\,f1$ * comes first. The same is true of the operands of the second *. If these transformations are carried out we get:

$$4{\cdot}0\,f1 * f0 + f2 + h * 3{\cdot}0\ /$$

As we have noted above the simple left-to-right algorithm will produce optimum code from this transformed expression.

What we are seeking in the transformation is a string which approximates as near as possible to an alternating sequence of operands and operators.

5.7 The relationship between binary trees and Reverse Polish strings

The re-ordering rule given above suggests that the binary tree and the Reverse Polish string are closely related. They are. Consider Fig. 5.3.

The binary tree for the integration expression has been distorted so all its left branches are much longer than its right branches. More precisely each right branch is shorter than the first level of the corresponding left branch. If the tree is projected on to the left hand margin, as shown, then the Reverse Polish results. From another point of view, the Reverse Polish results from an end-order traversal of the binary tree. Either way, as a one-dimensional projection of a two-dimensional tree or as a particular traversal of the tree, Reverse Polish is a less general representation than the binary tree. If the machine being compiled for is a stacking machine, then Reverse Polish accurately mimics its structure, and the loss of generality is not important.

Reverse Polish is useful, too, in other situations. Suppose that we are compiling for a mini-computer in which no hardware is provided to perform real arithmetic. The compiled program then must simulate this hardware: store locations to simulate the real accumulator (or stack of real accumulators), and procedures to simulate the instruction code. It turns out convenient to simulate a stacking machine because that separates out the functions of operand fetching from arithmetic. In this case, the integration expression:

$$h*(f0 + 4{\cdot}0*f1 + f2)/3{\cdot}0$$

which in Reverse Polish is:

$$h\,f0\;4{\cdot}0\,f1\;*\;+f2\;+\;*\;3{\cdot}0/$$

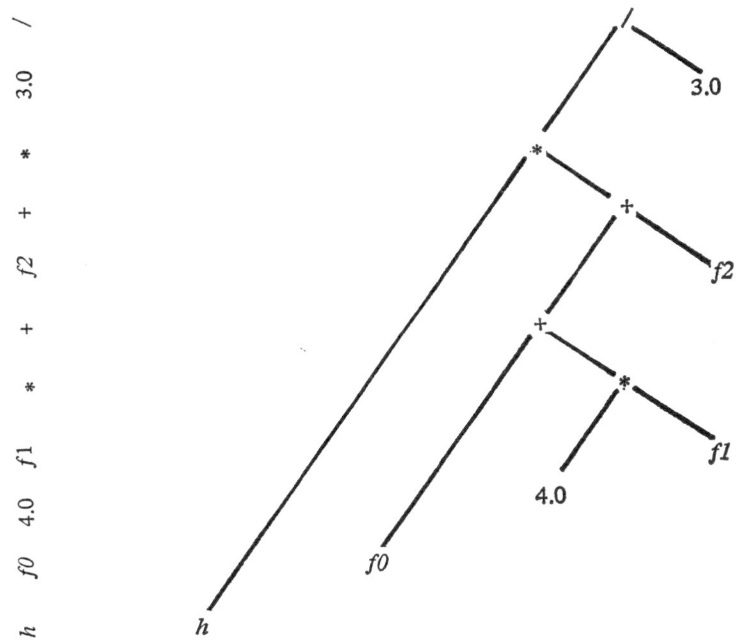

Fig. 5.3. The relationship between the binary tree and Reverse Polish string for: $h*(f0 + 4{\cdot}0*f1 + f2)/3{\cdot}0$

is effectively converted into the calls:

> fetch (*h*);
> fetch (*f*0);
> fetch (4·0);
> fetch (*f*1);
> mult;
> add;
> fetch (*f*2);
> add;
> mult;
> fetch (3·0);
> divide

Of course, this sequence could be compiled from the binary tree, as we have noted, by performing an end-order traversal.

6 A general tree structure

In this chapter we look at a much more general internal structure which allows all the possibilities of re-ordering. To see why consider an alternative way of evaluating Simpson's Rule:

$$\frac{h}{3}[f0 + 4f1 + f2]$$

This could have been evaluated:

$$h/3{\cdot}0*(f0 + 4{\cdot}0*f1 + f2)$$

The untransformed and transformed binary trees are shown in Fig. 6.1.

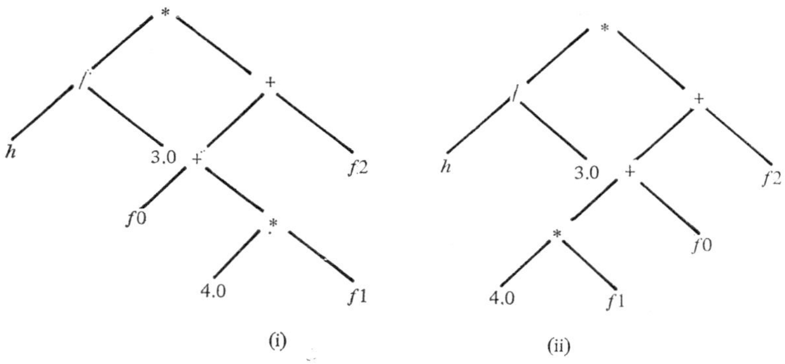

Fig. 6.1. Binary trees for h/3·0(f0 + 4·0*f1 + f2): (i) before transformation; (ii) after transformation*

The effect of the transformation is to convert the given expression into:

$$h/3{\cdot}0*(4{\cdot}0*f1 + f0 + f2)$$

The encoding of this clearly involves the (unnecessary) storing of $h/3{\cdot}0$ while evaluating the rest. Thus, the binary tree representation, including transformation, produces different (less efficient) code for:

$$h/3{\cdot}0*(f0 + 4{\cdot}0*f1 + f2)$$

from that produced for:

$$h*(f0 + 4{\cdot}0*f1 + f2)/3{\cdot}0$$

though the expressions are but different ways of saying the same thing.

6.1 N-ary trees

The essential problem with the binary tree structure is just that: it is binary. The (original) integration expression:

$$h*(f0 + 4{\cdot}0*f1 + f2)/3{\cdot}0$$

is regarded as the quotient of two quantities, on the one hand:

$$h*(f0 + 4{\cdot}0*f1 + f2)$$

and on the other:

$$3{\cdot}0$$

And the first of these is itself regarded as the product of:

$$h$$

on the one hand and:

$$f0 + 4{\cdot}0*f1 + f2$$

on the other. Thus, within the structure h is separated from $3{\cdot}0$.

An alternative interpretation of the expression is as the product of three quantities, h, $f0 + 4{\cdot}0*f1 + f2$, and $1/3{\cdot}0$, all of which are equally significant.

To adopt this interpretation we use a tree with a variable number of branches; we will call it an *n-ary tree*.

For example:

$$a + b + c$$

would be represented as:

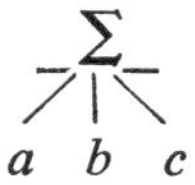

We will, however, use an alternative pictorial representation in which we foreshorten branches with leaves on them so that the leaves themselves appear at the node. This expression would then appear as in Fig. 6.2 (i).

With the n-ary tree it is convenient to regard a binary $-$ as a shorthand for $+-$, where this latter $-$ is a unary one. Thus:

$$a - b$$

is considered as:

$$a + - b$$

that is the sum of a and $-b$. Thus in this tree structure leaves may have associated with them a unary operator.

The tree for:

$$a - b + c$$

is given in Fig. 6.2 (ii). If any term is a product then the tree has a branch leading to a similar node which consists of quantities multiplied together. The tree for:

$$u + f{*}t$$

is given in Fig. 6.2 (iii).

In this context we often speak of *levels* rather than nodes. Fig. 6.2 (iv) contains three such levels: a π-level, followed by a Σ-level, followed by another π-level.

We also regard / as a shorthand for */ where this new / is an unconventional unary /; it gives the reciprocal of its operand.

Thus, we regard:

$$a \,/\, b$$

as $\qquad a \,{*}/\, b$

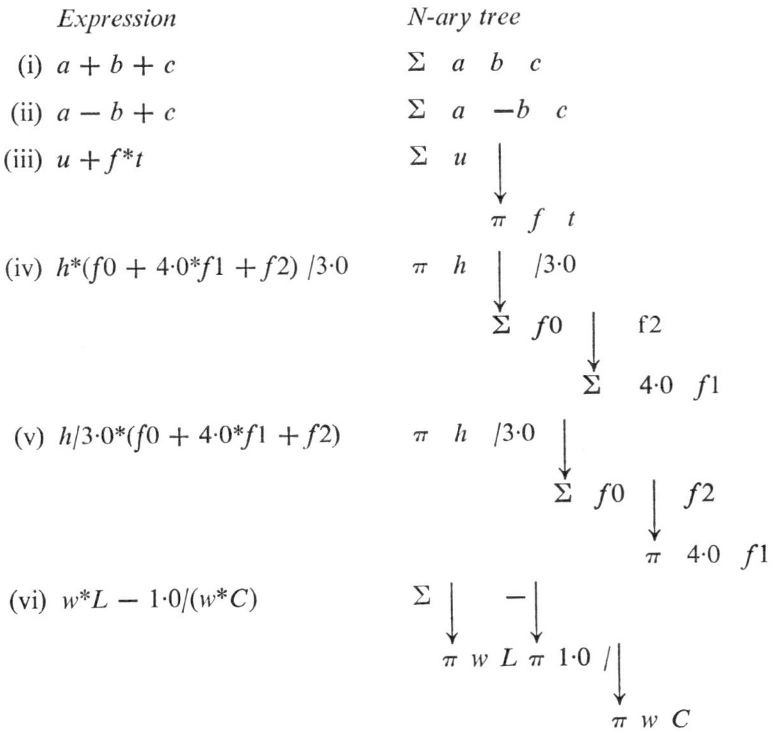

Fig. 6.2. N-ary trees for (i) $a + b + c$; (ii) $a - b + c$; (iii) $u + f*t$; (iv) $h*(f0 + 4{\cdot}0*f1 + f2)/3{\cdot}0$; (v) $h/3{\cdot}0*(f0 + 4{\cdot}0*f1 + f2)$; (vi) $w*L - 1{\cdot}0/(w*C)$

6.2 Creation of an n-ary tree

The creation of an *n*-ary tree is clearly closely related to the creation of a binary tree and the flow diagram of Fig. 4.7 is trivially modified. The changes are two-fold:

(i) The transition matrix is modified to ensure that consecutive operators of the same priority continue to be stacked. Unstacking takes place only when an operator of lower priority or a right bracket arrives.

(ii) The procedure for unstacking a node of a tree has to be generalised so that all operands or references to other nodes are unstacked and the negative terms appropriately marked.

6.3 Code generation from an n-ary tree

The encoding from the *n*-ary tree is also quite closely related to encoding from the binary tree. We merely extend the algorithm to process all branches, by an iterative loop. We would emphasise again that the algorithm processes the tree from left to right.

```
procedure encode nary (register, operation, expr, n);
string register, operation; tree expr; integer n;
    if datum is an operand then compile (register, operation,
                                                        datum)
    else if datum is an operator then
        begin
        if operation is '=' then
            begin
            encode nary (register, '=', left branch, n);
            while next branch exists do
                encode nary (register, datum, next branch, n)
            end
        else begin
            compile (register, '⇒', δn);
            encode nary (register, '=', left branch, n + 1);
            while next branch exists do
                encode nary (register, datum, next branch,
                                                        n + 1);
            compile (register, reverse (operation), δn)
            end
        end
```

In this algorithm it is understood that the operator referred to is a combination of the operator at the node (say + if it is a Σ-node) and the unary operator, if any, attached, to the operand (in this case the unary −).

It almost goes without saying that the algorithm produces exactly the same code as is produced from the binary tree.

6.4 Transformation of an n-ary tree

The reason for introducing *n*-ary trees is just that, since it gives a broader representation of an expression, it can be transformed in such a way that the encoding algorithm can produce optimum code. There are a number of transformations which can be performed. We will consider here the re-ordering of the operands. Note that this transformation (and some of the others) can only be applied after the tree has been produced and not during its creation.

All the operands at any level can be re-ordered at will. For the encoding algorithm to produce the optimum code, a simple re-ordering algorithm exists: if there is one operand which is a reference to a lower level it should be the first operand. We assume, for the moment, a simple interchange between the first operand and the 'complicated' one. In Fig. 6.3 we show how this algorithm would transform the trees of Fig. 6.2.

Again it is useful to talk as if the source string rather than the internal structure were transformed. We use the symbol ⇛ to mean 'is transformed to' as well as 'is compiled into'. Thus:

$$u + f*t \quad \Rrightarrow \quad f*t + u$$
$$h*(f0 + 4{\cdot}0*f1 + f2)/3{\cdot}0 \quad \Rrightarrow \quad (4{\cdot}0*f1 + f0 + f2)*h/3{\cdot}0$$
$$h/3{\cdot}0*(f0 + 4{\cdot}0*f1 + f2) \quad \Rrightarrow \quad (4{\cdot}0*f1 + f0 + f2)/3{\cdot}0*h$$
$$w*L - 1{\cdot}0/(w*C) \quad \Rrightarrow \quad w*L - /(w*C)*1{\cdot}0$$

Note that the alternative expressions for Simpson's rule both give rise to optimum code, though, because of the simple interchange used, they are slightly different.

This re-arrangement is likely to cause a unary operator (and its operand) to move to the front of its term in an expression, as the / has in the fourth example above.

This problem can be overcome by modifying that part of the encoding procedure which decides which operation a compiled instruction is to perform. The order now is defined by the type of node, the unary operator and whether or not there is an initial unary.

We will describe the technique for a π-node. There are two cases:

(i) If there is no initial unary then:

(*a*) For the first operand compile a load order.

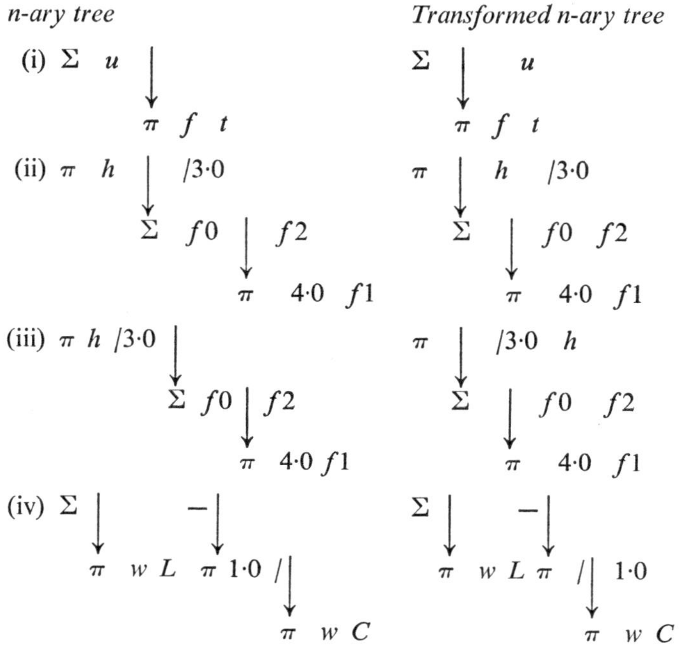

Fig. 6.3. Transformation of four of the n-ary trees of Fig. 6.2

(*i*) $u + f*t$	$\Rightarrow$	$f*t + u$
(*ii*) $h*(f0 + 4{\cdot}0*f1 + f2)/3{\cdot}0$	$\Rightarrow$	$(4{\cdot}0*f1 + f0 + f2)*h/3{\cdot}0$
(iii) $h/3{\cdot}0*(f0 + 4{\cdot}0*f1 + f2)$	$\Rightarrow$	$(4{\cdot}0*f1 + f0 + f2)/3{\cdot}0*h$
(*iv*) $w*L - 1{\cdot}0/(w*C)$	$\Rightarrow$	$w*L - /(w*C)*1{\cdot}0$

(*b*) For all subsequent operations if an operand has a unary operator compile a divide order.
(*c*) Else compile a multiply order.

(ii) If there is an initial unary then:

(*a*) For the first operand compile a load order.
(*b*) For all immediately following operands which have a unary operator compile a multiply order.
(*c*) For the first operand which has no unary operand compile a reverse divide order.
(*d*) Continue as in (*b*) and (*c*) of (i) above.

If we talk in terms of the equivalent transformation of the source string, and we consider first the transformation and then the encoding we have:

$$w*L - 1{\cdot}0/(w*C) \Rightarrow w*L - /(w*C)*1{\cdot}0$$
$$\Rightarrow w*L - w*C\phi 1{\cdot}0$$

There is a closely related algorithm for a Σ-node.

6.5 Unary operators

So far a unary — has appeared only as a result of our interpretation of the binary —. Of course, a (normal) unary — is treated similarly. Fig. 6.4 gives the n-ary trees for:

$$(-b + \text{disc})\ /a2$$
$$\text{and } (-b - \text{disc})\ /a2$$

The second example shows that the encoding algorithm above is incomplete. As it stands it would effectively transform the expression into:

$$(b + \text{disc})/a2$$

which is, of course, the negative of the answer. The solution is simple. If the expression is to be assigned to a variable (explicitly, in an assignment statement, or implicitly), and a 'store negative' order is available (i.e. one which stores the negative of the accumulator), it should be used. If not the expression must be explicitly negated by reverse subtracting 0·0.

Other unary operators (**sin**, **sqrt**) and so on give rise to their own levels (**sin**—level or **sqrt**—level). This level has of course only one operand. Fig. 6.4 also gives the trees for:

$$x + \textbf{sin}\ x$$
$$\text{and } (-b + \textbf{sqrt}\ (b*b - 4{\cdot}0*a*c))/(2{\cdot}0*a)$$

The reason for avoiding levels for — and / is just that orders exist on most machines for subtracting and dividing.

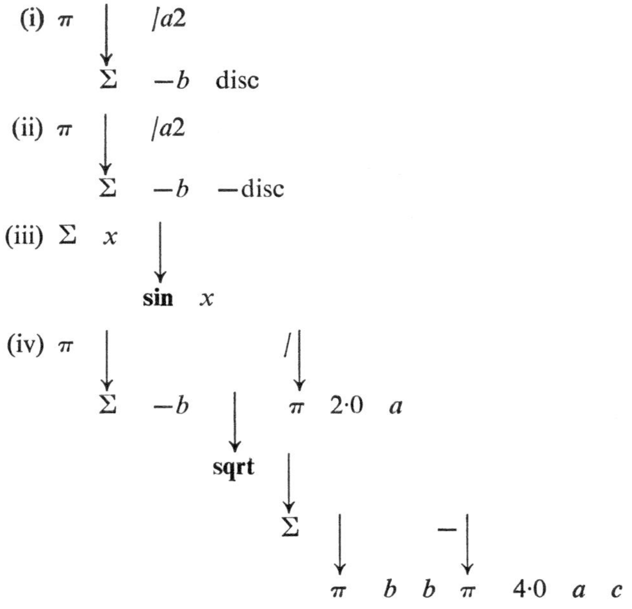

Fig. 6.4. Unary operators in n-ary trees: (*i*) $(-b + \text{disc})/a2$; (*ii*) $(-b - \text{disc})/a2$; (*iii*) $x +$ **sin** x; (*iv*) $(-b +$ **sqrt** $(b*b - 4{\cdot}0*a*c))/(2{\cdot}0*a)$

6.6 N-ary trees and Algol

We pointed out in Chapter 4 that Algol requires operands to be evaluated from left-to-right. We also noted that, provided there were no side-effects, the transformation of rotating a node is perfectly acceptable since the same numerical result is produced.

With the more general transformation we have introduced here this is no longer true. For example, if a and b are two large numbers of equal modulus but opposite sign and c is a much smaller number (say a factor of 10^p less, where p is the floating point precision of the machine) than evaluating

$$a + b + c$$
as $a + c + b$

will give significantly different results. [Whether either result is worth anything is not a question a compiler writer is allowed to ask himself.]

The definition of Fortran allows the compiler to perform this transformation even though different results are produced.

Algol on the other hand defines the evaluation to be left-to-right, and programmers are quite entitled to rely on this. As before, however, it is reasonable to give other programmers the benefit of this general optimisation. The only way this can be done is by asking the user to specify that such optimisation is allowed, since it is impossible for a compiler to tell which expression is sensitive to this re-ordering.

It is important to note that this problem is due to the *accuracy* of the floating point hardware. A similar problem exists in fixed point working due to its *range*. With a Boolean accumulator (see Chapter 7) there is no such problem.

6.7 An assessment of n-ary trees

There is no doubt that *n*-ary trees have a great potential since, because of their general structure, they allow the maximum optimisation to take place. There is, however, a price to be paid in the complexity of the algorithms especially when common subexpressions are to be catered for. For a compiler which seeks to provide the ultimate in optimisation then this form of tree will be a serious contender. The real question, however, is: how important is this degree of optimisation? There has been very little work done on this, so no answer can, as yet, be given. Intuitively though it seems that simple expressions are much more common than complicated ones in user programs, and Knuth's observations (see ref. 6.1) support this view, so that it may be that the simple optimisations obtained cheaply with the binary tree might well be adequate. Further, when a language allows a number of arithmetic types, the operations of addition and multiplication are defined as binary. We will generally use binary trees in what follows, making references to the *n*-ary tree only when it is particularly appropriate.

7 Booleans and conditions

We have spent three chapters exploring possible internal structures. As we shall see in this and later chapters they have a rather wider applicability than just to arithmetic expressions with scalar operands. We now return to our basic language and ease another restriction: the form of conditional facilities allowed.

7.1 Boolean expressions

Suppose that instead of being restricted simply to the relation between two simple operands we expand the form of the conditional statement to approach the full power of the Algol *Boolean expression* or the Fortran *logical expression*. We will ignore the Algol Boolean operators $\equiv$ and $\supset$, and restrict ourselves to $\wedge$ (.AND.), $\vee$ (.OR.) and $\neg$ (.NOT.). The relations themselves are between two expressions. Thus, we allow *Boolean expressions* such as:

$$x \geqslant 0{\cdot}0 \wedge y \geqslant 0{\cdot}0$$
$$b \uparrow 2 \geqslant 4{\cdot}0 * a * c$$
$$\text{height} \geqslant 1{\cdot}1*\text{average} \wedge \neg\,(\text{age} < 18{\cdot}0 \vee \text{age} > 65{\cdot}0)$$

We introduce at the same time the concept of the *Boolean variable*, declared, for example, by:

Boolean tall, under 18, over 65, tall adult

which can be assigned **Boolean** values in *assignment statements* such as:

$$\text{tall adult} := \text{height} \geqslant 1{\cdot}1*\text{average} \wedge \neg\,(\text{age} < 18{\cdot}0 \vee \text{age} > 65{\cdot}0)$$
$$\text{tall adult} := \text{tall} \wedge \neg\,(\text{under 18} \vee \text{over 65})$$

We assume that the machine can store and access Boolean variables, ideally using one bit per variable. The modifications to the procedure for dealing with declarations are trivial.

Further we will allow the full Algol conditional statement such as:

$$\textbf{if } P > P\text{crit} \textbf{ then } T := T\text{crit} \textbf{ else } T := T\text{calc}$$

Let us concentrate on the Boolean expression itself.

The interpretation of a Boolean expression is based, like that of an arithmetic expression, on the precedence of the operators. Since the Boolean expression includes the arithmetic operators we include them in the precedence table as shown in Table 7.1.

$\uparrow$
$*$ /
$+$ $-$
$=$ $\neq$ $<$ $\geqslant$ $\leqslant$ $>$
$\neg$
$\wedge$
$\vee$

Table 7.1. Precedence of operators

7.2 Internal representation

All three internal structures described for arithmetic expressions can be extended to cater for Boolean expressions as illustrated in Fig. 7.1.

The algorithm for the creation of each of these structures follows immediately from the similar algorithms for arithmetic expressions. For the binary tree, the algorithm of Fig. 4.7 is sufficiently general as it stands: only the transition matrix needs expanding in the light of Table 7.1; for Reverse Polish we need only update the precedence table; and for the *n*-ary trees the extensions are similarly trivial.

We will concentrate on the binary tree for the rest of the chapter.

7.3 Code generation from a binary tree with no relations

In order to deal with Boolean expressions it is convenient to introduce a new register, the Boolean register BN, with the appropriate operational orders. First, we consider $\wedge$, $\vee$ and $\neg$, together with load and store orders. We restrict ourselves, for this section only, to expressions containing only Boolean variables.

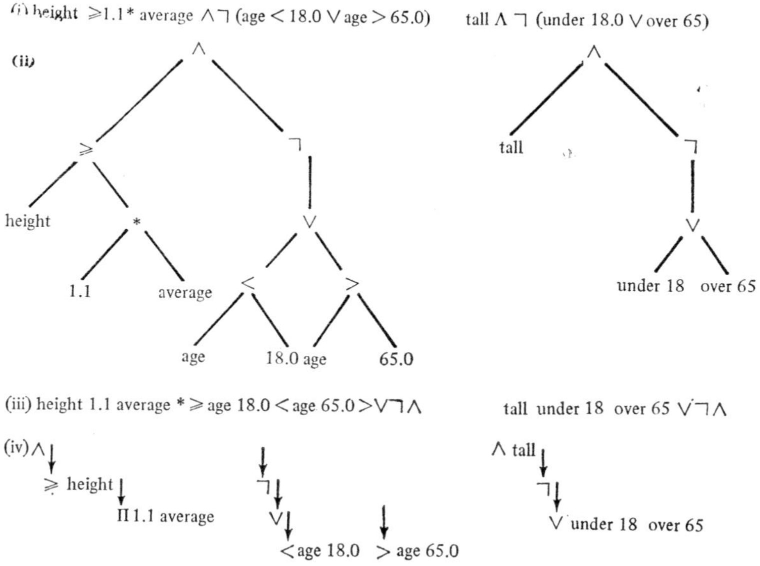

Fig. 7.1. Representation of source expressions (i) as: (ii) binary trees; (iii) Reverse Polish; (iv) n-ary trees

Given these orders, we can use the transformation algorithm and the left-to-right encoding algorithm of Chapter 4 as they stand. The effect of the transformation is simply:

tall $\wedge \neg$ (under 18 $\vee$ over 65) $\Rightarrow$ $\neg$ (under 18 $\vee$ over 65) $\wedge$ tall

The encoding algorithm would then produce the optimal sequence:

BN = under 18
BN $\vee$ over 65
BN $\neg$
BN $\wedge$ tall

Although it is not relevant here, we note that each of the operations $\wedge$ and $\vee$ is commutative and so its reverse is the same as itself.

7.4 Code generation from a binary tree with relations

Let us now consider the more frequent case in which, instead of Boolean variables, we have relations for the basic operands as in:

$$\text{height} \geqslant 1{\cdot}1*\text{average} \wedge \neg\,(\text{age} < 18{\cdot}0 \vee \text{age} > 65{\cdot}0)$$

whose tree is given in Fig. 7.1 (ii).

The transformation (rotating about the $\geqslant$-node) produces:

$$1{\cdot}1*\text{average} \leqslant \text{height} \wedge \neg\,(\text{age} < 18{\cdot}0 \vee \text{age} > 65{\cdot}0)$$

since the reverse of $\geqslant$ is $\leqslant$.

We have already introduced orders to effect the comparison. For example:

AFL = *x*
AFL COMPARE *y*

These cause the comparison register to be set appropriately. [In Chapter 2 we used orders which jumped on the state of this register.] There is also a reverse compare order, REV COMP, defined by the relation:

$$\begin{array}{l} \text{AFL} = b \\ \text{AFL REVCOMP } a \end{array} \equiv \begin{array}{l} \text{AFL} = a \\ \text{AFL COMPARE } b \end{array}$$

We now expand the address part of the orders available for operating on BN to include not only Boolean operands (as above) but also the state of the comparison register. For example:

BN = IF <

which sets BN **true** if the result of the previous comparison (as shown by the comparison register) was <; and sets BN **false** otherwise. Thus:

$$\text{age} < 18{\cdot}0$$

in the above would be compiled into:

AFL = age
AFL COMPARE 18·0
BN = IF <

Thus, the encode procedure must now discriminate on the type of node. In the following we have again inserted a redundant if-clause for clarity.

```
procedure encode (register, operation, expr, n);
string register, operation; tree expr; integer n;
    if datum is an operand then compile (register, operation,
                                                         datum)
    else if datum is a unary operator then
        begin
        if operation is '=' then
            begin
            encode (register, '=', left branch, n);
            compile (register, datum)
            end
        else begin
            compile (register, '⇒', δn);
            encode (register, '=', left branch, n + 1);
            compile (register, datum);
            compile (register, reverse (operation), δn)
            end
        end
    else if datum is an arithmetic or Boolean operator then
        begin
        if operation is '=' then
             begin
             encode (register, '=', left branch, n);
             encode (register, datum, right branch, n)
             end
        else begin
             compile (register, '⇒', δn);
             encode (register, '=', left branch, n + 1);
             encode (register, datum, right branch, n + 1);
             compile (register, reverse (operation), δn)
             end
        end
    else if datum is a relational operator then
        begin
        encode ('AFL', '=', left branch, n);
        encode ('AFL', 'COMPARE', right branch, n);
        compile ('BN', operation, 'IF', datum)
        end
```

This produces the code of Table 7.2, where we assume the rotation around the $\geqslant$-node referred to earlier.

```
AFL = 1·1
AFL * average
AFL COMPARE height
BN = IF ⩽
BN ⇒ δ0
AFL = age
AFL COMPARE 18·0
BN = IF <
AFL = age
AFL COMPARE 65·0
BN ∨ IF >
BN ¬
BN ∧ δ0
```

Table 7.2. Simple encoding of height $\geqslant$ 1·1*average $\wedge\ \neg$ (age $<$ 18·0 $\vee$ age $>$ 65·0)

[On many machines the orders typified by BN = IF $\leqslant$ do not exist, and up to four orders are required to do the same job. This makes a considerable difference to the size of code and reinforces some of the observations made in later sections.]

Perusal of this code shows some inefficiencies:

(i) If we rotate the tree about the $\wedge$-node then we no longer need to store BN in $\delta 0$. [The structure of the tree is essentially that of tall $\wedge\ \neg$ (under 18 $\vee$ over 65).] This implies that the transformation algorithm must be more sophisticated: it must treat as a leaf any branch of an $\wedge$-node or an $\vee$-node which points to a relational operator. We leave this as an exercise for the reader.

(ii) We unnecessarily reload AFL with age before comparing it with 65·0. We have discussed how this redundant order may be deleted in Chapter 2 and will return to it in Chapter 9.

(iii) We can utilise DeMorgan's Laws:

$$\neg (p \wedge q) \equiv \neg p \vee \neg q$$
$$\neg (p \vee q) \equiv \neg p \wedge \neg q$$

If the operands p and q are Boolean variables these laws are of no help since they actually introduce another operation. If the operands are both relations on the other hand, it is possible to absorb the $\neg$ by negating the relational operators. Table 7.3 gives the relational operators with their reverses and their negatives.

Operator	*Reverse*	*Negative*
$=$	$=$	$\neq$
$\neq$	$\neq$	$=$
$<$	$>$	$\geqslant$
$\geqslant$	$\leqslant$	$<$
$>$	$<$	$\leqslant$
$\leqslant$	$\geqslant$	$>$

Table 7.3. Relational operators with their reverses and negatives

Thus, we can transform:

$$\neg\,(\text{age} < 18{\cdot}0 \vee \text{age} > 65{\cdot}0)$$

into:

$$\text{age} \geqslant 18{\cdot}0 \wedge \text{age} \leqslant 65{\cdot}0$$

These three techniques lead to the optimal code of Table 7.4.

```
AFL = age
AFL  COMPARE 18·0
BN = IF ⩾
AFL  COMPARE 65·0
BN ∧ IF ⩽
AFL = 1·1
AFL * average
AFL  COMPARE height
BN ∧ IF ⩽
```

Table 7.4. Optimal coding of height $\geqslant$ 1·1*average $\wedge\ \neg$ (age $<$ 18·0 $\vee$ age $>$ 65·0)

It is interesting to reflect on the extent of the transformation.

$$\text{height} \geqslant 1{\cdot}1{*}\text{average} \wedge \neg\,(\text{age} < 18{\cdot}0 \vee \text{age} > 65{\cdot}0)$$

has been effectively transformed to:

$$\text{age} \geqslant 18{\cdot}0 \wedge \text{age} \leqslant 65{\cdot}0 \wedge 1{\cdot}1{*}\text{average} \leqslant \text{height}$$

7.5 Conditional statements

More often than not, Boolean expressions are used in conditional statements. We discuss these now before we go on to discuss an alternative approach to Booleans. Suppose we introduce a conditional statement of the form:

<conditional statement> :: = <if clause> **then** <statement1> **else** <statement2>

where:

<if clause> :: = **if** <Boolean expression>

This is compiled as:

```
     if ¬ <Boolean expression> then go to λ0;
     <statement1>;
     go to λ1;
λ0:  <statement2>;
λ1:
```

So the compiler will need to create some temporary labels as previously it has created some temporary variables. We will use λ0, λ1, . . . for these labels.

We introduce two further orders which jump on the state of the Boolean register typified by:

```
IF BN JUMP end
IF NOT BN JUMP λ0
```

Thus, the statement:

if tall ∧ ¬ (under 18 ∨ over 65) **then** total1 := total1 + weight
else total2 := total2 + weight

is considered:

```
        if ¬ (tall ∧ ¬ (under 18 ∨ over 65)) then go to λ0;
        total1 := total1 + weight;
        go to λ1;
    λ0: total2 := total2 + weight;
    λ1:
```

and compiled (after rotation about the ∧-node):

```
        BN = under 18
        BN ∨ over 65
        BN ¬
        BN ∧ tall
        IF NOT BN JUMP λ0
        AFL = total1
        AFL + weight
        AFL ⇒ total1
        JUMP λ1
    λ0: AFL = total2
        AFL + weight
        AFL ⇒ total2
    λ1:
```

If either of the statements is a go to statement then the coding is modified to avoid jumping to a jump order.

For example:

if tall ∧ ¬ (under 18 ∨ over 65) **then go to** pass 1 **else** total := total + weight

should be treated as:

if tall ∧ ¬ (under 18 ∨ over 65) **then go to** pass 1; total := total + weight

[It would probably have been better to write it this way in the first place if it had to be written at all.] This is compiled, of course, into:

```
BN = under 18
BN ∨ over 65
BN ¬
BN ∧ tall
```

```
IF BN JUMP pass 1
AFL = total
AFL + weight
AFL ⇒ total
```

The omission of an else-clause is dealt with in a fairly obvious way in both cases, and we leave all these as exercises.

The second statement can itself be conditional and so may require its own labels. The whole procedure, then, must have as a parameter the number of the first of the two labels.

The introduction of the conditional statement has meant, as some of our examples show, that statements often now need more than one line, so that a statement-by-statement compiler is no longer a line-by-line one. Consequently, the read-a-line process of the compiler must be replaced by a procedure which reads enough lines to include a statement (into an expanded source line area). This can be trivially done by making it read lines until it finds one with a semicolon or **end** in it. Once we do this we can trivially allow more than one statement to a line. Both of these relaxations we now assume.

[It is possible to define a language in which semantically similar facilities are allowed and which can be compiled line-by-line. We will not go into the question here beyond noting that Fortran achieves this with loops (see section 9.10) and could easily be upgraded to allow conditional facilities. We will continue to expand our language in an Algol-like way.]

7.6 An alternative encoding

The $\wedge$ and $\vee$ operations have particularly simple characteristics. For example, using the symbol $\emptyset$ to stand for **true** or **false**.

$$\textbf{true} \vee \emptyset = \textbf{true}$$

Thus, if the first operand is **true**, there is no point evaluating the second, since the value of the total expression is that of the first operand.

Similarly:

$$\textbf{false} \vee \emptyset = \emptyset$$

and so if the first operand is **false** there is no point storing it while evaluating the second operand, since the value of the total expression is that of the second operand.

Similar observations can be made about $\wedge$ since:

true $\wedge\ \emptyset = \emptyset$
false $\wedge\ \emptyset =$ **false**

We can take advantage of this to avoid unnecessary computation at run time by altering the encoding which takes place at $\wedge$- and $\vee$-nodes.

We use the $\vee$-node as an example, and consider first the general case. With the current algorithm we:

compile ('BN', '⇒', δn)
encode ('BN', '=', left branch, n + 1)
encode ('BN', '$\vee$', right branch, n + 1)
compile ('BN', reverse (operation), δn)

In the light of the above we could, instead, use the following approach:

encode ('BN', '=', left branch, n)
compile ('IF', 'BN', 'JUMP', λ1)
encode ('BN', '=', right branch, n)
label next order (λ1)

This resulting sequence is statically shorter. Even if both branches have to be evaluated at run time it is dynamically faster; and if the evaluation of the right branch is avoided it can be significantly faster, expecially if that branch is in any sense complicated.

In the simpler case, where the expression is to be loaded into BN, instead of:

encode ('BN', '=', left branch, n)
encode ('BN', '$\vee$', right branch, n)

we could:

encode ('BN', '=', left branch, n)
compile ('IF', 'BN', 'JUMP', λ1)
encode ('BN', '=', right branch, n)
label next order (λ1)

Statically, this sequence is one order longer. Dynamically, it may be one order slower (if both branches have to be evaluated) though, if the right-hand branch is complicated (a function call, say) and is skipped, it can be significantly faster.

Similar changes are required at the $\wedge$-node.

Note that this produces a nested structure of jumps since encoding a left or right branch is done in an exactly similar way to that of its parent node.

For example, the expression:

tall $\wedge$ thin $\vee$ short $\wedge$ fat

whose tree is given in Fig. 7.2 (i) would be compiled:

```
     BN = tall
     IF NOT BN JUMP λ1
     BN = thin
λ1:  IF BN JUMP λ0
     BN = short
     IF NOT BN JUMP λ0
     BN = fat
λ0:
```

Perusal of the chain of jump orders shows that this code still has inefficiencies, which we will return to in section 7.7.

The re-ordering rule we have been using for binary trees: rotating a subtree around its node, if necessary, to put a leaf on the right branch, is concerned with eliminating redundant store and load orders. Since this new algorithm avoids storing, the rule is no longer relevant. Indeed since it is the code of the right branch that may be skipped at run time, the rule should be reversed!

We have illustrated this algorithm with respect to Boolean operands; it is equally valid, of course, for operands which are relations, and the potential gains are greater because of the evaluation of the relations.

Consider the expression:

height $>$ 6·0 $\wedge$ weight $<$ 10·5 $\vee$ height $<$ 5·5 $\wedge$ weight $>$ 12·0

which is closely related to the previous example. Its tree is given in Fig. 7.2 (ii).

The code produced would be:

```
     AFL = height
     AFL COMPARE 6·0
     BN = IF >
     IF NOT BN JUMP λ1
     AFL = weight
     AFL COMPARE 10·5
     BN = IF <
λ1:  IF BN JUMP λ0
     AFL = height
     AFL COMPARE 5·5
     BN = IF <
     IF NOT BN JUMP λ0
     AFL = weight
     AFL COMPARE 12·0
     BN = IF >
λ0:
```

We notice, as well as the jumps to tests which cannot possibly be true, that there are pairs of orders which first of all set BN after a comparison and then jump on the state of BN. There is a set of orders which jump on the state of the comparison register directly. Since Boolean expressions occur far more frequently in conditional statements or conditional expressions than in Boolean assignments we ask whether the Boolean register is required at all. In the next section we illustrate a technique to overcome these last two problems.

7.7 The conditional approach

Let us concentrate on conditional statements, and to underline this fact we will call the Boolean expression a condition. The construct:

if <condition> **then** <statement 1> **else** <statement 2>

we will compile as before into:

```
     if ¬ <condition> then go to λ0;
     <statement1>;
     go to λ1;
λ0:  <statement2>;
λ1:
```

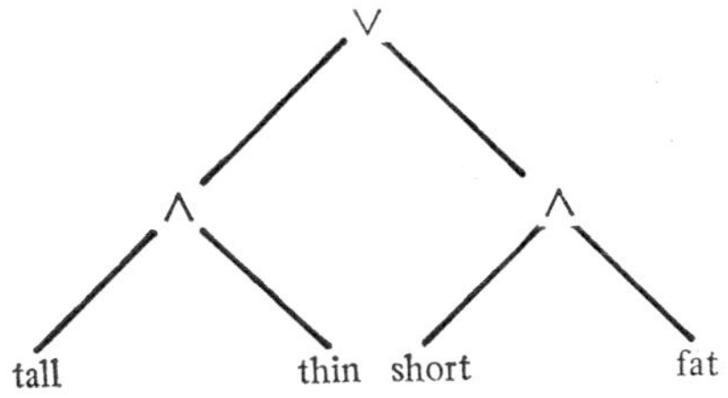

(i)

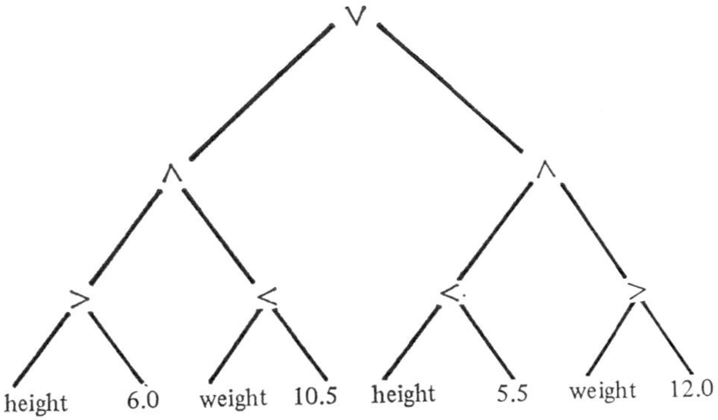

(ii)

Fig. 7.2. Binary trees for: (i) tall $\wedge$ thin $\vee$ short $\wedge$ fat
(ii) height $>$ 6·0 $\wedge$ weight $<$ 10·5 $\vee$ height $<$ 5·5 $\wedge$ weight $>$ 12·0

The problem then is to encode the <condition> (from the binary tree structure), to jump to $\lambda 0$ **if false**. If the top-most node of the condition is an $\wedge$-node of the form:

A $\wedge$ B

then the encoding is simple: we encode A to jump to $\lambda 0$ if it is **false** and then encode B to jump to $\lambda 0$ likewise if it is **false.** The structure is illustrated in Fig. 7.3 (i).

The structure when the top-most node of the condition is an $\vee$-node is shown in Fig. 7.3 (ii). Note that if this node is:

A $\vee$ B

then we encode A so that a jump is made (to a different label) if A is **true**, not **false**. Since A itself might be an $\wedge$-node, or an $\vee$-node we need further structures which jump if the condition is **true**. These are given in Fig. 7.3 (iii) and (iv).

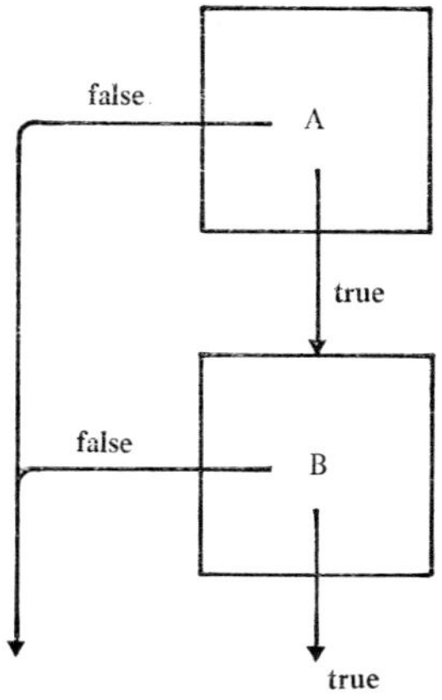

(i) A $\wedge$ B (jumping if **false**)

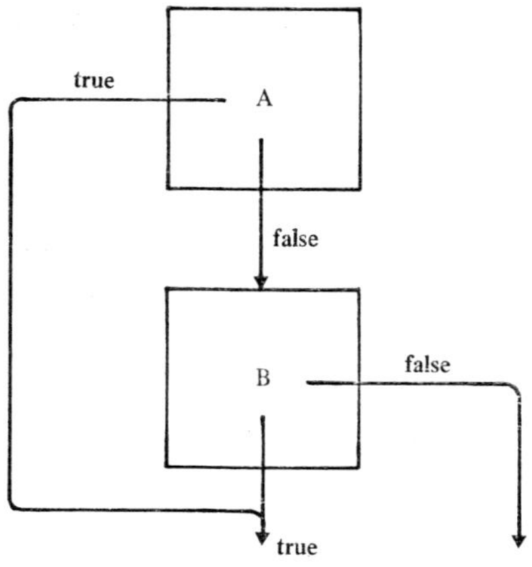

(ii) A $\vee$ B (jumping if **false**)

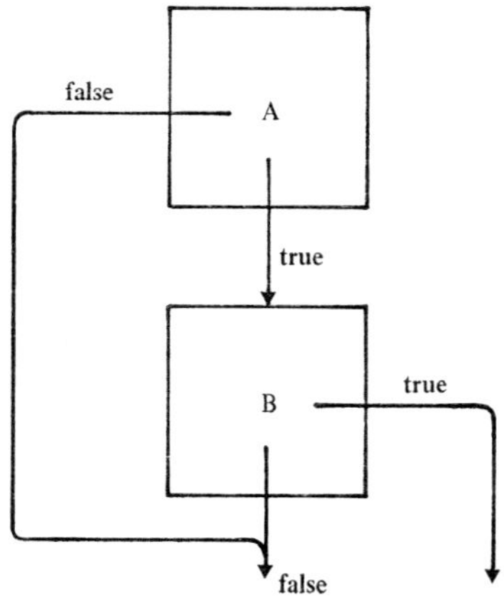

(iii) A $\wedge$ B (jumping if **true**)

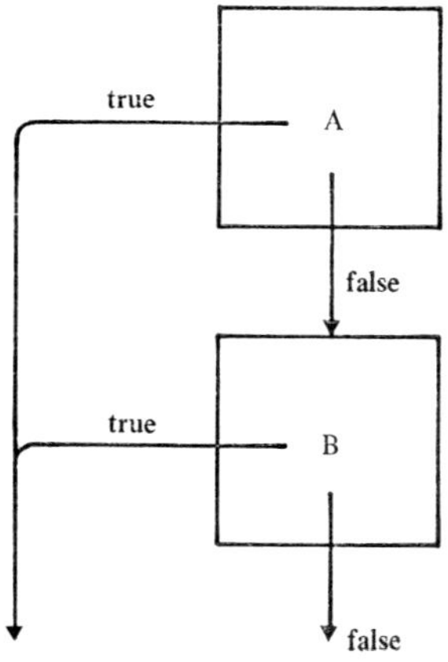

(iv) A $\vee$ B (jumping if **true**)

Fig. 7.3. Conditional structures

The expression of Fig. 7.2 (ii):

$$\text{height} > 6{\cdot}0 \wedge \text{weight} < 10{\cdot}5 \vee \text{height} < 5{\cdot}5 \wedge \text{weight} > 12{\cdot}0$$

is now compiled (jumping to λ0 if **false**):

```
     AFL = height
     AFL COMPARE 6·0
     IF ≤ JUMP λ2
     AFL = weight
     AFL COMPARE 10·5
     IF < JUMP λ1
λ2:  AFL = height
     AFL COMPARE 5·5
     IF ≥ JUMP λ0
     AFL = weight
     AFL COMPARE 12·0
     IF ≤ JUMP λ0
λ1:
```

Clearly although Boolean expressions are related to arithmetic expressions and so can be compiled by the same algorithm (the encode algorithm of section 7.4), when we consider them as conditions, the similarity begins to wane. We will give an algorithm for encoding conditions along the lines of this section in a moment, which will use the simple encode procedure as a subroutine to encode any arithmetic expressions. Clearly the encode condition procedure requires as its parameters:

(i) The address of the tree.
(ii) Whether the jump is to be on the condition's being **true** or **false**.
(iii) What label to jump to.

The ¬ node, which we have so far ignored is simply included. No code is planted; instead, when encoding the node which is its left (and only) branch, we negate the condition on which a jump is to be made.

The procedure is given below. We would call it initially:

encode condition (condition, **false**, 0)

to cause the condition to be compiled to jump to λ0 if **false**.

```
procedure encode condition (condition, true or false, l);
tree condition; Boolean true or false; integer l;
    if datum is an operand then
        begin
        compile ('BN', '=', datum);
        compile ('IF', if true or false then 'BN' else 'NOT BN',
                                                    'JUMP', l)
        end
    else if datum is a Boolean operator then
        begin
        if datum is '¬' then encode condition (left branch, ¬
                                                true or false, l)
        else if datum is '∧' then
             begin
             if true or false then
                  begin
                  encode condition (left branch, false, l + 1);
                  encode condition (right branch, true, l);
                  label next order (l + 1)
                  end
             else begin
                  encode condition (left branch, false, l);
                  encode condition (right branch, false, l)
                  end
             end
        else if datum is '∨' then
             begin
             if true or false then
                  begin
                  encode condition (left branch, true, l);
                  encode condition (right branch, true, l)
                  end
             else begin
                  encode condition (left branch, true, l + 1);
                  encode condition (right branch, false, l);
                  label next order (l + 1)
                  end
             end
        else if datum is a relational operator then
```

```
begin
encode ('AFL', '=', left branch, 0);
encode ('AFL', 'COMPARE', right branch, 0);
compile ('IF', if true or false then datum else
                     negative (datum), 'JUMP', 1)
end
```

The code produced by this procedure for the original Boolean:

$$\text{height} \geqslant 1{\cdot}1*\text{average} \wedge \neg\,(\text{age} < 18{\cdot}0 \vee \text{age} > 65.0)$$

is given in Table 7.5 where, again, we have assumed rotation about the ⩾-node and the ability to avoid reloading AFL with age.

```
AFL = 1·1
AFL * average
AFL COMPARE height
IF > JUMP λ0
AFL = age
AFL COMPARE 18·0
IF < JUMP λ0
AFL COMPARE 65·0
IF > JUMP λ0
```

Table 7.5. Encoding of height ⩾ 1·1*average ∧ ¬ (age < 18·0 ∨ age > 65·0) *treated as a condition* (*jumping to* λ0 *if* **false**)

Using this approach we transform a Boolean assignment such as

```
<variable> := <condition>
```

into:

```
    if ¬ <condition> then go to λ0;
    <variable> := true;
    go to λ1;
λ0: <variable> := false;
λ1:
```

7.8 An appraisal of the approaches

We will compare only the first (pure Boolean) and the third (pure conditional) algorithms. The second lies somewhere in between.

If we consider first of all size, then the number of orders compiled for the Boolean expression or condition is approximately equal under both techniques.

In most machines in use, however, there is no order equivalent to:

BN $\wedge$ IF $\geqslant$

which is central to the Boolean approach and quite often up to four orders are required instead (though coding tricks are often used to reduce this). In this case the Boolean approach when the operands are relations can produce quite an excessive amount of code.

If the Boolean expression, compiled as a Boolean, is used in a conditional statement, then a further order to test BN must be compiled. Conversely, of course, if the Boolean expression, compiled as a conditional, is being used in an assignment, extra orders must be compiled to load BN.

On balance then, it is probably preferable (from the point of view of the compiled code) to encode as a Boolean when the context is a Boolean assignment and the operands are Boolean and encode as a condition when the context is a conditional statement and the operands are relations.

If we consider speed, then the observations applied to size above are also relevant, as is the comment that the conditional approach is designed to avoid unnecessarily obeying parts of the compiled sequence. [But note that with machines which overlap or pipeline instructions, jump instructions can sometimes be very expensive indeed, and so it may actually be faster to obey unnecessary orders than to jump round them.]

Finally we should mention that it is impossible to tell at compile time which of the orders compiled under the conditional approach will be obeyed at run time. This places constraints on the over-all optimisation as we shall see later.

7.9 The conditional approach and Algol

We said in section 7.6 with respect to an $\vee$-node that 'if the first operand is **true**, there is no point evaluating the second . . .'. What we have done is transform:

if $\neg$ (A $\vee$ B) **then go to** $\lambda 0$

into:

```
      if    A then go to λ1;
      if ¬ B then go to λ0;
λ1:
```

So that if A is **true,** B is never evaluated. This, of course, is the point of the transformation. However, as we have seen with respect to arithmetic expressions, Algol places restrictions on the transformations that a compiler can perform. Algol specifies that the operands of a Boolean expression must, like those of an arithmetic expression, be evaluated from left-to-right. All the observations of section 4.6 are relevant. The observations of section 6.6 are, however, not relevant because Booleans are always accurately represented within a machine.

A new observation is relevant, though. The conditional approach seeks to omit the evaluation of operands—and accordingly may produce incorrect results in the case where the omitted operand is a function call which has side effects.

It is interesting to note that the conditional approach may cause incorrect programs to give 'correct results'. Consider the following Algol procedure (taken from a set of university lecture notes on the theory of computation) which purports to determine whether its argument is both positive and even:

Boolean procedure poseven(n); **value** n; **integer** n;
if n $\geqslant 0 \wedge (n = 0 \vee$ poseven $(n - 2))$ **then** poseven :=
true else poseven := **false**

[In the original, the body was phrased in terms of a conditional expression rather than a conditional statement.]

Clearly, this never terminates if evaluated, in accordance with the Algol Report, as a Boolean.

If evaluated using the conditional approach it is effectively transformed into:

```
Boolean procedure poseven(n); value n; integer n;
     begin
     if n < 0 then go to λ0;
     if n = 0 then go to λ1;
     if ¬ poseven (n − 2) then go to λ0;
λ1:  poseven := true;
     go to λ2;
λ0:  poseven := false;
λ2:  end
```

which gives (what I imagine to be) the desired result.

Of course, it is as important that a compiler does not give answers to an incorrect program as it is that it gives the correct answers to a correct program.

7.10 Conditional expressions

We now consider conditional expressions such as those of Algol 60; for example:

if $P \geqslant P\text{crit}$ **then** $T\text{crit}$ **else** $T\text{calc}$

This is essentially a ternary rather than a binary construct, since there are three operands, the Boolean expression, and two other expressions which we will assume, as in the example above, are arithmetic but which may well be Boolean. It is most naturally represented as an *n*-ary tree as in Fig. 7.4 (i), in which Γ represents a conditional expression.

It can be represented as a binary tree as in Fig. 7.4 (ii), though this is straining the concept a little. We will not consider this in depth; instead, we make a few pertinent observations.

Let us consider first the generation of the tree. The delimiter **if** does not appear in the tree. (The reader might prefer the **then**-node to be renamed **then-if**, but that is not the point.) The point is that there are two 'operators' (if we expand the conventional meaning of the word); one whose 'operands' are the Boolean expression and the first expression; and the other whose 'operands' are this result and the second statement. The delimiter **if** is quite redundant. If we modify the precedence algorithm of Fig. 4.7 to deal with conditional expressions we will have to include a sequence which will delete the **if** from the stack, as well as expand the transition matrix. We leave that as an exercise.

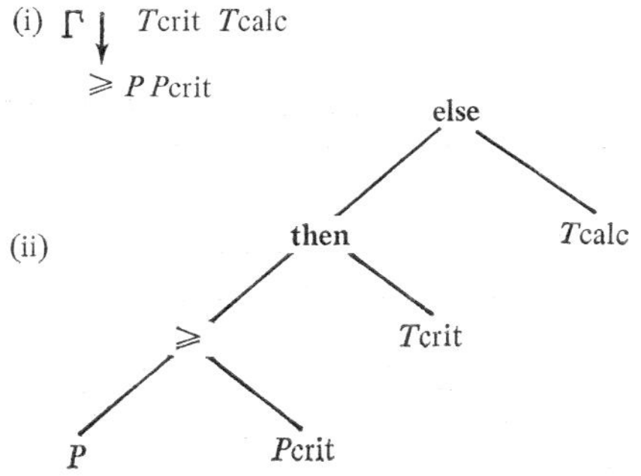

(iii) P *P*crit $\geqslant$ *T*crit **then** *T*calc **else**

Fig. 7.4. Representation of **if** $P \geqslant$ *P*crit **then** *T*crit **else** *T*calc as: *(i) n-ary tree; (ii) binary tree; (iii) Reverse Polish*

[We also note in passing that the **if** is quite redundant in the source language; no ambiguity would arise if it were deleted. It does have some mnemonic significance to a programmer though, and can be utilised by a compiler since any expression after an **if** must be Boolean. Further, if we allow the Boolean expression itself to be conditional as in Algol, then the **if** is no longer redundant.]

Now consider encoding from the tree. We would clearly produce code closely related to that discussed with respect to conditional statements.

if $P \geqslant$ *P*crit **then** *T*crit **else** *T*calc could be compiled into:

AFL = *P*			AFL = *P*
AFL COMPARE *P*crit			AFL COMPARE *P*crit
BN = IF $\geqslant$			
IF NOT BN JUMP λ0	or		IF < JUMP λ0
AFL = *T*crit			AFL = *T*crit
JUMP λ1			JUMP λ 1
λ0: AFL = *T*calc			λ0: AFL = *T*calc
λ1:			λ1:

The algorithms can be modified quite easily to do this—again it is left as an exercise. However, if we consider the first encoding above (the pure Boolean one), and consider that this expression could be part of a larger arithmetic expression if it were enclosed in brackets, then as we move from the top level of the tree downwards we find that the register required alternates AFL, BN, AFL and could go on indefinitely since the operands of the Boolean expressions could themselves be conditional expressions. Thus, the simple technique of section 7.4 for eliminating an unnecessary storing of BN fails. The simplest solution is to make a preliminary pass through the tree to determine what registers are required by the sub-trees of each node. This information can be used during the encoding to ensure no register is stored unnecessarily. Alternatively, we may adopt a completely different strategy. If we are about to compile an order which uses a register and if at run time that register will contain useful information we first of all compile an order to store it; later, when it can resume its original function, we compile an order to restore its value. This implies that we maintain a list of the states of the registers during compilation. It also means a fundamental change to the structure of the encoding procedure.

8 Mixed expressions and assignments

All the expressions we have used so far have been homogeneous in that all the operands are of the same type, generally **real**. It was this that obliged us to write 4·0 and 3·0 in the integration expression when we might have preferred to write 4 and 3 as in:

$$h*(f0 + 4*f1 + f2)/3$$

In this chapter we explore the problems that arise from allowing *mixed expressions*, that is expressions whose operands may be of different types. We also expand our view to include assignments.

8.1 Explicit type conversion

To confine expressions to be homogeneous does not affect the range of programs that can be written, though it can be tedious. Variables which ought to be of type **integer** have sometimes to be **real** (for example, counters which are used as operands within the loop); at worst, two variables have to be used, one **integer**, one **real**, both of which have to be kept at the same value. Consequently all real languages allow values of one type to be converted to associated values of another type. This can be done by means of *type conversion functions* (such as IFIX and FLOAT of Fortran and entier of Algol) or by *type conversion operators*. [Conceptually there is very little difference between unary operators and functions of one variable; in a compiler, though, operators are easier to handle.]

Suppose we expand our language to include two unary operators, **float** which converts an integer into a real and **fix** which does the reverse. Thus we allow expressions such as:

float nominal + 0·001
fix $(x/y) + 1$

The **float** operator is quite straight forward: it converts an integer into a real of the same value. We assume that our machine has an (operandless) order FLOAT which converts the integer in AFX into a real of the same value in AFL. Thus, the first expression would be compiled into:

AFX = nominal
FLOAT
AFL + 0·001

Likewise, our machine has a FIX order so that the second expression is compiled into:

AFL = *x*
AFL / *y*
FIX
AFX + 1

We have not, as yet, defined the meaning of the **fix** operation. Since it operates on a real variable which, in general, will not have an integer value there are three possible definitions:

(i) The value is rounded to the nearest integer.
(ii) The value is rounded down (towards $-\infty$).
(iii) The value is rounded towards zero.

This is not a compiler writer's decision: it is the language designer's. However, the compiler writer must be sure that he does implement a correct conversion, and if the FIX order in the hardware performs a different conversion, he must program his way round it. For example, if the **fix** operator is defined as rounding to the nearest integer, and the FIX order rounds down, then:

fix $(x/y) + 1$

would be compiled as:

AFL = *x*
AFL / *y*
AFL + 0·5
FIX
AFX + 1

The two operators **fix** and **float** fit neatly into all three forms of internal representation. Fig. 8.1 shows the binary trees for:

float nominal + 0·001
fix (x/y) + 1

The re-ordering algorithm is appropriate too. We would re-order:

1 + **fix** (x/y)

into:

fix (x/y) + 1

to avoid storing AFX (which would have 1 in it) while performing the FIX operation.

The encoding algorithm has to be expanded to include this new class of operator, the type conversion. It has the characteristic that the operator at the node (say, **fix**) determines the register (here, AFL) to be used in the code compiled for the tree which is its left branch.

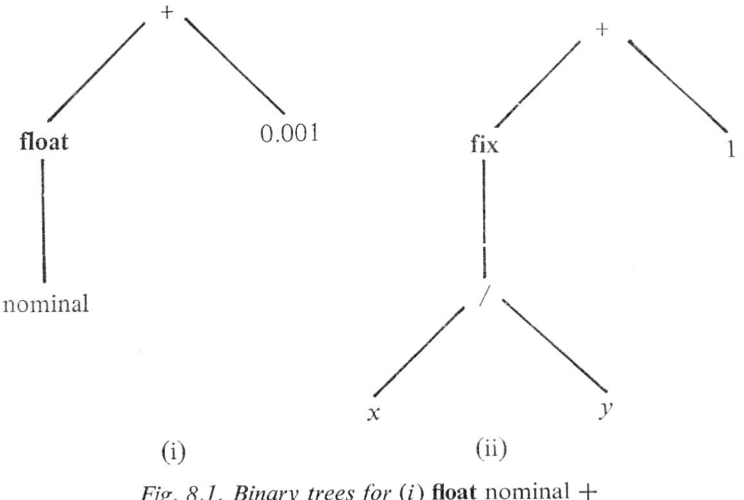

(i) (ii)

Fig. 8.1. Binary trees for (i) **float** nominal + 0·001; *(ii)* **fix** (x/y) + 1

There is no need, of course, to use type conversion operators to change the type of a constant; we merely write the constant in the correct form. We write:

1·0

say, instead of:

float 1

8.2 Implicit type conversion

Having to specify explicitly the type conversion operators is often considered tiresome especially when the operator could be deduced from the expression. For example, as we have already noted, it might be preferable to write:

$$h*(f0 + 4*f1 + f2)/3$$

instead of:

$$h*(f0 + 4{\cdot}0*f1 + f2)/3{\cdot}0$$

and:

$$x + i$$

instead of:

x + **float** i

Most languages allow this, the expressions then being said to be *mixed*. (One exception is Standard Fortran.) Let us expand our language in this way.

Two problems arise. First, the language designer's problem, which of the conversions is to be made implicit: **fix** or **float**? That both can't be implicit can be seen by considering:

x + **float** i
fix $x + i$

both of which would reduce to:

$$x + i$$

if both conversions could be implicit. In practice it is always **float** that is implicit (the class of integers being a subset of the class of reals); **fix** then must be explicit.

The second problem is the compiler writer's. Fig. 8.2 (i) gives the binary tree for $x + i$, as produced by the syntactical analysis procedure.

If x were of type **real**, and i of type **integer**, then the underlying tree is that of:

$x +$ **float** i

given in Fig. 8.2 (ii). If this tree were produced by the syntactical analyser it would, of course, be transformed to that of:

float $i + x$

given in Fig. 8.2 (iii) before encoding.

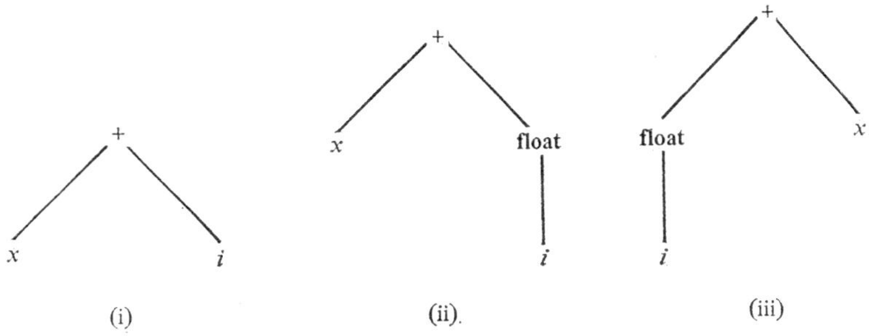

Fig. 8.2. Trees for x + i: (i) syntax tree; (ii) underlying tree; (iii) transformed underlying tree

Thus, to produce optimum code the compiler must contain another procedure between the syntactical analysis and transformation procedures to expand the tree as produced into the underlying tree. Note that this procedure is a semantic one (it needs to know the properties of the operands) whereas the syntactical analysis and transformation procedures are both syntactical ones. So mixed expressions cause the syntactical and semantic phases to become less separate than before.

Alternatively the compiler writer may decide (hopefully on a statistical basis) that mixed expressions are relatively infrequent, and accept the price involved in not producing the underlying tree, that is in failing to produce some simple optimisations. This is the usual solution since it preserves the separation of the syntactical and semantic phases.

8.3 Constants

We noted earlier that we do not use conversion operators for constants. The underlying expression for:

$$x + 1$$

is:

$$x + 1{\cdot}0$$

and both trees have the same structure. During the encoding the procedure has to take a diversion to access the constant 1 (using the pseudo-constant on the tree), float it on the spot, add the floated value 1·0 to the constants list, and proceed as if the pseudo-constant for 1·0 had been present. Note that this means that the encoding procedure updates the constants list, a function previously reserved for the lexical analysis procedure. Note, too, that the constants list, at the end of compilation, may well contain constants which are not used at run time.

An alternative approach is to modify the lexical analysis procedure so that any constant with an integral value is put on the constants list both as an integer and as a real value, the pseudo-constant being the index of, say, the integer value. The encoding procedure may then regard the pseudo-constant as referring to either value as appropriate.

8.4 Assignments

We have not considered assignments since Chapter 2; we now return to them. Their form is simply:

<variable> := <expression>

For example:

$$v := u + f^*t$$

The notion of assignment can be included within expressions (in all three internal structures) quite simply by considering := as an operator of the lowest priority. Fig. 8.3 gives the three structures for:

$$v := u + f^*t$$

We concentrate on the binary tree. The curious characteristic of the := -node is that the transformation procedure should always reverse its operands since we clearly must evaluate the expression before we assign. If we use ⇒ as the reverse of := we convert:

$$v := u + f^*t$$

into:

$$u + f^*t \Rightarrow v$$

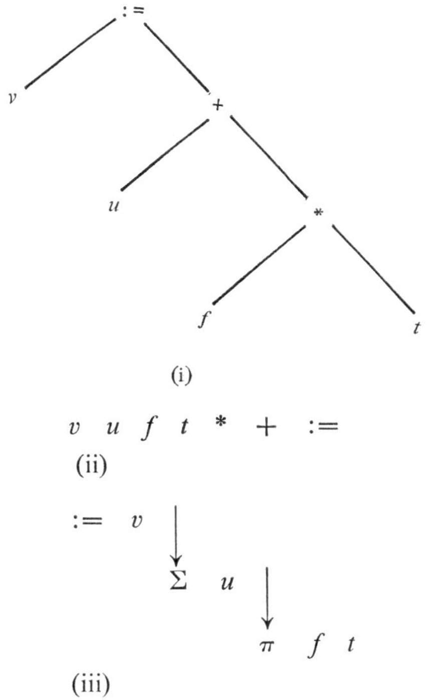

*Fig. 8.3. Representation of v: = u + f*t: (i) as a binary tree; (ii) in Reverse Polish; (iii) as an n-ary tree*

It has often been suggested that this be the form of the expression as written, though the suggestion has made little progress in practice.

Even where mixed expressions are not allowed, *mixed assignments* (assignments in which the types of the expression and the variable differ) almost always are. The value of the expression is merely type-converted before assignment. This causes no problems of optimisation because the assignment must be the last operation.

8.5 Types of expression

We have so far carefully avoided saying how we determine which register should be used when encoding a complete expression. The reason is simply that it depends on whether expressions are mixed or not, and, when we consider a large range of types, how the semantics of an expression are defined.

If expressions may not be mixed, the type of an expression is the same as the type of any of its operands, in particular the first. Thus the encode procedure may merely look at the first operand to decide which accumulator to use for the evaluation. [Remember that the encode procedure we have been using has been shorn of those parts which check for semantic errors, such as an operand's not having been declared, and operands' not being consistent.] Thus if an expression was meant to be say real, and, by mistake, its first operand was of type integer, then it would not be faulted but all the other operands would.

If expressions may be mixed, the problem is more complicated. The type of an expression is real if any one of its operands is real. [Note that in this context:

$$\textbf{fix}\ (x/y)$$

is of type integer, that being, of course, the purpose of the **fix** operator.]

A compiler then could scan the syntactical tree to determine the type of the expression; process the tree by inserting all the implicit **float** operators if appropriate, and then encode the tree. Thus, if i, j, k are integer and x real, the expression:

$$i + j + k + x$$

is of type real and is a contraction of:

$$\textbf{float}\ i + \textbf{float}\ j + \textbf{float}\ k + x$$

It is tempting to consider this as equivalent to:

$$\textbf{float}\ (i + j + k) + x$$

especially on a machine in which floating point operations are much slower than fixed point ones (such as those with no floating point hardware).

This leads us to an interesting new approach for the encoding procedure: it may start off assuming the type of the expression to be that of the first operand and use the appropriate accumulator, changing only if it has to. (That is, if it has assumed type integer and meets an operand of type real.)

Note that there is a subtle difference between:

float i + **float** j + **float** $k + x$
float $(i + j + k) + x$

It is possible for the latter to cause AFX to overflow when the former would not. Conversely, the former might be subject to rather greater rounding errors.

Again what a compiler writer is allowed to compile depends on how the language is defined and on what extra information the programmer is willing to provide.

8.6 Further types of variable

Most languages provide further types of variable: complex, double-length real and so on. When these are considered, the problems multiply. Should there be explicit type conversion operators between all pairs of types? Which type conversions are to be implicit? And so on.

If the language contains a hierarchical set of types such as integer, real and complex then a simple solution is possible: allow implicit conversion from integer to real, integer to complex, and real to complex; provide explicit operators for converting from real to integer and complex to real.

If the language contains a less convenient set of types (for example, integer, real, complex and double length real), a completely different solution is generally resorted to. So far the two operands of an operator have been of the same type, and the result was of that type, too. [An implicit type transfer function may have been inserted in some cases though.] The new solution defines in a tabular form the type of the result for all possible combinations of the operands.

Table 8.1 gives the table of the arithmetic operators (except exponentiation) for Standard Fortran.

First operand	Integer	Real	*Second operand* Double precision	Complex
Integer	integer	—	—	—
Real	—	real	double precision	complex
Double precision	—	double precision	double precision	—
Complex	—	complex	—	complex

Table 8.1. Standard Fortran table for arithmetic operators

As can be seen some combinations are not allowed.

Note that this solution leans heavily towards a binary tree structure (rather than an *n*-ary tree structure) as the internal form. The notion of a sum of a number of quantities no longer exists: it is replaced by the notion of a sum of just two quantities. This is a pity from the run-time efficiency point of view, limiting as it does the amount of optimisation possible.

On the other hand, the notion of implicit type conversions is removed and so the clear distinction between the syntactical and semantic parts of the compiler is retained. It should be said that although Fortran is defined in this way, it also allows expressions to be re-ordered at will as we have indicated in earlier chapters.

Even with this solution explicit type conversion operators are required: Fortran allows those given in Table 8.2 (or, more precisely, the type conversion function equivalents):

Function	*Conversion*	*Comment*
IFIX	real → integer	rounding towards 0
SNGL	double precision → real	taking the most significant part
REAL	complex → real	taking the real part
AIMAG	complex → real	taking the imaginary part
FLOAT	integer → real	
DBLE	real → double precision	
CMPLX	real → complex	

Table 8.2. Fortran explicit conversion functions

The meaning of mixed assignments has to be specified, too. This is often in tabular form. Table 8.3 refers to Standard Fortran.

	Type of expression			
Type of variable	Integer	Real	Double Precision	Complex
Integer	assign	IFIX, assign	REAL, IFIX, assign	—
Real	FLOAT, assign	assign	SNGL, assign	—
Double precision	FLOAT, DBLE, assign	DBLE, assign	assign	—
Complex	—	—	—	assign

Table 8.3. Fortran assignments

This notion can be extended to provide a table like that of Table 8.1 for each operator or groups of operators. Table 8.4 gives a table for division from the definition of Algol-W. In this language the types integer, real and complex can all be held double-length, in which case the type is preceded by 'long'.

	Second operand		
First operand	Integer	Real	Complex
Integer	long real	real	complex
Real	real	real	complex
Complex	complex	complex	complex

The result has the quality 'long' if both operands have the quality or if one has the quality 'long' and the other is 'integer', or if both are 'integer'.

Table 8.4. Algol-W table for / operator

8.7 Multiple assignments

Most programs start with an initialisation sequence. Quite often a number of variables have to be cleared. Many languages allow the assignments:

$$i := 0;$$
$$j := 0$$

to be condensed into:

$$i := j := 0$$

This is called, for obvious reasons, *multiple assignment*. It looks innocuous enough, but it is important to understand its meaning. Let us consider the more general case:

<variable1> := <variable2> := <expression>

Is it equivalent to:

<variable2> := <expression>;
<variable1> := <expression>

or:

<variable1> := <expression>;
<variable2> := <expression>

or:

<variable1> := <expression>;
<variable2> := <variable1>

or:

<variable2> := <expression>;
<variable1> := <variable2>

or even, as in Algol, something else? With the simple example:

$$i := j := 0$$

it does not matter, but consider:

$$i := I\,[i] := \text{read}$$

where the four alternatives give four different results.

For reasons of efficiency it should certainly be one of the last two; and from considering the binary tree such as that of Fig. 8.4 (i) it should be the last. But, as we have noted with respect to Algol, it may not be.

It is pertinent to note that if assignments were written as suggested in section 8.4:

$$0 \Rightarrow j \Rightarrow i$$
$$\text{read} \Rightarrow i \Rightarrow A[j]$$

and the ⇒ operator assumed, like the other operators, to associate from the left then the problem would disappear.

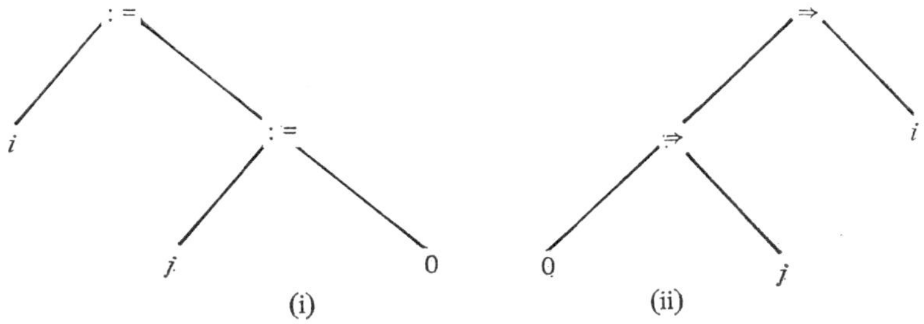

Fig. 8.4. Binary tree for i:= j: = 0: (i) before transformation; (ii) after transformation

8.8 A comment on this chapter

Much of this chapter has been concerned with language design, not compiler writing. There are two reasons for this.

First, it is important that a compiler writer appreciate the necessity of implementing the language as defined. It is important, too, that he realise what alternatives are available to him, and under what conditions they are valid.

Secondly, it seems reasonable to assume that all future languages will be designed by teams which include compiler writers. To make an adequate contribution the compiler writer must understand all the available possibilities. We have not covered them all here, of course, but we hope there have been sufficient to give food for thought.

9 Optimisation

We have, throughout this book, quite often referred to 'optimisation'. Perhaps now is the time to be more precise about the notion. To talk about optimisation on its own does not really make sense: we can optimise only with respect to some criterion. It could be size of object code, speed of compilation and so on, but it normally is the speed of the object program. We will, therefore, continue to use the term 'optimisation' to mean 'maximisation of the run time speed'.

Even so, there is no guarantee that the techniques will produce the best possible code and so we really ought to use the term 'amelioration'. (Nobody does and so we will not.) Optimisation consists of a *pot-pourri* of different techniques each designed to optimise with respect to more specific criterion such as minimising unnecessary storing of partial results, optimising the use of registers and so on. Some of these techniques, particularly those which are machine-dependent, conflict as we shall see.

It is the *ad hoc* nature of optimisation that makes a description of it so difficult. Techniques may be classified on the basis of:

(i) Their generality (machine-dependent as against machine-independent).
(ii) The region of a program over which they are applicable (within a statement, across small groups of statements, or rather more globally).
(iii) The parts of the compiler which are involved (the transformation of the internal structures or the encoding) and so on.

We will concern ourselves mainly with optimisation within a statement such as can be carried out in a one-pass, statement-by-statement compiler. Some reference, however, must be made to multi-pass compilers (that is, compilers which process the complete source program in a number of stages, the input to one stage being the output from the previous) since it is in these compilers that the greatest optimisation has so far been achieved.

We have already noted with respect to both binary and *n*-ary trees that transformation of the internal structure can lead to improved code. We now consider these transformations in more detail starting with the one discussed earlier.

9.1 Elimination of unnecessary store and load orders

In section 4.10 we showed how, with a binary tree, operands may be re-ordered to eliminate unnecessary storing and loading orders. For example:

$$h*(f0 + 4*f1 + f2)/3 \quad \Rightarrow \quad (4*f1 + f0 + f2)*h/3$$

This transformation is shown in Fig. 9.1.

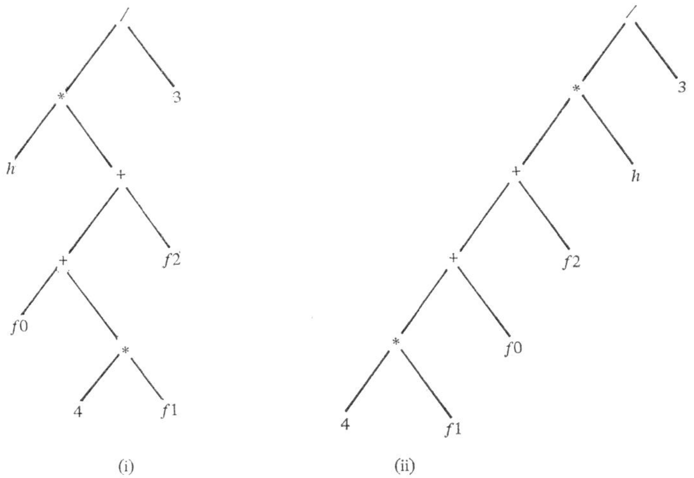

Fig. 9.1. Saving unnecessary stores and loads with a binary tree: (i) tree for $h*(f0 + 4*f1 + f2)/3$*; (ii) tree for* $(4*f1 + f0 + f2)*h/3$

9.2 Evaluation of constant expressions at compile time

Simpson's rule is often derived in the form:

$$\int_a^b f(x)\,\mathrm{d}x \approx \frac{2h}{6}\,[f0 + 4f1 + f2]$$

To evaluate this we might well write the expression:

$$2*h/6*(f0 + 4*f1 + f2)$$

Clearly, it would be desirable for 2/6 to be evaluated at compile time. This process is called *folding* the constants. Suppose we make the (mildly ridiculous) assumption that the expression was written:

$$2/6*(f0 + 4*f1 + f2)*h$$

Fig. 9.2 (i) shows the tree. The constants 2 and 6 may be folded as shown in Fig. 9.2 (ii)

Note that re-ordering should be postponed until after folding takes place, since folding often reduces a 'complicated' node to a leaf. Fig. 9.2 shows this effect.

This example is rather synthetic; more practical examples do arise.

(i) Suppose a programmer as a matter of style 'parameterises' his program by assigning constants to identifiers at the start of a program. He may change these values later, if necessary, just by changing these assignment statements.

```
min := 0;
max := 100;
width := 10;
     .
     .
     .
     .
no of bands := (max−min)/width;
```

Provided the compiler can establish (by means as yet unspecified) that max, min and width are unchanged, it can effectively convert the last statement into:

no of bands := 10

by replacing min, max and width in the tree with 0, 100 and 10 respectively, and then folding the constants.

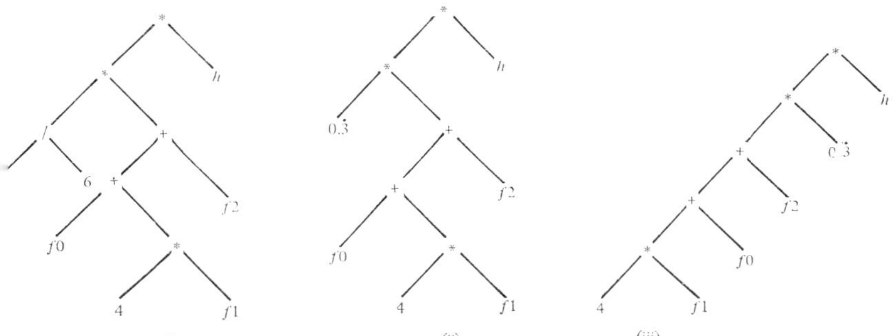

Fig. 9.2. Folding of constants with binary trees: tree for 2/6*(*f*0 + 4**f*1 + *f*2)**h*: *(i) initially; (ii) after folding; (iii) after folding and re-ordering*

That variables remain unchanged can be established in one of two ways. Firstly, the compiler can keep a record of the variables and how they change as it compiles. In a statement-by-statement compiler the appearance of a label inhibits further optimisation since the compiler cannot determine whether the values of the variables will be altered in parts of the program which end with a go to statement referring to the label.

On the other hand, a multi-pass compiler can perform quite a sophisticated analysis along these lines in an early pass.

Secondly, the language may contain a construct such as:

min ≡ 0;
max ≡ 100;
width ≡ 10;

which defines min, say, to be a pseudonym for 0 (and not a variable). This construct appears in Algol 68.

(ii) Folding may also be important where a programmer does not wish to evaluate a constant himself, either because he may do it incorrectly (and the characteristic of a computer is its ability to do arithmetic accurately), or because he wants the result to the accuracy of whatever machine he runs it on.

Consider the following assignment:

horizon := height/((1 + **sqrt** 5)/2)

which calculates where the horizon should be in a picture of a given height according to the classical golden section. Folding will effectively transform this to:

horizon := height/1·618033988 . . .

or even:

horizon := height*0·618033988 . . .

if we allow folding to convert a division into a multiplication by the reciprocal.

(iii) Suppose our language is expanded to include a macro facility which allows us to write, among the declarations, a macro definition such as:

macro polar (**real** *r*, *t*, *x*, *y*);
r := **sqrt** ($x \uparrow 2 + y \uparrow 2$);
t := **arctan** *y*/*x*
end macro

A reference to this in the source program, such as:

polar (*r*1, *t*1, *x*1, *y*1)

is replaced by the body of the macro with the formal parameters *r*,*t*,*x* and *y* replaced by the actual parameters:

*r*1 := **sqrt** ($x1 \uparrow 2 + y1 \uparrow 2$);
*t*1 := **arctan** *y*1/*x*1

and this sequence is then compiled.

If this macro is referenced, as it well might be:

polar (*r*1, *t*1, 1, 1)

then it is replaced by:

$$r1 := \textbf{sqrt}\ (1 \uparrow 2 + 1 \uparrow 2);$$
$$t1 := \textbf{arctan}\ 1/1$$

Folding would reduce this to:

$$r1 := 1{\cdot}4142135623\ \ldots$$
$$t1 := 0{\cdot}7853816339\ \ldots$$

(iv) As we shall see in the next chapter, accessing matrix element $m[i, j]$ is done by accessing an element of an equivalent vector $m'[i*c + j]$ where c is often a constant. If i and j are also constants then the subscript expression can be folded to produce a constant subscript.

9.3 Elimination of common sub-expressions

Consider the evaluation of the annual repayment £P on a mortgage of £A taken out over n years at an annual rate of interest of r. (Here r is a fraction, e.g. 0·095 if the rate of interest is $9\frac{1}{2}$ per cent.)

$$P := A*r*(1 + r) \uparrow n/((1 + r) \uparrow n - 1)$$

The binary tree is given in Fig. 9.3 (i).

Clearly, it would be advantageous to evaluate $(1 + r) \uparrow n$ once only (assuming, as here, that this is allowable, i.e. that r and n are not liable to side-effects). To enable us to do this we need an internal structure which can indicate common sub-expressions. The representation usually used is the *directed graph*. This is obtained from the binary tree by pruning second and subsequent appearances of a common node and arranging for the superior nodes to refer to the original appearance. The directed graph for the mortgage repayment assignment is given in Fig. 9.3 (ii). The conversion of the tree to the directed graph is quite simple: it is merely a question of comparing each node with all those created before it. Indeed the directed graph is often created directly.

Let us first of all consider encoding this directed graph. It is interesting to note that the algorithm we have used for encoding a tree will actually work with the directed graph (but will of course compile orders to evaluate $(1 + r) \uparrow n$ twice). This encoding is shown in Table 9.1.

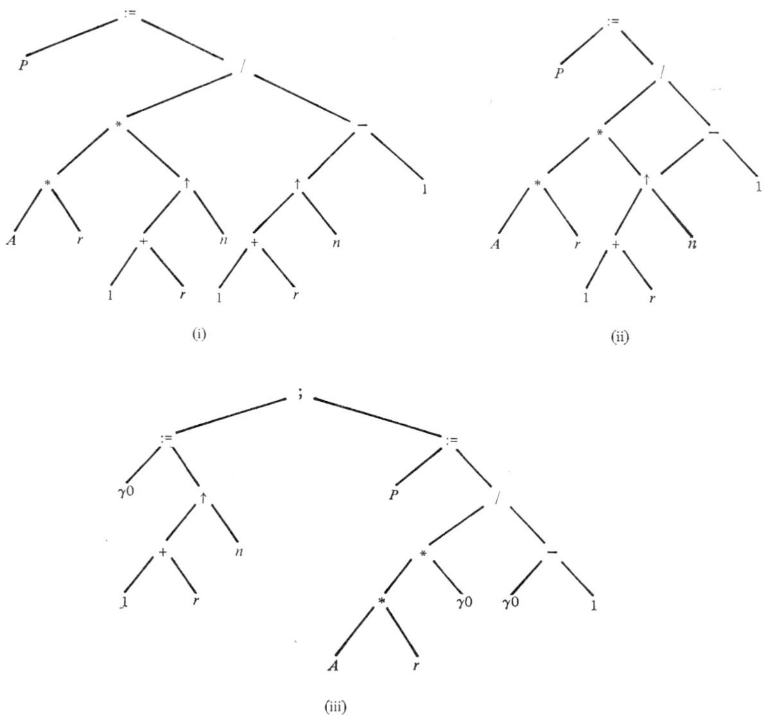

Fig. 9.3. Common sub-expressions:
P: = $A*r*(1 + r) \uparrow n/((1 + r) \uparrow n - 1)$:
(i) binary tree; (ii) directed graph; (iii) separated tree

What we seek to do is modify that algorithm so that it will encode the directed graph causing $(1 + r) \uparrow n$ to be evaluated once. There are two problems.

(i) We must be able to tell whether any node has two branches referring to it, so that after the node has been encoded we can compile an order to store the value in a temporary location.

Binary tree	*Directed graph*	*Separated tree*
AFL = A	AFL = A	AFL = 1·0
AFL * r	AFL * r	AFL + r
AFL ⇒ $\delta 0$	AFL ⇒ $\delta 0$	AFL ↑ n
AFL = 1·0	AFL = 1·0	AFL ⇒ $\gamma 0$
AFL + r	AFL + r	AFL = A
AFL ↑ n	AFL ↑ n	AFL * r
AFL * $\delta 0$	AFL ⇒ $\gamma 0$	AFL * $\gamma 0$
AFL ⇒ $\delta 0$	AFL * $\delta 0$	AFL ⇒ $\delta 0$
AFL = 1·0	AFL ⇒ $\delta 0$	AFL = $\gamma 0$
AFL + r	AFL = $\gamma 0$	AFL − 1
AFL ↑ n	AFL − 1	AFL ϕ $\delta 0$
AFL − 1	AFL ϕ $\delta 0$	AFL ⇒ P
AFL ϕ $\delta 0$	AFL ⇒ P	
AFL ⇒ P		

Table 9.1. Encoding of P: $= A*r*(1 + r) \uparrow n/((1 + r) \uparrow n - 1)$*: (i) from the binary tree; (ii) from the directed graph; (iii) from the separated tree*

(ii) When we are encoding subsequent nodes whose branches refer to this node we must remember to access the temporary variable rather than encode the whole node again.

What this implies is that when we store a directed graph we require five words for each node; as well as operator, left branch and right branch of the binary tree, we need two extra quantities: a Boolean, which we shall call *multiple*, indicating whether the node is referred to by more than one branch, and an integer, denoted by *location*, which is initially null, but which during encoding will contain the name of the temporary variable used to hold the value represented by the node.

This temporary variable has rather different characteristics from those encountered previously in encoding trees. In the earlier case the variable arose in a regular pattern (reflecting the regular structure of the tree). The $n + 1^{\text{th}}$ variable had always served its purpose before the nth and so it was possible to use the same variable a number of times in the one expression using a trivial algorithm. Indeed, we suggested that these variables could be held in a stack. With this new type of temporary variable, we find a much less regular structure and certainly the life of the mth variable is quite unrelated to that of the $m + 1^{\text{th}}$. Accordingly we use a different set of temporary variables, $\gamma 0$, $\gamma 1$, . . . which we will allocate serially but which we will not re-use within the same expression. (More sophisticated algorithms do exist for re-using them.)

```
procedure encode graph (register, operation, expr, n, m);
string register, operation; tree expr; integer n, m;
    begin
    if location is not null then compile (register, operation,
                                                  γ location)
    else if datum is an operand then compile (register, operation,
                                                        datum)
    else if datum is a unary operator then
        begin
        if operation is '=' then
            begin
            encode graph (register, '=', left branch, n, m);
            compile (register, datum)
            end
        else begin
            compile (register, '⇒', δn);
            encode graph (register, '=', left branch, n + 1,
                                                          m);
            compile (register, datum);
            compile (register, reverse (operation), δn)
            end
        end
    else if datum is a binary operator then
        begin
        if operation is '=' then
            begin
            encode graph (register, '=', left branch, n, m);
            encode graph (register, datum, right branch, n, m)
            end
        else begin
            compile (register, '⇒', δn);
            encode graph (register, '=', left branch, n + 1,
                                                          m);
```

```
            encode graph (register, datum, right branch,
                                                n + 1, m);
            compile (register, reverse (operation), δn)
            end
        end;
    if multiple ∧ location is null then
        begin
        compile (register, '⇒', γ m);
        location := m;
        m := m + 1
        end
    end
```

The coding produced by the call:

encode graph ('AFL', '=', tree, 0, m)

where m has previously been set to zero is given in Table 9.1 which shows it to be shorter than that obtained from the binary tree. The table is deceptive in that the significant order saved is:

AFL $\uparrow n$

which, in practice, has to be simulated by a loop sequence which is statically longer and dynamically much slower than, say, a multiplication or division order.

A directed graph is a much more complicated structure than a binary tree as the above encoding procedure suggests. We note two things in particular:

(i) We sometimes, as here, find that we already have information in the register at the point at which we start to evaluate the common sub-expression, and so we have to store this information. In this situation it would be advantageous to evaluate the common sub-expression first.

(ii) The transformation of a directed graph is more complicated because a common sub-expression behaves, at its second and subsequent appearances, as a simple leaf.

An alternative representation arises by considering the statement as equivalent to a series of statements, one to evaluate each common sub-expression and one to evaluate the original expression in terms of these sub-expressions:

$$\gamma 0 := (1 + r) \uparrow n; P := A*r*\gamma 0/(\gamma 0 - 1)$$

If we regard ; as a binary operator then a single tree structure arises, called a *separated tree*. Fig. 9.3 (iii) shows the tree for this expression. The usual encoding algorithm can be used, the ;-node giving rise to no code at all. [As in Algol 68, the semicolon can be thought of as a 'carry-on' operator: that is, do the left branch and then do the right branch.]

As shown in Table 9.1 this can produce better code.

However, as it stands the technique of the separated tree can, itself, produce inefficiencies because by separating out the sub-expression we have severed some important links. Consider the following statement which calculates the number of bands of a given width in a histogram whose upper and lower limits are given by max and min respectively:

> no of bands := **if** width*((max − min)/width) = (max − min) **then** (max − min)/width **else** (max − min)/width + 1

The separated-tree technique effectively transforms this into:

> γ0 := max − min;
> γ1 := γ0/width;
> no of bands := **if** width* γ1 = γ0 **then** γ1 **else** γ1 + 1

The resulting encoding would include the following sequence of orders:

```
AFL ⇒ γ1
AFL = width
AFL * γ1
AFL COMPARE γ0
```

which could be more efficiently encoded as:

```
AFL ⇒ γ1
AFL * width
AFL COMPARE γ0
```

which would be the case if the last of the separate assignments were transformed to:

no of bands := **if** $\gamma 1$*width = $\gamma 0$ **then** $\gamma 1$ **else** $\gamma 1 + 1$

To do this we need to extend the criteria by which the re-ordering procedure rotates a node. It is also usual to re-order so that the sub-expressions:

*a***b* and *b***a*

are recognised as being common.

The re-ordering algorithm then is:

(i) If neither branch is a leaf, do nothing.
(ii) If only one branch is a leaf and it refers to a normal operand, rotate if necessary to make it the right branch.
(iii) If one branch is a leaf and it refers to a sub-expression, rotate if necessary to make it the left branch (although this may not bring any improvement).
(iv) If both branches are leaves referring to sub-expressions leave alone (since it is difficult to determine which, if either, would be able to benefit from being on the left branch).
(v) If both branches are leaves referring to operands rotate, if necessary, to put them in a standard order.

Note that the elimination of common sub-expressions is possible only as long as the side-effects problem is absent. The discussions of sections 4.6 and 6.6 are relevant. Note, too, that the elimination of common sub-expressions may not bring any improvement. If the common sub-expression is the sum of two scalars, the transformation quite often merely replaces a load order and an add order with a store order and a load order. [If the machine has a pipelined instruction unit the store order may cause the 'optimised' code to run slower!]

9.4 Are these simple optimisations worth it?

The optimisations we have performed so far could all have been done by the programmer: the fact that we have been able to define the transformations in terms of the source language shows that. In fact, most programming language teachers insist that their students perform the optimisations described themselves, especially those related to folding and common sub-expressions. It is worthwhile pausing for a moment to answer the question that often is asked: Does the compiler have to do it? Should the compiler do it?

The answer is simple: no, the compiler does not have to do it, but yes, it should do it. There are three reasons.

(i) The first, the most important, is quite simply that a programmer should be allowed to write his program in a way that is as meaningful as possible to him. He should not have to break down what is a coherent unit to him, for example,

$$P := A*r*(1 + r) \uparrow n/((1 + r) \uparrow n - 1)$$

into two less meaningful units, for example,

$$\text{comp} := (1 + r) \uparrow n;$$
$$P := A*r*\text{comp}/(\text{comp} - 1)$$

especially as this involves him in the creation of, to him, totally meaningless quantities, for example, comp.

(ii) As we shall see in the next chapter with respect to arrays it is often impossible for a programmer to perform some optimisations without seriously transforming the structure of his program.

(iii) The folding of constants often allows a programmer to specify irrational constants such as:

$$1 + \frac{\sqrt{5}}{2}$$

in terms of exact quantities, here 1, 5 and 2 which are folded to produce an answer which is as accurate as the machine will allow. Thus, the program will run with maximum accuracy on any machine. It is quite common for programmers to use:

4 * **arctan** 1

for π.

There are, of course, situations in which there is no need for the optimisation to be done at all, either by programmer or compiler. The classical case is the student teaching load. Here there is the possibility that, since many programs do not run at all, and the rest have very short run-times, the time spent by the compiler in performing its optimisations might exceed any time saved during the running of its optimised object program. If this is the case, then the compiler can be written so that the optimisation can be switched off for such runs.

9.5 Remembering the contents of registers within statements

So far we have considered the transformation of the tree. Let us now consider the encoding algorithm. In Chapter 2 we noted that by remembering what quantity will be in BM at run time we could often eliminate unnecessary orders which load BM. The example we used there was:

$$p[j] := q[j] \Rightarrow \begin{array}{l} \text{BM} \;\; = j \\ \text{AFL} = q[\text{BM}] \\ [\text{BM} \;\; = j] \\ \text{AFL} \Rightarrow p[\text{BM}] \end{array}$$

where, as in earlier chapters, the order enclosed in square brackets can be omitted.

This principle can be expanded to include all registers. (So far we have introduced only BM, AFL, AFX and BN, but more will appear in subsequent chapters.) For example:

$$\textbf{if } a > b \textbf{ then } \text{max} := a \textbf{ else } \text{min} := a \Rightarrow \begin{array}{rl} & \text{AFL} = a \\ & \text{AFL COMPARE } b \\ & \text{IF} \leqslant \text{JUMP } \lambda 0 \\ & [\text{AFL} = a] \\ & \text{AFL} \Rightarrow \text{max} \\ & \text{JUMP } \lambda 1 \\ \lambda 0: & [\text{AFL} = a] \\ & \text{AFL} \Rightarrow \text{min} \\ \lambda 1: & \end{array}$$

Note that within a statement we often do not know what will be in a register. Two cases are important:

(i) If a statement contains a function call (see Chapter 12) then at run time the evaluation of the function will cause the values in (at least some of) the registers to be altered.

(ii) If we use the conditional approach in dealing with conditional expressions and if the Boolean expression contains $\wedge$ or $\vee$ then what is in the registers after the evaluation of the condition might well be unpredictable.

9.6 Remembering the contents of registers across statements

The technique can be extended across adjacent statements.
For example:

$x := p[i]$	BM $= i$ AFL $= p$[BM] AFL $\Rightarrow x$
$p[i] := q[i]$ $\Rightarrow$	[BM $= i$] AFL $= q$[BM] [BM $= i$] AFL $\Rightarrow p$[BM]
$q[i] := x$	AFL $= x$ [BM $= i$] AFL $\Rightarrow q$[BM]

There are a number of situations in which what will be in the registers at run time is unknown:

(i) If a statement is labelled then because there may be a subsequent go to statement which refers to the label, it is impossible to say what will be in the registers at run time when the labelled statement is obeyed.

(ii) If a statement is conditional then what will be in some of the registers after the statement is obeyed may not be determinable.

9.7 Common sub-expressions across consecutive statements

If we ignore questions of accuracy, the following statements evaluate the two real roots of the quadratic $ax^2 + bx + c = 0$:

$x1$:= $(- b +$ **sqrt** $(b \uparrow 2 - 4*a*c))/(2*a)$;
$x2$:= $(- b -$ **sqrt** $(b \uparrow 2 - 4*a*c))/(2*a)$

We would like this to be evaluated as:

$\gamma0$:= **sqrt** ($b \uparrow 2 - 4*a*c$);
$\gamma1$:= $2*a$;
$x1$:= $(-\ b + \gamma0)/\gamma1$;
$x2$:= $(-\ b - \gamma0)/\gamma1$

without having to write it that way. That is we would like to be able to eliminate common sub-expressions across statements. If we allow a ;-node to be produced by the appearance of a semicolon in the source text then clearly a single tree similar to the separated tree can be used to represent these statements. This implies that the compiler must be expanded to deal with say, two or three statements at a time. We will not pursue this any further, preferring to consider the effect of the optimisation rather than its implementation. Fig. 9.4 (i) shows the tree for the quadratic statements above.

The common sub-expressions can now be recognised and separated as described earlier (Fig. 9.4 (ii)).

We have already noted with respect to optimisation within a statement that common sub-expressions can be dealt with in this way only so long as the side-effects problem is absent; that is provided the evaluation of the expression does not cause a change in the environment such that second or subsequent evaluations of the sub-expression produce a different answer from the first (generally due to the evaluation of a function).

When we consider common sub-expressions across statements a further problem is superimposed. By definition the first statement alters the environment of the second since it assigns a value to some variable. Thus a further limitation is placed on the elimination of common sub-expressions: the left hand side variable of the first must not appear in the sub-expression.

9.8 Re-ordering statements

The use of the binary tree suggests that the ;-node can be rotated: that is, that statements can be interchanged. This is so, provided, of course, that the results are identical; provided, that is, that the changes to the environment produced by the evaluation of each statement do not effect the values required by the other. One example

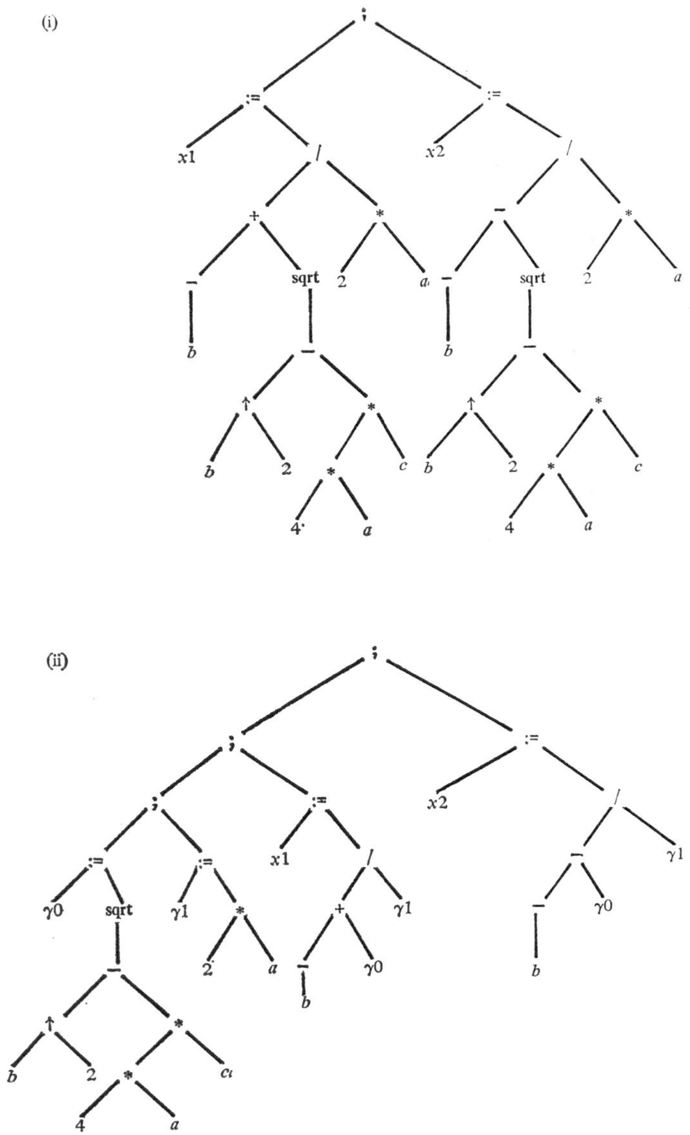

Fig. 9.4. Trees for statements: $x1: = (-b + \textbf{sqrt}\ (b \uparrow 2 - 4*a*c))/(2*a)$; $x2: = (-b - \textbf{sqrt}\ (b \uparrow 2 - 4*a*c))/(2*a)$
(i) initially; (ii) after common sub-trees have been recognised and separated

can be found in the four orders into which we transformed the quadratic evaluation. The first two statements might be interchanged giving (with a consequent re-ordering of the operands of the third):

$$\begin{aligned} y1 &:= 2*a; \\ y0 &:= \textbf{sqrt}\ (b \uparrow 2 - 4*a*c); \\ x1 &:= (y0 - b)/y1; \\ x2 &:= (-\,b - y0)/y1 \end{aligned}$$

producing slightly better code. We can, of course, use a binary tree for a series of statements though this limits the amount of re-ordering which may take place in the same way as it does for the operands of an expression. We will not, however, follow this up. The *n*-ary tree obviously gives greater flexibility.

9.9 N-ary trees again

We introduced the *n*-ary tree in Chapter 6 as a more general form of internal structure, one which was amenable to more transformations than the binary tree; that is as a structure more suitable to optimisation. All the transformations of binary trees discussed in this chapter are applicable to *n*-ary trees. As with binary trees, we generalise the re-ordering rule from the simple one given in section 6.4. The operands of a level should be in the following order:

(i) Branches referring to lower levels.
(ii) Leaves which refer to sub-expressions.
(iii) Leaves which refer to simple operands all in some standard order.
(iv) Leaves which refer to constants.

We now look at five transformations corresponding to those discussed earlier with reference to binary trees.

(i) Elimination of unnecessary store and load orders. This has already been discussed in Chapter 6 where we showed that both:

$$h*(f0 + 4*f1 + f2)/3$$
$$\text{and}\quad h/3*(f0 + 4*f1 + f2)$$

were effectively transformed into:

$$(4*f1 + f0 + f2)*h/3$$

The above re-ordering criterion ensures this, or more precisely:

$$(f1*4 + f0 + f2)*h/3$$

(ii) Folding of constant sub-expressions. As we suggested in section 9.2, the expression:

$$2*h/6*(f0 + 4*f1 + f2)$$

might well be written to evaluate an integral by Simpson's rule. The re-ordering criterion ensures that the constants 2 and /6 will be moved

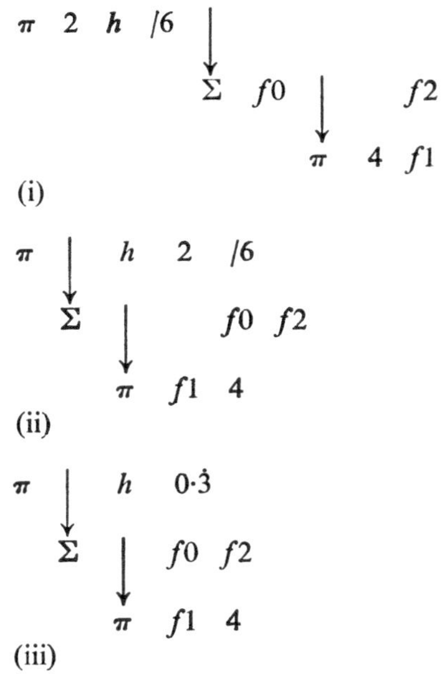

Fig. 9.5. Reordering and folding in n-ary trees: $2*h/6*(f0 + 4*f1 + f2)$: (*i*) *untransformed;* (*ii*) *re-ordered;* (*iii*) *with constants folded*

to the end, where they may be folded to give $0{\cdot}\dot{3}$. This is illustrated in Fig. 9.5.

This example illustrates the fact that in an *n*-ary tree folding constants does not necessarily involve elimination of a level.

(iii) Elimination of common sub-expressions within a statement. Similar techniques are applicable to those described for binary trees.

Similar structures are used too: directed graphs and separated trees. They are, though, more general. (Whether this generality is useful is open to question.) For example, due to the re-ordering:

$$a + b + c$$
$$b + a + c$$
$$a + c + b$$
$$c + a + b$$
$$b + c + a$$
$$c + b + a$$

are all recognised as being the same sub-expression. If we were to use binary trees the first pair would be recognised as being the same expression; so, too, would the second pair though it would be a different sub-expression from the first one. The last pair would be recognised as a third sub-expression. Finding common sub-expressions can be slow though, since each might be embedded in the middle of the operands of a level, and a considerable amount of comparison might be required to isolate them.

(iv) Elimination of common sub-expressions across statements. By connecting a sequence of consecutive statements through a ;-node it is possible to eliminate common sub-expressions from them along the lines described for binary trees.

(v) Re-ordering statements. If statements are connected via a ;-node then they can be re-ordered in a more general way than allowed with binary trees. A reason why we might want more general re-ordering will appear in a subsequent section.

Other transformations are possible. For example:

(vi) Elimination of redundant brackets. Consider the expression:

$$(x11 - x12) - (x21 - x22)$$

where the first set of brackets are purely redundant, and the second redundant in the sense that they could be dropped if the signs of the enclosed operands are changed. The tree for this is given in Fig. 9.6.

All the levels are Σ-levels. Clearly the lower Σ-levels can be absorbed into the upper level provided that the effect of an upper-level unary operator is transferred to the operands of the lower level.

Before we leave *n*-ary trees we must re-emphasise again that the more general transformations of *n*-ary trees may cause different results to be produced due to round-off in the floating-point accumulator and so on; and so in many languages under many conditions their use might be precluded.

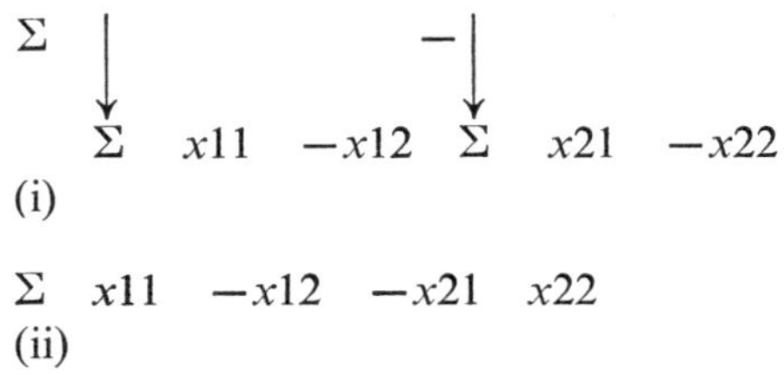

Fig. 9.6. Elimination of 'redundant' brackets: $(x11 - x12) - (x21 - x22)$: *(i) initially; (ii) after transformation*

9.10 Loops

So far we have not introduced the notion of a loop to our language—and this is a very convenient point to do it. In most languages loops are not a basic concept, being defined in terms of simpler concepts. In this they are like the general form of conditional statement (section 7.5). [In many people's view this is unfortunate: the notions of looping and conditional statements are thought to be fundamental, and the jump order a relic of the past. Even so, until the structure of machines is radically altered, the compiler writer has still to map the looping and conditional statements onto simpler statements including the conditional jump.] Suppose then we introduce a looping facility by allowing any statement to be preceded by a *for clause*:

<looping statement> :: = <for clause> <statement>

For simplicity we consider only a simple form of for clause reminiscent of Algol's step-until element:

<for clause> ::= **for** <variable> := <expression1>
step <expression 2>
until <expression 3> **do**

There are a number of ways in which a language designer can define the meaning of this statement: he can choose whether the expressions are to be evaluated once only on entry to the loop, or once on each traverse (or twice on each traverse as the second expression is in Algol!); he can choose whether, like Algol, the statement is to be skipped when the expressions are not compatible with obeying the statement a sensible number of times, or whether, like Fortran, the loop is to be obeyed at least once; he can choose whether the expressions are to be integer or real; he can choose whether the variable has a defined value on completion of the loop or is undefined. We will ignore this area, being the province of the designer and not the compiler writer and use the simplest possible definition, in which all the expressions are integer, and in which we assume that the expressions have sensible values:

```
     <variable> := <expression1>;
λ0:  <statement>;
     if <variable> = <expression3> then go to λ1;
     <variable> := <variable> + <expression2>;
     go to λ0;
λ1:
```

9.11 Optimisation over simple loops

Consider the following statement for evaluating the reactance of a series *L-C* circuit at a fixed frequency but over a linear range of inductance.

```
for L := 1 step 1 until n do
            X[L] := 2*pi*f*L − 1/(2*pi*f*C)
```

Recognition of 2*pi*f as a common sub-expression would cause the statement to be compiled as:

```
     L := 1;
λ0:  γ0 := 2*pi*f;
     X[L] := γ0*L − 1/(γ0*C);
     if L = n then go to λ1;
     L := L + 1;
     go to λ0;
λ1:
```

Now the value of $\gamma 0$ remains constant over all traverses of the loop, and so it would be preferable to have it evaluated once only. This can be done by moving the label $\lambda 0$ down to the next statement (and, in general, down over all those statements which evaluate a constant quantity). What we have done effectively is to transform the statement into:

$\gamma 0 := 2*pi*f$;
for $L := 1$ **step** 1 **until** n **do** $X[L] := \gamma 0*L - 1/(\gamma 0*C)$

That is, we have removed the constant (common) sub-expression from the loop. More importantly, we may remove any sub-expression which remains constant within the loop such as $1/(\gamma 0*C)$ in the above:

$\gamma 0 := 2*pi*f$;
$\gamma 1 := 1/(\gamma 0*C)$;
for $L := 1$ **step** 1 **until** n **do** $X[L] := \gamma 0*L - \gamma 1$

This is the more usual case and it involves a process of scanning the tree to find sub-trees which are independent of the controlled variable and of the variable on the left hand side of the assignment statement. To do this it is sometimes convenient to revert to the equivalent assignment form of representation used initially in Chapter 4.

9.12 Compound statements and optimisation over larger loops

In practice, of course, the body of a loop comprises more then one statement. We can allow this by defining a *compound statement*, a series of statements separated by semicolons and surrounded by brackets, and allowing it to be qualified by a for clause. The introduction of the compound statement radically affects the statement-by-statement structure of a compiler, since a statement can be a compound statement which is made up of other statements some of which may be compound statements and so on. Indeed, the whole program can be a single statement as is the case with Algol. We can still write a compiler which processes the program in a single pass by having it process a *unit* at a time where a unit is either a simple statement, a clause or a bracket. Once again, the read-a-line procedure must be expanded. We will continue to use the phrase *statement-by-statement* giving it this more general meaning. [Of course, we could have retained the full statement-by-statement nature by adding looping facilities like Fortran's but again we prefer to move towards Algol.] Conventionally, the brackets are written as '**begin**' and '**end**' and we will conform to this convention here, though alternatives such as '(' and ')' as allowed in Algol 68, and '§' and '$' of CPL have their attractions. As an example, consider the following loop for evaluating the length of the third side and the area of a series of triangles, in which two sides *a* and *b* are kept constant and the included angle varies from 10° to 90° in steps of 10°.

```
for C := 10 step 10 until 90 do
    begin
    c[C] := sqrt (a ↑ 2 + b ↑ 2 - 2*a*b*cos(pi*C/180));
    area [C] := 0·5*a*b*sin (pi*C/180)
    end
```

In the spirit of the previous section this should be compiled:

```
γ0 := a ↑ 2 + b ↑ 2;
γ1 := a*b;
γ2 := pi/180;
for C := 10 step 10 until 90 do
    begin
    γ3 := γ2*C;
    c[C] := sqrt (γ0 - 2*γ1*cos γ3);
    area [C] := 0·5* γ1*sin γ3
    end
```

or even:

```
γ0 := a ↑ 2 + b ↑ 2;
γ1 := 2*a*b;
γ2 := pi/180;
for C := 10 step 10 until 90 do
    begin
    γ3 := γ2*C;
    c[C] := sqrt (γ0 - γ1*cos γ3);
    area [C] := 0·25*γ1*sin γ3
    end
```

To achieve this optimisation involves compiling a group of statements at one time, and so clearly involves the use of a multi-pass compiler. The techniques involved in such compilers are quite sophisticated and outside the scope of this book. Those interested are referred to the work of Frances Allen (see refs. 9.1 and 9.2). We will make a few observations for the sake of completeness.

(i) If we treat the complete body of the loop at once, then the *n*-ary tree is the more appropriate internal representation of the statement, since sub-expressions from all parts of the body may benefit from being removed from the loop. Complete (programmer-written) statements may also be moved but this is much less likely. With an *n*-ary tree representation the technique is to move a statement up the loop as far as possible—that is, until a statement is reached which redefines the value of any of its operands, or vice-versa.

A statement-by-statement compiler will, of course, be able to optimise only those loops whose bodies are a single statement. A sensible compromise is to allow the compiler to digest a few units at a time. The compiler can then process loops of two or three statements as a whole and, from Knuth's observations, (see ref. 9.4) this seems to cater for most optimisable cases.

(ii) Loops, of course, may be nested within loops. An algorithm for performing optimisations over general loops will move statements outside all the loops over which they are constant.

(iii) Loops in programs are not always explicitly indicated by means of formal constructs such as the for clause used above. In Fortran, for example, there is no construct which allows a loop to be repeated while a condition is true (the while clause of Algol); and so a programmer must create such loops out of the simpler constructs. These loops are as susceptible to optimisation as the formal loops. Recognition of what actually constitutes a loop is a major part of any optimisation procedure. (This is one of the reasons for advocating the addition of the appropriate constructs to Fortran.)

(iv) So far we have described techniques which operate on constant sub-expressions, but consider the following statement (which might arise from accessing matrices as we shall see in the next chapter):

for j := 1 **step** 1 **until** n **do**
    sum := sum + $a[i*c + j]$

and, in particular, the operand $a[i*c + j]$. In our basic language the subscript of an array was simply a variable. We will reconsider the whole problem of arrays in the next chapter, but, for the moment, we note that to deal with expressions as subscripts merely requires the expression to be evaluated in BM, and we assume the appropriate set of orders. As it stands, the evaluation of $a[i*c + j]$ requires a multiplication and an addition. On successive iterations of the loop the values of the subscript vary by 1, and so each value may be obtained from the previous one by a simple addition of 1. Effectively we would like to transform the statement into:

```
γ0 := i*c;
for j := 1 step 1 until n do
    begin
    γ0 :=γ0 + 1;
    sum := sum + a[γ0]
    end
```

This process, which involves the recognition of sub-expressions which are linear functions of the controlled variable, is called *strength reduction.*

9.13 Is this more general optimisation worth it?

Very little work has done in determining the efficiency of any of the techniques so far discussed (or those discussed in subsequent sections). However, it seems likely that the old computing adage: that you can gain 90 per cent of the effect for 10 per cent of the effort is probably valid here. That is, in most cases, a statement-by-statement compiler (or one that processes two or three statements together) will produce code of sufficiently high quality. This situation should improve further as machine design starts to reflect the requirements of high-level languages.

Of course, there will always be cases in which the maximum possible optimisation is required and then the more extensive loop optimising techniques will be required.

In what follows we will return to our simple, one-pass, statement-by-statement compiler.

9.14 Delaying the storage of registers

So far we have not considered which register to use for testing and incrementing the controlled variable. As we have constrained it to be an integer, we could have used AFX. However, since the controlled variable is almost invariably used as a modifier and only as a modifier there is an advantage in using BM, which, as we have noted has all the appropriate operations available. For example the loop:

for i := 1 **step** 1 **until** n **do** $a[i]$:= 0

would be compiled (remembering the state of BM across statements and taking the loading of AFL with 0 out of the loop):

```
      BM = 1
      BM ⇒ i
      AFL = 0
λ0:   AFL ⇒ a[BM]
      BM COMPARE n
      IF = JUMP λ1
      BM + 1
      BM ⇒ i
      JUMP λ0
λ1:
```

A further principle is applicable here: postpone the storing of a register until absolutely necessary, that is, until the register is required for another purpose. The objective of this principle is to move the storing order outside the loop. In this example, BM contains the value of i continuously; the first store order can be eliminated, and the second store planted outside the loop at a point (if any) at which BM is required.

```
      BM = 1
      AFL = 0
λ0:   AFL ⇒ a[BM]
      BM COMPARE n
      IF = JUMP λ1
      BM + 1
      JUMP λ0
λ1:
```

The register involved is usually BM, but may be one of the accumulators. Consider a loop for the evaluation of a polynomial by nested multiplication:

```
y := 0;
for i := 1 step 1 until n do y := y*x + a[i]
```

This could be compiled:

```
     AFL = 0
     BM = 1
λ0:  AFL * x
     AFL + a[BM]
     BM COMPARE n
     IF = JUMP λ1
     BM + 1
     JUMP λ0
λ1:
```

.15 Recognition of special cases

The translation of any construct must deal with the most general of cases. Often some efficiency can be gained by recognising common cases (which are often quite simple examples of the general case) and dealing with them specially.

For example, consider a loop in which the increment is the constant 1.

Then the construct:

```
for <variable> := <expression 1> step 1 until
                  <expression 3> do <statement>
```

is compiled, using the general definition given earlier:

```
     <variable> := <expression 1>;
λ0:  <statement>;
     if <variable> = <expression 3> then go to λ1;
     <variable> := <variable> + 1;
     go to λ0;
λ1:
```

This is equivalent to the simpler alternative:

<variable> := <expression 1>;
λ0: <statement>;
<variable> := <variable> + 1;
if <variable> ⩽ <expression 3> **then go to** λ0;
<variable> := <variable> − 1

where the body of the loop is one order shorter due to the elimination of one of the jumps. [The final statement, outside the loop, is required to ensure that the variable has the same value after completion of the loop in both cases. This illustrates why Algol in fact left the value undefined: the compiler writer then omits this statement.] All the examples of section 9.14 would benefit from this technique.

The loop is a rich source of such special cases. If, like Algol, the loop is defined in such a way that all three expressions are to be evaluated on each traverse, then it is possible to recognise those expressions which remain constant (most of them in practice) and evaluate them once. Again, if the controlled variable is not used within a loop then the loop may be transformed to take advantage of this. For example, the loop for calculating the square root of a number using five iterations of Newton's Approximation (assuming an appropriate initial approximation y):

for i := 1 **step** 1 **until** 5 **do** y := 0·5*(y + a/y)

may be transformed:

for i := −4 **step** 1 **until** 0 **do** y := 0·5*(y + a/y)

Why this last transformation might be desirable will be described in the next section.

We will have cause to mention further examples of this technique in subsequent chapters.

9.16 Machine-dependent optimisation

All the techniques discussed so far have been machine independent: we have discussed their effects in source language terms except when discussing the storage delay technique. Such techniques should be relevant to all machines. There is another class of techniques, the machine-dependent techniques which seek to take advantage of the characteristics of the machine for which the compiler is compiling. Each machine has a different set of relevant characteristics and so it is pointless trying to review all possible techniques. Instead we give three examples.

(i) Our machine has only special purpose registers. Most machines on the other hand are provided with a set of more general registers. For example, the ICL 1900 has 8, IBM 360 has 16 and Atlas had 128. Some of the registers will be allocated by the compiler writer to the functions of the special purpose registers. The rest are then available for use. They have two significant characteristics. Firstly, the order code is often geared to their use so that fewer orders are required to operate on quantities held in registers than those held in store. Often one order is required to increment a quantity held in a register as against three if held in the store. Secondly, the registers can often be accessed faster (flip-flop speed as against core speed). Consequently, some importance is attached to using the registers to the full.

If there were more registers than scalar quantities the solution would be simple: allocate each variable to a register for the duration of the program. [This solution was used with Mercury Autocode on Atlas.] Generally speaking, though, there are more variables than registers; and so some strategy must be adopted for allocating a variable to a register as required. The goal is to ensure that a variable remains in a register while it still has operations to be done on it. The classical solution requires a multi-pass compiler. It is described by Hopgood (see ref. 9.4) who attributes it to Belady. Clearly, if all the registers are allocated and a new variable occurs and is to be allocated a register, then some other variable must relinquish one. Belady's algorithm chooses from the variables allocated the one which will be the last to be subsequently operated on.

In a one-pass system, this solution is inapplicable. As a variable requires a register, the register to be used and the variable to be displaced must be chosen on a simpler basis: either by an algorithm which allocates the registers serially, or one which allocates them at random. It is not clear by how much this solution falls short of Belady's, if any.

(ii) Some machines such as the ICL 1900 have a set of orders which leave the result not in the register but in the store location which holds the operand. For example, in a notation resembling the one we have used for our machine:

AFX $+\Rightarrow$ i

adds the values in i and AFX and stores the results in i: it adds AFX to i.

Statements like:

$i := i + 1$

which we have compiled as:

AFX $=$ i
AFX $+$ 1
AFX $\Rightarrow$ i

can be compiled:

AFX $=$ 1
AFX $+\Rightarrow$ i

The simplest technique for achieving this is to combine the order pair:

AFX operator operand
AFX $\Rightarrow$ operand

into:

AFX operator $\Rightarrow$ operand

This can be done immediately after the store order is compiled, or it can be done instead of compiling the store order.

Note that this technique requires the transformed tree for $i := i + 1$ to be as shown in Fig. 9.7 (i).

This conflicts with the requirements for capitalising on the values already in registers, for which the tree of Fig. 9.7 (ii) is applicable. [Simple incrementing orders are quite common and in a machine with a number of registers it is often thought desirable to reserve a register which permanently holds the value 1. Then the incrementing statement above is compiled into a single order.]

(iii) Machines are often provided with a special looping order which:

(*a*) adds 1 to a register,
(*b*) tests that register against zero,
(*c*) if not equal to zero jumps to the label specified as its operand.

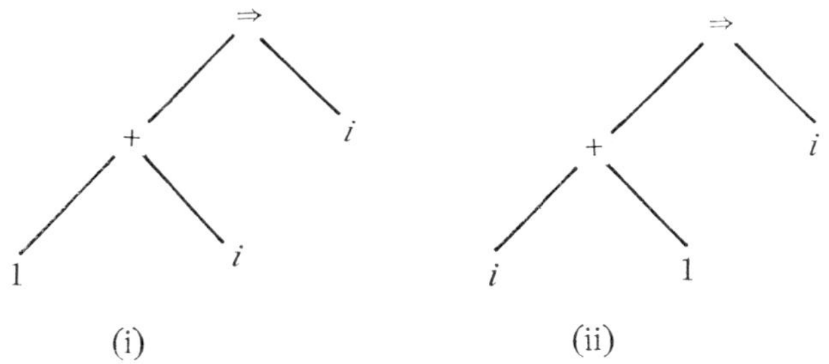

Fig. 9.7. Transformed tree for $i := i + 1$: (i) as required to capitalise on orders which leave their result in store; (ii) as required to capitalise on the contents of AFX from previous order

This is the rationale behind the transformation of:

for i := 1 **step** 1 **until** 5 **do** $y := 0{\cdot}5*(y + a/y)$

into:

for i := −4 **step** 1 **until** 0 **do** $y := 0{\cdot}5*(y + a/y)$

where the loop can be mapped directly onto this one order.

As we shall see in section 10·4, the use of the strength reduction technique often removes all references to the controlled variable within the loop and the above transformation can subsequently be applied.

9.17 The place of optimisation

The very existence of the notion of optimisation arises from the incompatibilities between the structure of the languages that programmers write in and the structure of the machines that engineers build. This situation is changing and as it does the importance of optimisation techniques will decline. We cite two examples.

(i) If general purpose registers are provided in hardware to achieve speed, then they can be made invisible to the programmer and variables can be allocated to them by hardware. The register allocation problem then disappears.

(ii) Most machines recognise in the hardware only scalars and vector elements (in engineering terms unmodified and modified addresses). As we shall see in the next chapter, matrices and higher order arrays must be mapped onto these simple structures. This gives rise to subscripts inside loops which are linear functions of the controlled variable, and to the technique of strength reduction. As machines are provided with more comprehensive data structure facilities, so this optimisation technique becomes redundant.

Even so, other techniques such as re-ordering the operands of an expression and the elimination of common sub-expressions are likely to be relevant for some time yet.

As we have commented throughout this chapter, very little is known about the relative importance of the different techniques. Most compiler writers have included the techniques that they thought were useful and found that the over-all result was an improvement; very few have had the time to do detailed experiments measuring the utility of each technique and matching it against the cost (in terms of compile time, or compiler size, or object program size). There remains a lot of work to be done here. Even the view stated above that 90 per cent of the effect can be gained for 10 per cent of the cost by means of a statement-by-statement compiler is only an opinion.

Before we leave this subject we should mention the conflict between large-scale optimisation and fault monitoring and detection, a subject we will return to in Chapter 14. If an object program has resulted from significant transformations of the source text, by moving invariant expressions outside a nest of loops, then there is some difficulty, both for the compiler writer to compile appropriate checking sequences and for the programmer to reconcile fault information produced about this program with the original source text.

0 Arrays

In dealing with expressions so far, we have considered only scalars and constants as operands. Array elements are, of course, quite important as the examples of the previous chapter reminded us. In this chapter we consider the range of array facilities.

0.1 Static vectors

The basic language contains *static vectors* (i.e. vectors whose bounds are static or constant) declared for example:

array $v[0:10]$

In all accesses to an array, the subscript is constrained to be either an integer variable or an integer constant as in:

$v[1] := v[2]$
$v[\mathrm{i}] := v[\mathrm{i}] + 1$

although in the last chapter we indicated how we might deal with expressions as subscripts.

Let us consider just the loading of $v[i]$ into the accumulator. The code compiled for this is simply:

BM $= i$
AFL $= v$[BM]

The binary tree representation is fairly straightforward.

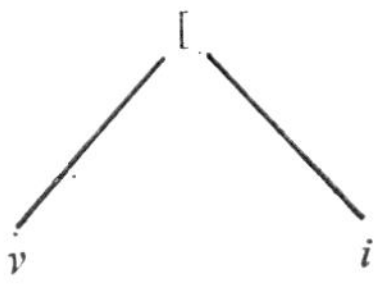

where, in the tree, [is regarded as a non-commutative operator which modifies its left branch by its right branch. More meaningfully, we might use a new operator $\downarrow$.

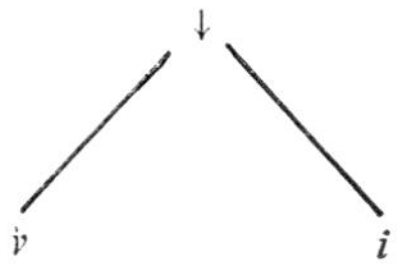

The right bracket does not appear on the tree. Unlike the **if** of a conditional expression it is not redundant though in the source code, since both of the following:

$$x := v[i + 1]$$
$$x := v[i] + 1$$

would produce:

$$x := v[i + 1$$

if the] were omitted.

Another sequence must be added to the generating algorithm of Fig. 4.7 to ensure that the [is deleted from the stack; and the transition matrix must be expanded by a row (for [) and a column (for]). The [is regarded as a bracket and always stacked.

There is an interesting point of language design here. We could have arranged to omit the] by regarding [as an operator and giving it, say, a high priority. Then

$$x := v[i + 1$$

or as would be more meaningful here as well:

$$x := v \downarrow i + 1$$

would represent in algebraic terms:

$$x = v_i + 1$$

Then we would represent:

$$x = v_{i+1}$$

by using brackets:

$$x := v \downarrow (i + 1)$$

This would have lead to a pleasing symmetry in dealing with:

$$v_i \text{ and } v^i$$

However, even in computer science, old conventions die hard. From this point of view the square bracket convention can be thought of as:

(i) Insisting on the brackets around all subscripts even scalars;
(ii) Rewriting the pair of symbols $\downarrow$ (as [and the symbol) as].

Consequently, we might arrange for the lexical analysis procedure to reverse the process, converting [to $\downarrow$ (, and] to). This would then avoid the necessity of adding the extra sequence to the generating algorithm mentioned above. However, this is not generally done—the error in $v[i)$ would be undetected.

The inclusion of array elements further expands both the transformation and the encoding algorithms. Two points are of interest.

(i) Since we will always evaluate the subscript first, it is convenient to automatically rotate a $\downarrow$-node (as it was for a := -node).
(ii) Since such a node requires the modifier rather than the accumulator (or sometimes both) the criterion for re-ordering is further complicated.

Consequently, we will, in future, discuss only the code to be generated, leaving it as an exercise to expand the algorithms accordingly.

Let us expand our language by allowing the lower bound to vary from 0 but remaining a constant. As we noted in Chapter 2, an array has two properties: its mode and its address.

The address we store is not that of the initial element of the array since that would lead to poor coding. Consider the array declared:

array $v[l{:}u]$

where l and u represent some constants. Then the dispacement of element $v[i]$ from the initial element $v[l]$ is $i - l$, and so that after loading BM with the subscript i a constant l must be subtracted. It would be preferable to perform the subtraction once only by storing l less than the address of the initial element $v[l]$, that is the address of $v[0]$. This address is called the *base address* (b). Note that there may not, in fact, be an element $v[0]$, nevertheless, the base address does exist (l less than the address of the initial element) and it is convenient to think of it as if the element $v[0]$ existed.

To load $v[i]$ we compile:

BM = i
AFL = b[BM]

For a number of reasons not least the desire to minimise notational complexity, we will continue to write the name of the array instead of b in examples:

BM = i
AFL = v[BM]

10.2 Checking vector accesses

In Chapter 14 we will investigate faults and fault monitoring in detail but it is important here to notice that one of the most common sources of error lies in attempting to access an array element which does not exist—that is, one in which the subscript lies outside the bounds given in the declaration. Since the effect is unpredictable (especially in higher order arrays accessed by Iliffe vectors—see section 10.8) it is desirable to prevent it—or, at least, to terminate the running of the program as soon as it occurs. We do this by compiling extra orders into the code. For example, to load $v[i]$ where v had been declared, as before:

array $v[l:u]$

we would compile:

BM = i
BM COMPARE l
IF < JUMP fault monitor
BM COMPARE u
IF > JUMP fault monitor
AFL = v[BM]

where fault monitor is the address of the appropriate fault monitoring sequence.

Clearly we need to store both bounds during compilation as properties of the array. Thus, the vector v has four properties:

(i) mode
(ii) base address (b)
(iii) lower bound (l)
(iv) upper bound (u)

Note that the increased number of properties for an array is another reason for separating, as we did, the identifiers list from the properties list. During lexical analysis we do not know (or at least we choose not to know) what type of quantity the identifier refers to and so we do not know how many properties to attribute to it.

As we have already suggested, to allow subscripts to be general expressions is trivial. The subscript is evaluated in BM. For example to load $v[2*i + j]$ into the accumulator, ignoring subscript checking, we compile:

BM = 2
BM * i
BM + j
AFL = v[BM]

It is possible to coalesce additive constants in the subscript into the base address. That is to load $v[i + 1]$, instead of compiling:

BM = i
BM + 1
AFL = v[BM]

we compile:

BM = i
AFL = v'[BM]

where v' stands for the base address, $b + 1$. Effectively, we map the vector v onto the vector v':

array $v'[l - 1:u - 1]$

For different constants, of course, we use different mappings. If the subscript is just a constant, such as in $v[3]$, then we do not use BM at all, effectively converting the element into a scalar.

If we consider subscript checking, then the use of this optimisation implies that we check the subscript against the constants $l - 1$ and $u - 1$ which clearly are folded at compile time. Note, again, the influence of optimisation on fault monitoring.

10.3 Static matrices

Let us now consider *matrices* whose subscript bounds are constant, typified by:

array $m[l1:u1, l2:u2]$

The classical technique, called the *multiplication method*, is to consider this declaration as a mapping onto an *equivalent vector*:

array $m'[l':u']$

where l' and u' are constants which will be determined below. Suppose we store the array by row, that is in the order $m[l1, l2]$, $m[l1, l2 + 1]$, $m[l1, l2 + 2]$ . . . then the displacement of $m[i, j]$ beyond the initial element $m[l1, l2]$ is:

$$
\begin{aligned}
&(i - l1)*(u2 - l2 + 1) + (j - l2)\\
&= i*(u2 - l2 + 1) + j - \{l1*(u2 - l2 + 1) + l2\}\\
&= i*c + j - l'
\end{aligned}
$$

where $c = (u2 - l2 + 1)$ and $l' = l1*c + l2$ and these are both constants.

In terms of the equivalent vector this is the displacement of $m'[i*c + j]$ from $m'[l']$. Thus, the equivalent vector is:

array $m'[l':u']$

where $\quad l' = l1*c + l2$

and $\quad u' = u1*c + u2$

and to access $m[i, j]$ we access $m'[i*c + j]$.

We call $[i*c + j]$ the *equivalent subscript* to $[i, j]$. Thus, to load the accumulator with $m[i, j]$ we compile:

BM $= i$
BM * c
BM $+ j$
AFL $= m'$[BM]

This mapping causes $m[0, 0]$ and $m'[0]$ to coincide and so it is meaningful to talk of the base address of m. Consequently, we will use m rather than m' in subsequent code sequences.

Since this is an essentially tertiary construct the binary tree is, like that of the conditional expression, a little contrived. It is:

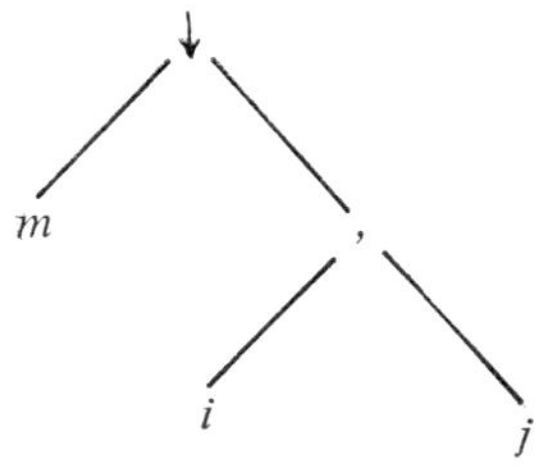

As the discussion shows, the meaning of the ,- node is very dependent on m.

In fact, the tree is really a shorthand for:

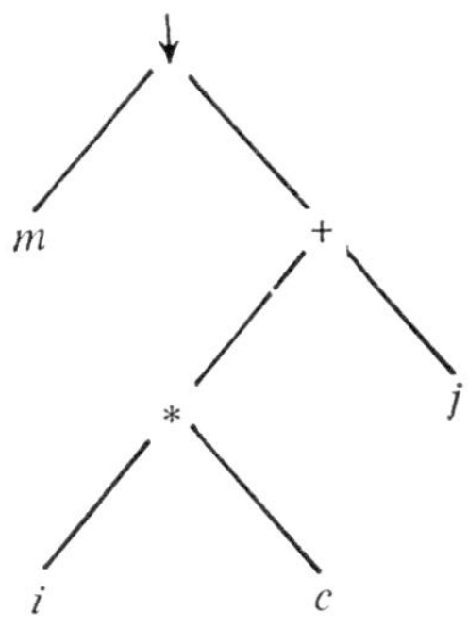

Note that this complete tree cannot be produced by a purely syntactical process. The syntactical process produces the shorthand tree; and some semantic processing is required (to find c) before the complete tree is produced.

10.4 Optimisation of matrix accesses

Within a single statement a number of optimisations are available.

(i) Since $m[i, j]$ is mapped onto $m'[i*c + j]$ any additive constants in j may be coalesced into the base address, thus, effectively performing a second mapping.

(ii) If either i or both i and j are constants then, since c is constant, the equivalent subscript $i*c + j$ may be folded to give a constant subscript which may be coalesced as above to produce a scalar quantity.

(iii) Within a statement common subscript lists may be eliminated.

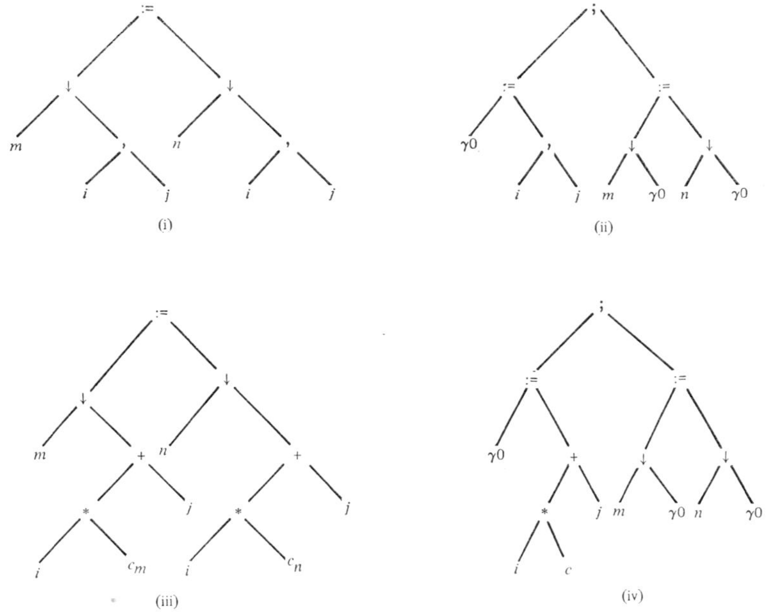

Fig. 10.1. Representations of m $[i,j]:= n[i,j]$: (*i*) *simple tree;* (*ii*) *tree with the sub-expression eliminated;* (*iii*) *expanded tree;* (*iv*) *expanded tree with the sub-expression eliminated* $(c_m = c_n = c)$

Consider the statement:

$$m[i, j] := n[i, j]$$

which we map onto:

$$m'[i*c_m + j] := n'[i*c_n + j]$$

The simple syntax tree is given in Fig. 10.1 (i).

The algorithm of section 9.3, which eliminates common sub-expressions would produce the tree of Fig. 10.1 (ii). [Often the directed graph representation is used.] This means that the evaluation of:

$$i^*c_n + j$$

to produce the equivalent subscript of n is avoided. As can be seen from the expanded tree of Fig. 10.1 (iii) this is valid only if $c_m = c_n$ $(=c)$. It almost invariably is, of course, and so statement-by-statement compilers generally use the simple tree, checking during the encoding that the optimisation is valid, thus retaining the separation of syntactical and semantic processing.

The matrix facility, or at least this implementation of it, is one of the conventional justifications for requiring compilers to eliminate common sub-expressions: that the user is quite unable to do this optimisation himself (unless he chooses always to treat his matrices as vectors!)

Because this treatment of matrices regards:

$$m[i, j] := n[i, j]$$

as:

$$m'[i^*c + j] := n'[i^*c + j]$$

and because such statements invariably appear in loops, the strength reduction techniques are also applicable: indeed, they have been developed purely for this situation.

Consider matrix copying:

```
for i := 1 step 1 until p do
    for j := 1 step 1 until q do
        m[i, j] := n[i, j]
```

This is treated as:

```
for i := 1 step 1 until p do
    for j := 1 step 1 until q do
        m'[i*c + j] := n'[i*c + j]
```

Elimination of the common sub-expression $i*c + j$ produces:

```
for i := 1 step 1 until p do
    for j := 1 step 1 until q do
        begin
        γ0 := i*c + j;
        m'[γ0] := n'[γ0]
        end
```

Subsequent strength reduction on $\gamma 0$ produces:

```
for i := 1 step 1 until p do
    begin
    γ0 := i*c;
    for j := 1 step 1 until q do
        begin
        γ0 := γ0 + 1;
        m'[γ0] := n'[γ0]
        end
    end
```

One of the consequences of strength reduction is that references to the controlled variable of a loop are removed. In this example, no reference is left and so we could transform the for clause to take advantage of the special looping order described in section 9.16.

A second level of strength reduction is applicable to $\gamma 0 := i*c$ giving:

```
γ1 := 0;
for i := 1 step 1 until p do
    begin
    γ1 := γ1 + c;
    γ0 := γ1;
    for j := 1 step 1 until q do
        begin
        γ0 := γ0 + 1;
        m'[γ0] := n'[γ0]
        end
    end
```

With our machine this second strength reduction makes little, if any, improvement: within the loop, we have replaced a multiplication by an addition, a load and a store. However, in a machine with a number of general purpose registers, it is likely that $\gamma 0$ and $\gamma 1$ will be held in registers and the comparison is between a multiplication and an addition; and in a machine with the special looping order, the for clause can be mapped onto a single order.

Regardless of the machine used, if q is replaced by a constant equal to c the variable $\gamma 1$ can be eliminated since at the end of the j-loop $\gamma 0$ will already be c greater than its value on entry.

10.5 Checking matrix accesses

Checking the access to matrix elements can be considered in one of two ways. First we can check that the equivalent subscript of the vector lies within range, so that in the absence of optimisation the code for loading $m[i, j]$ would be:

```
BM = i
BM * c
BM + j
BM  COMPARE l'
IF < JUMP fault monitor
BM  COMPARE u'
IF > JUMP fault monitor
AFL = m[BM]
```

This is the cheaper option and the less satisfactory. It is, however, obligatory in Fortran. (Fortran also insists that the array should be stored by column but that is a minor alteration.) If strength reduction is applied then bound checking, if done at all, must be done this way.

With this approach we need five properties for a matrix:

(i) mode
(ii) base address (b)
(iii) multiplier (c)
(iv) equivalent lower bound (l')
(v) equivalent upper bound (u')

The alternative approach to subscript checking is to check each individual subscript. This involves, in this example, storing $i*c$ while we test j.

The complete sequence to load $m[i, j]$ is:

```
BM = i
BM COMPARE l1
IF < JUMP fault monitor
BM COMPARE u1
IF > JUMP fault monitor
BM * c
BM => δ0
BM = j
BM COMPARE l2
IF < JUMP fault monitor
BM COMPARE u2
IF > JUMP fault monitor
BM + δ0
AFL = m[BM]
```

This is quite a long sequence compared with the non-checking sequence and explains the general reluctance to provide full array bound checking that still exists amongst compiler writers. If we perform this full checking then we need seven properties:

(i) mode
(ii) base address (b)
(iii) multiplier (c)
(iv) first lower bound ($l1$)
(v) first upper bound ($u1$)
(vi) second lower bound ($l2$)
(vii) second upper bound ($u2$)

Static arrays, which is one aspect of a completely static allocation of storage as we shall see later, is a characteristic of Fortran. Indeed whether the allocation is static or dynamic (which we describe in the following sections) is one of the major criteria for classifying programming languages. We shall use this broad distinction in later chapters.

As we have hinted there are other ways of accessing arrays, which we will consider later, since they are better described in the context of the dynamic arrays.

0.6 Dynamic vectors

Let us now expand our language to include the much more general case of an array whose bounds are known only at run time. First we consider the *dynamic vector* and ignore array bound checking. Consider, for example:

array $v[l:u]$

where l and u now are integer variables or expressions.

The problem is that we do not know at compile time the base address of the array and so cannot store it in the properties list. And, of course, we do not know its bounds. Thus we can draw a distinction between those quantities whose address we know at compile time (the scalars), which we call the *static variables*, and those whose address is known only at run time (array elements) called the *dynamic variables*.

Since we do not know the base address at compile time (and so cannot store it in the properties list, and so cannot compile it as the address part of an order) we must calculate it and store it at run time. The technique is to allocate another static variable (whose address we do, of course, know at compile time) to hold the base address at run time. We call this word a *descriptor*.

So, for example, the declarations:

integer l, u;

.

.

.

array $v[l:u]$, w . . .

would result in the store being allocated as in Fig. 10.2.

(Note that for this example to make sense, some imperatives must appear between the integer and array declarations to ensure that l and u have values. There are no compelling reasons for insisting, as Algol 60 does, that all declaratives should precede all imperatives. It is sufficient to insist, as Algol 68 does, that there should be no control transfers across the array declaration.)

Now we have made a significant qualitative change here: previously the run time store was a simple linear affair and we almost passed over mention of it. Now we have a structure to be maintained at run time. (A simple one yet, but more detailed ones will appear over the next few chapters.)

To set up this structure, code must be compiled for the array statement. The dynamic array declaration is a hybrid imperative/ declarative. It causes code to be compiled to set up the run time structure, and it inserts properties into the properties list.

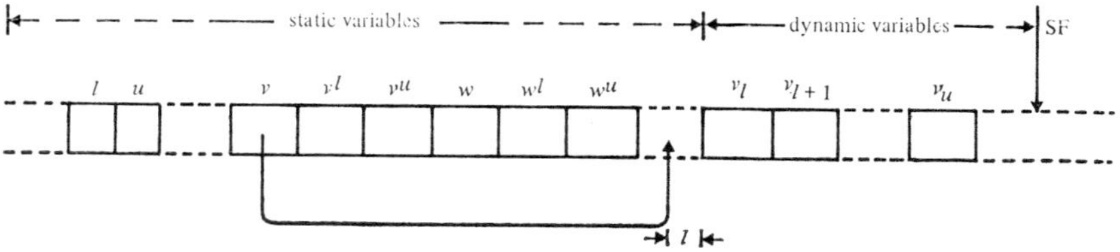

Fig. 10.2. Layout of the store after the declarations:
integer *l*, *u*;
.
.
.
array *v*[*l*:*u*], *w* . . .

To implement this we introduce a new register called the stack front, SF, (the reason for this terminology will become obvious in the next chapter) with the appropriate operations. For the present, these operations are loading, storing and simple arithmetic. On entry to the compiled program, it is set to point to the end of the static variables. The orders compiled for the array declaration:

array *v*[*l*:*u*]

then perform the following operations:

(i) evaluate lower bound (*l*)
(ii) store SF-*l* in the descriptor (*v*)
(iii) evaluate upper bound (*u*)
(iv) Add $u - l + 1$ to SF so that SF always points to the next word of store available for dynamic variables

Let us now consider how to access these dynamic array elements. To do this we will introduce another new register, the descriptor register, DR, which holds descriptors and enables them to be used.

(For the moment DR can be thought of as an ordinary register.) The code to load $v[i]$ is:

DR $= v$
BM $= i$
AFL = DR[BM]

Clearly DR may be loaded and stored; the appearance of DR[BM] as an operand causes the descriptor in DR to be modified by the index in BM (it is sufficient for the moment to regard this as simple addition) and the operand at the resulting address to be accessed. Thus AFL = DR[BM] in the above causes the element $v[i]$ to be loaded into the accumulator.

To perform bound checking we compile similar orders to those for static vectors, in similar places. Of course the bounds are not known at compile time and so are not stored in the properties list. Like the base address they must be evaluated at run time and stored in two extra static variables, the lower limit v^l and the upper limit v^u, which can be conveniently placed after the descriptor v as shown. With bound checking, to load $v[i]$ we compile:

DR $= v$
BM $= i$
BM COMPARE v^l
IF $<$ JUMP fault monitor
BM COMPARE v^u
IF $>$ JUMP fault monitor
AFL = DR[BM]

Clearly the sequence compiled for the array declaration must be extended to store l in v^l and u in v^u.

If we regard the descriptor as containing all three quantities: base address, lower limit and upper limit then the interesting possibility arises that DR can be provided with extra hardware to check the access automatically along the following lines. The order AFL = DR[BM] causes the index in BM to be compared with the upper and lower limits of the descriptor in DR. If it is outside the limits an interrupt occurs; otherwise the base address part of the descriptor in DR is modified by the index in BM and the operand at the resulting address loaded into the accumulator. This is the reason for our machine's inclusion of DR as a special register. There is a trend in modern machines towards this structure.

10.7 Dynamic matrices

Dynamic matrices are dealt with in a similar way. We need to compile further orders to store, as a static variable, the number of

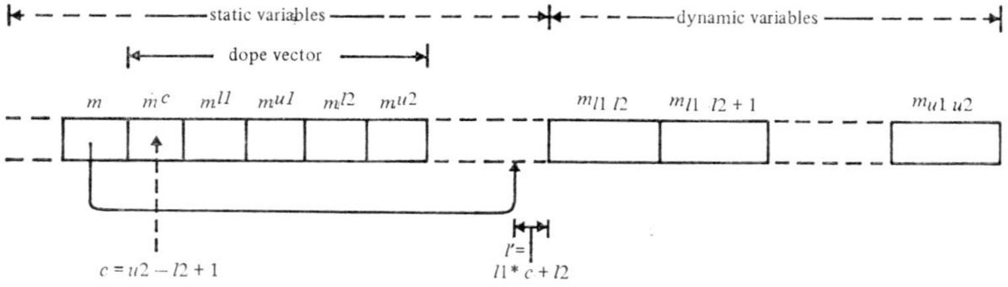

Fig. 10.3. Layout of the store after declaration:
array *m*[*l*1:*u*1, *l*2:*u*2]
using the multiplication method

columns *c* (to be used as a multiplier) as well as the base address (and, for bound checking, the bounds). For example, the array:

array *m*[*l*1 : *u*1, *l*2 : *u*2]

would require the run time structure of Fig. 10.3 which includes all four bounds.

The coding (again ignoring bound checking) to load *m*[*i*, *j*] is:

DR = m
BM = i
BM * m^c
BM + j
AFL = DR[BM]

As in the static case we have two options when we consider subscript checking: either we can check each subscript, which requires us to store four bounds (as shown in Fig. 10.3) and compile ten extra orders; or we can check on the equivalent subscripts which requires us to store two equivalent bounds ($m^{1'}$, $m^{u'}$) and compile four extra orders. We will not give the details. The collection of information needed for accessing and checking is often called a *dope vector*.

The multiplication method is often modified to store the dope vector with the dynamic variables, with a descriptor of the dope vector being stored with the static variables. That is, an array has two descriptors, one of the array itself and one of its dope vector.

Note that the special DR hardware we mentioned in an earlier section is quite sympathetic to the second form of subscript checking described above (the one which regards the matrix as a vector) and so we do not get complete bound checking.

This highlights the main characteristic of the way we have been considering a matrix—we have mapped it on to an equivalent vector. In other words the vector of numbers has been our only data structure, and we have used arithmetic operations (multiplication and addition) to map other data structures (matrices and arrays of higher dimensions) onto it.

10.8 Iliffe vectors

An alternative approach first suggested by Iliffe (see ref. 10.1), is to regard a matrix as a *vector of vectors*. Thus we have a descriptor pointing to a vector of descriptors (called an *Iliffe vector*) each of which points to a row of the matrix. Thus, the declaration:

array $m[l1:u1,\ l2:u2]$

produces the structure of Fig. 10.4.

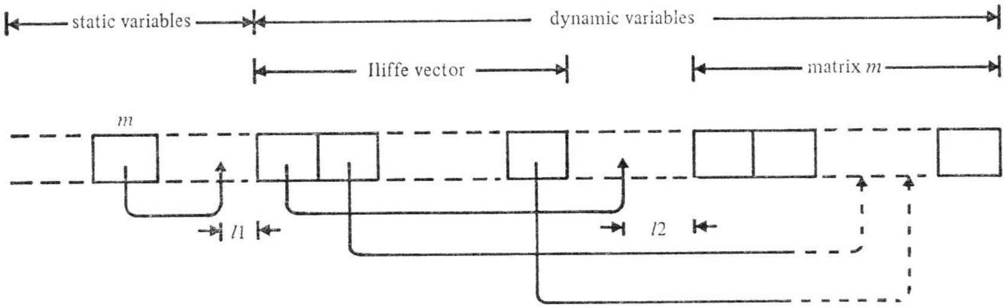

Fig. 10.4. Layout of store after the declaration:
array $m[l1:u1,\ l2:u2]$
using Iliffe vectors

The sequence compiled to load $m[i, j]$ is:

DR = m
BM = i
DR = DR[BM]
BM = j
AFL = DR[BM]

This sequence is much more amenable to individual subscript checking since the subscripts are loaded individually into BM. Two options are available for storing the bounds. We may store all four bounds as a dope vector, placing it beside the descriptor. Alternatively we may, as suggested earlier, expand the descriptor to include one pair of bounds. The Iliffe vector then becomes a vector of descriptors, each descriptor containing the second bounds ($l2$, $u2$), while the main descriptor contains only the first bounds ($l1$, $u1$). With this latter solution the hardware suggested will perform complete subscript checking automatically, (though at the price of storing the second bounds ($l2$, $u2$) once for each row). We assume this solution in what follows.

The sequence compiled for the array declaration now is quite involved since it needs to set up this complete structure. In practice it is often made into a subroutine.

This form of accessing regards $m[i, j]$ as $m[i]$ $[j]$ or $m \downarrow i \downarrow j$ applying the subscripting operations from left to right.

Thus we really require a different tree structure:

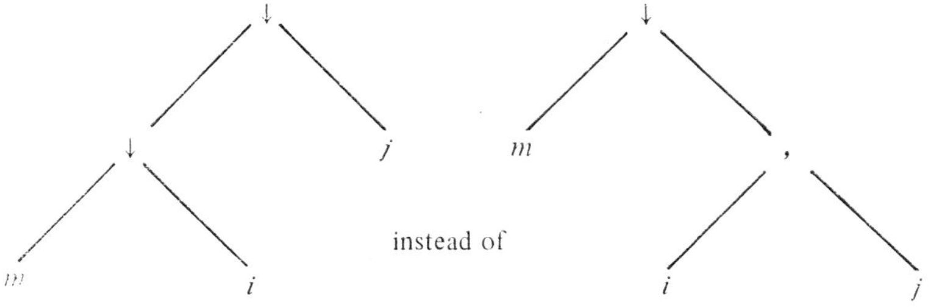

This can be produced quite simply by changing some of the entries of the transition matrix.

Considering optimisation within a statement we cannot, with this structure, optimise:

$$m[i, j] := n[i, j]$$

because, as it is regarded as:

$$m \downarrow i \downarrow j := n \downarrow i \downarrow j$$

there is no common sub-expression. We can, however, optimise:

$$m[i, j] := m[i, k]$$

(which is regarded as:

$$m \downarrow i \downarrow j := m \downarrow i \downarrow k)$$

by storing DR when it contains $m \downarrow i$. That is, we convert it to:

$$\gamma 0 := m \downarrow i$$
$$\gamma 0 \downarrow j := \gamma 0 \downarrow k$$

where $\gamma 0$ is a variable of type descriptor.

A similar operation is required when optimising across loops. Consider again matrix copying:

```
for i := 1 step 1 until p do
    for j := 1 step 1 until q do
        m[i, j] := n[i, j]
```

This is treated as:

```
for i := 1 step 1 until p do
    for j := 1 step 1 until q do
        m ↓ i ↓ j := n ↓ i ↓ j
```

The expressions $m \downarrow i$ and $n \downarrow i$ are constant within the inner loop and can be moved outside:

```
for i := 1 step 1 until p do
    begin
    γ0 := m ↓ i; γ1 := n ↓ i;
    for j := 1 step 1 until q do
        γ0 ↓ j := γ1 ↓ j
    end
```

This is a purely syntactical process. Compare this with the multiplication method where common sub-expression recognition (which requires some semantic processing) is required followed by two levels of strength reduction to produce comparable code. Indeed using Iliffe vectors effectively eliminates the necessity of strength reduction procedures at all.

More significantly, building on the DR mechanism previously described, we can arrange for the optimisation to be done by the hardware rather than the software. The code compiled by the simplest compiler for:

$$m \downarrow i \downarrow j := n \downarrow i \downarrow j$$

is:

DR = n
BM = i
DR = DR[BM]
BM = j
AFL = DR[BM]
DR = m
BM = i
DR = DR[BM]
BM = j
AFL ⇒ DR[BM]

Four descriptors are involved, n, $n \downarrow i$, m and $m \downarrow i$. If the hardware associated with DR is arranged to remember, say, the last 16 descriptors it has accessed, then after the first traverse of the loop, all four descriptors will be in its private memory. Consequently subsequent references will not need to access the main store, referring instead to the private memory, which can be made significantly faster. Note that with this form of optimisation, the compiler does not plant any fewer orders, and the machine does not obey fewer orders; instead it obeys some orders much faster than usual.

10.9 Three and higher dimensional arrays

The extension to three and more dimensions is quite straightforward. Consider the array:

array $t[l1:u1, l2:u2, l3:u3]$

The multiplication method maps this onto a vector:

array $t'[l':u']$

and accesses $t[i, j, k]$ as $t'[i*c1 + j*c2 + k]$

where $c2 = (u3 - l3 + 1)$
$c1 = c2*(u2 - l2 + 1)$
$l' = l1*c1 + l2*c2 + l3$
$u' = u1*c1 + u2*c2 + u3$

The dope vector is extended to include $c2$ and, if desired, the third pair of bounds. The techniques of common sub-expression elimination and strength reduction are applicable. In a compiler which attempts no optimisation it may be preferable to access $t[i, j, k]$ as $t'[(i*c3 + j)*c2 + k]$
where:

$$c3 = (u2 - l2 + 1)$$

to allow the subscript to be evaluated without storing partial results.

With the Iliffe vector method, the primary descriptor points to an Iliffe vector, each element of which points to a row of an Iliffe matrix, each element of which points to a row of the array t.

).10 A comparison of Iliffe vectors and the multiplication method

It is interesting to review the characteristics of the two methods. We do so using the Iliffe vector as the basis.

(i) It uses store accesses instead of multiplications. This might be important for a machine without an integer multiplier (Atlas, CDC 7600).

(ii) It is very sympathetic to checking individual array bounds (and hardware can be provided to do it), whereas the multiplication method favours over-all bound checking.

(iii) It requires extra store for the Iliffe vectors, each matrix requiring its own. For arrays of higher dimensions we require more store.

(iv) Optimisation across loops is much more easily implemented; strength reduction techniques are unnecessary. Further, hardware can be provided to do it automatically.

(v) It is asymmetrical: it regards a matrix as a row of rows rather than a column of columns. Thus, the optimisation techniques are strongly dependent on the order of access to elements of a matrix. Access by rows is optimisable; access by columns is not. Suppose the matrix copy statement were written:

> **for** i := 1 **step** 1 **until** p **do**
>   **for** j := 1 **step** 1 **until** q **do**
> $m[j, i] := n[j, i]$

There is nothing constant within the inner loop and so no optimisation is possible.

On the other hand, the multiplication method is invariant to the order of access, the above matrix copy statement being equally susceptible to common sub-expression elimination and strength reduction.

(vi) No spatial relation is assumed between one row and another. They may be stored consecutively: they need not be. They need not even be of the same length. Although languages do not generally provide them, this technique is applicable to triangular and jagged arrays.

(vii) On a more philosophical plane it regards operand accessing as operand accessing and not as arithmetic. It is this which creates the possibility of hardware optimisation.

10.11 Storing a multiplication vector

In a machine with no integer multiplier the use of the Iliffe vector scheme is sometimes thought too expensive in terms of storage. Accordingly a hybrid technique is sometimes used. For each matrix we store two vectors, first the equivalent vector, second a vector containing all relevant multiples of the multiplier. Thus the array declaration:

> **array** $m[l1:u1, l2:u2]$

produces the structure of Fig. 10.5.

To access $m[i, j]$ we compile:

> BM = i
> DR = m^*
> BM = DR[BM]
> BM + j
> DR = m
> AFL = DR[BM]

As with the multiplication method, checking individual bounds is tedious. The most convenient check to perform (and the one the special harware would do) is on the first subscript and on the equivalent subscript, which still is not completely satisfactory.

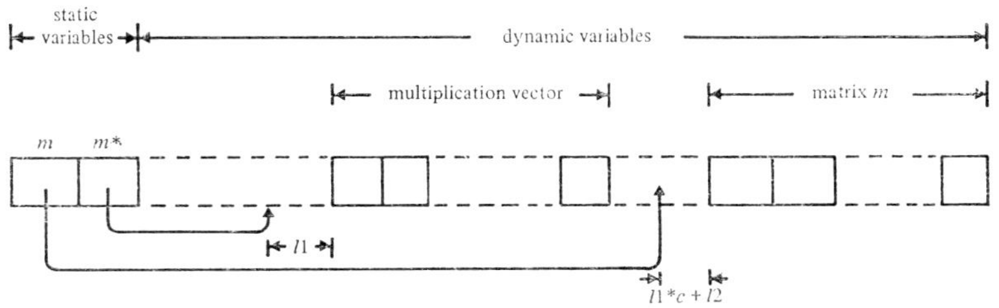

Fig. 10.5. Layout of the store after the declaration:
array *m*[*l*1 : *u*1, *l*2 : *u*2]
using the multiplication vector method

The characteristic of this solution is that the multiplication vector can be shared amongst all matrices of the same size.

10.12 A comment on this chapter

Within this chapter we have made a number of comments on machine design. This is because it seems reasonable to suppose that, just as future language design teams will contain compiler writers, so too will future machine design teams. The compiler writer, to make an adequate contribution, must understand how changes in architecture will affect the nature of the orders he compiles. He must be aware that many of the existing compiler writing techniques arise directly from the deficiencies of existing hardware, and are in no way fundamental. Clearly this philosophy has a very wide application; we have chosen to illustrate it in this chapter, purely because array accessing provides a realistic example.

11 Block structure

In Chapter 3 we briefly introduced blocks as part of the argument for separating out lexical analysis from syntactical analysis. We now consider them in more detail. We will consider their effects on both static and dynamic allocation languages, though in practice the notion has no relevance to Fortran. (There is no reason why it could not be added however.)

11.1 Blocks

Blocks are essentially devices for enabling parts of a program to share store at run time, and share identifiers at compile time. Syntactically, a block consists of a series of declarations separated by semicolons, followed by a series of statements separated by semicolons, the whole enclosed within brackets which we will again represent as **begin** and **end**. A compound statement can be considered as a degenerate block in which no declarations appear.

Consider the skeletal program of Fig. 3.3, which is reproduced as Fig. 11.1.

Within any block, it is possible to refer to the variables declared within the block (we will call them the *variables of the block*) and to the variables of any blocks enclosing that block. Thus, within block 3 of Fig. 11.1, we can refer to the variables of blocks 3 and 1 but not block 2. Similarly, within block 2 we can refer to the variables of blocks 2 and 1 but not 3. Thus, blocks 2 and 3 can share the same storage space for variables. As we progress through a program the accessible variables change and the allocation of storage must accurately reflect this. This change takes place only at **begin**s and **end**s and is illustrated in Fig. 11.2. Note that this figure and subsequent ones in this chapter are quite schematic; nothing should be read into the fact all the boxes are of the same size.

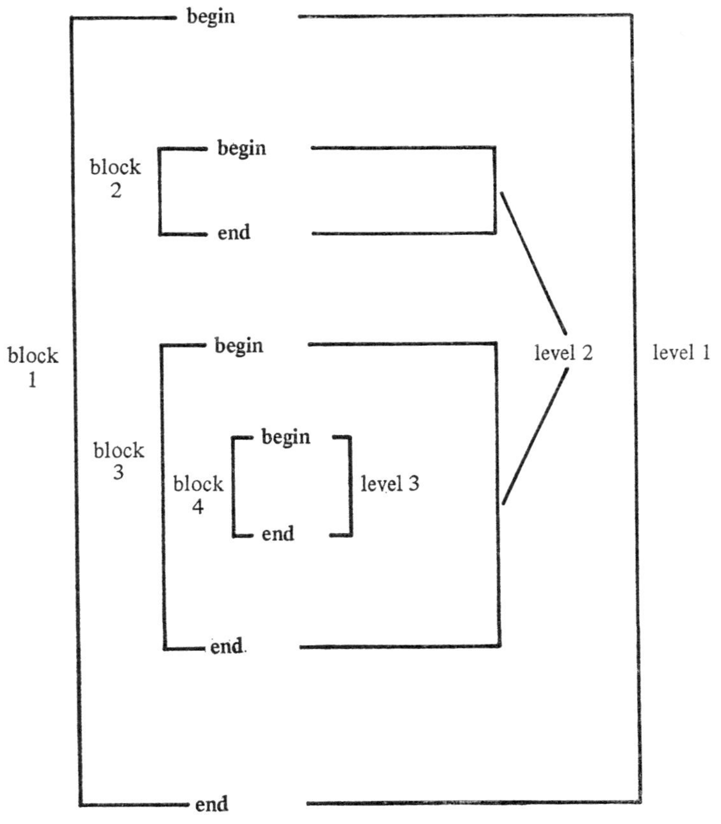

Fig. 11.1. A skeleton of a block structure program

11.2 Blocks in a language with static storage allocation

Note that the storage space expands and contracts from one end: it is a grander version of the simple stack discussed earlier. It is for this reason that SF is so named: it marks the *f*ront of the *s*tack as it expands and contracts.

In a language with static storage allocation, we always know at compile time how many variables there are in a block; and so we always know where the variables of any enclosed block will start;

and so we know the address of every variable. Thus we require no run time structures to be maintained, and no orders to be compiled for **begin** and **end**. Indeed, SF itself is quite unnecessary. We do need some compile time structures, though as we shall see in section 11.7.

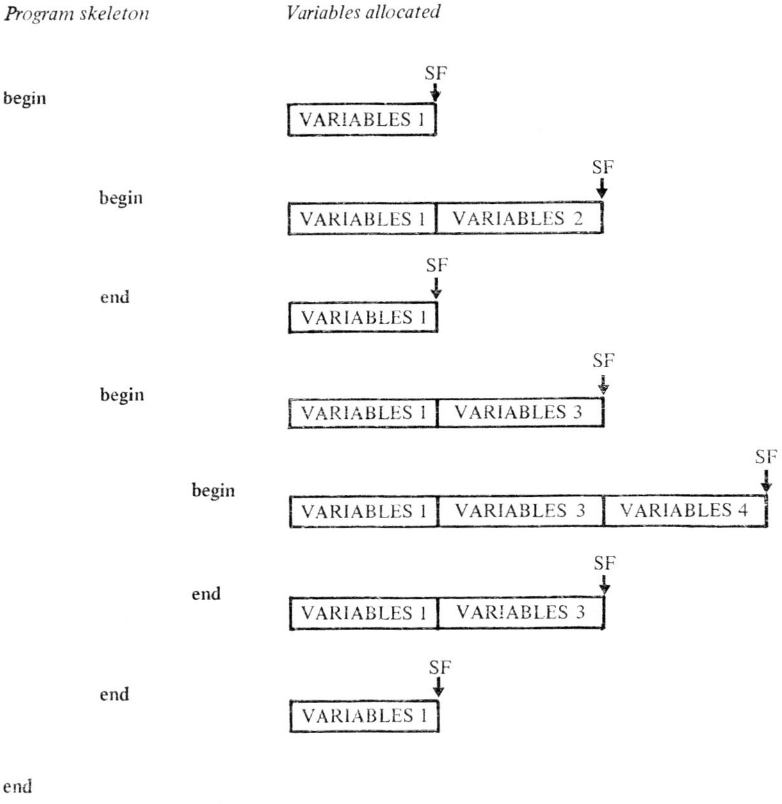

Fig. 11.2. The allocation of variables of the program of Fig. 11.1.

11.3 Blocks in a language with dynamic storage allocation

In a language with dynamic storage allocation, on the other hand, we do not know, at compile time, how many variables there are in a block; and so we do not know where the variables of any enclosed block will start; and so we do not know the address of every variable. Within each block, of course, the situation is as described in Chapter 10. Their variables are of two classes: the *static variables*, whose address *relative to the start of the variables* of the block, we know at compile time, and the *dynamic variables*, whose address we do not know.

Thus at run time, when, of course, we do know where the variables of a block start, we must arrange to add this value to the relative address of the variable within the block. We introduce a further register, the *stack base register* (SB) which is arranged always to contain the address of the start of the variables of the block currently being obeyed.

Suppose block 4 started:

> **begin**
> **real** *a*, *b*, *c;*

The variables *a*, *b*, *c* will have relative addresses 0, 1 and 2. The statement:

> $a := b$

is compiled, going back to lowest level of machine order, into:

> AFL = {1/SB}
> AFL ⇛ {0/SB}

where '/SB' means 'relative to SB'. The SB register then behaves just like a conventional modifier, though we will continue to regard it as a special purpose register.

How do we access variables that are in enclosing blocks? Clearly we need to maintain a whole series of stack bases, one for each enclosing block. In this context we talk of the *textual level* of a block. This is a measure of the depth to which it is nested within enclosing blocks. The outer block, block 1, is at textual level 1; the blocks immediately within it, blocks 2 and 3, are at textual level 2; and any blocks within them, here only block 4, are at textual level 3; and so on. The level numbers for the skeletal program have been added to Fig. 11.1. Since blocks at the same textual level cannot be active at the same time, we need only to associate stack bases with textual levels rather than with blocks. We call the collection of stack bases, a *stack base directory*, or a *display*. Within block 4 we would have the structure of Fig. 11.3.

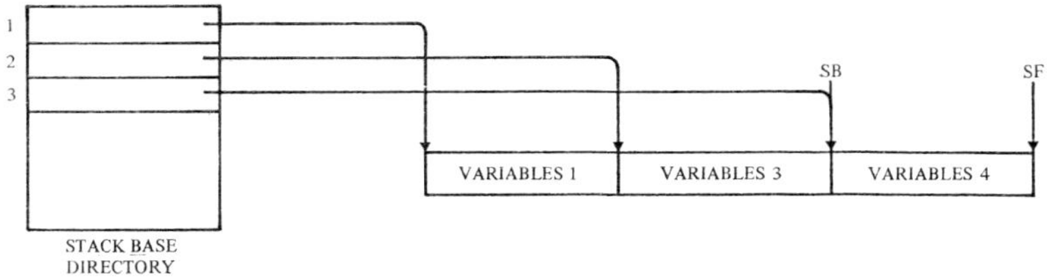

Fig. 11.3. The stack and stack base directory within block 4 of the skeletal program of Fig. 11.1

We have assumed here that the stack base directory is held in the store. It might well be held as a set of special registers (as in the Burroughs B6000 machines), or in a group of modifier registers (as on Atlas). If it is held in the store it is convenient to have an *extra stack base register* (XSB) which can be set to the stack base of an enclosing block so that its variables may be accessed.

If blocks 3 and 4 had the structure:

```
begin
real x, y, z;
      .
      .
      .
      begin
      real a, b, c;
      .
      .
      .
      end
          .
          .
          .
end
```

Then within block 4 the statement:

$x := a*y$

would be compiled:

AFL = {0/SB}
XSB = Stack base directory entry 2
AFL * {1/XSB}
AFL ⇒ {0/XSB}

It is fairly uncommon for programs to access variables of different blocks at random; indeed, most access variables of the current block and only one enclosing block. In this situation XSB is infrequently loaded though perhaps frequently used.

In future we will revert to:

AFL = *a*
AFL * *y*
AFL ⇒ *x*

for the compiled code leaving the loading of XSB implicit.

Clearly **begin** and **end** are compiled into instructions to maintain this structure. A **begin** at textual level *n* is compiled into orders to:

(i) Set SB to SF.
(ii) Store SB as entry n in the stack base directory.
(iii) Advance SF over static variables of the block.

The second order is required in case there is an enclosed block (at level n + 1) which will later on use the variables of this current block. This order is redundant in blocks which have no blocks embedded in them. If we can detect this case (in a multi-pass compiler) then the order can be deleted.

The third order above involves a simple case of the same problem as that encountered when processing go to statements before the label has appeared. Here we have to compile an order whose address part is not known until further statements have been compiled. The solution is to compile the order with zero as the address part; remember the address of the order using *bp* (the *begin pointer*), say; and correct the address part at the corresponding **end**, (or some other convenient place) when the number of static variables is known.

The **end** compiles into *two* orders:

(i) Reset SF to SB.
(ii) Reset SB from entry n-1 in the stack base directory.

Note that this implies that the stack base directory often contains entries to non-existent blocks since such entries are not erased at the **end** of a block. Such entries are never accessed and so no problems arise.

11.4 Storing temporary variables

When dealing with expressions we introduced temporary variables, $\delta 0$, $\delta 1$, etc., for holding partial results. The compiler may well allocate space within the variables of the block for these. However, with a nested block structure (and with procedures, see Chapter 12) this is wasteful of store, each block being provided with its own set. The variables occur in a regular pattern and we suggested in Chapter 4 that they might be held in a stack. We can maintain such a stack by using SF. There are two possibilities:

(i) The variables $\delta 0$, $\delta 1$ ... are associated with addresses SF, SF + 1 and so on, the stack being effectively maintained at compile time. In the lowest level of machine code:

AFL ⇒ $\delta 2$

is:

AFL ⇒ {2/SF}

(ii) A stack can be maintained at run time by orders to stack and unstack. For example, we could add to our machine, orders typified by:

STACK AFL

which is equivalent to:

AFL ⇒ {SF}
SF + 1

and add a special operand as in:

AFL + STACK

which is equivalent to:

SF − 1
AFL + {SF}

Because of the way δs are accessed, all orders to store them map onto the STACK order and all orders to access them use STACK as an operand.

11.5 Coalescing blocks

The orders required to enter and leave a block (five in a simply block-structured situation, more when the block structure is superimposed on to a procedure-structure) together with the increase in size of the stack base directory that each level implies has lead compiler writers to consider the *coalescing of blocks.*

Suppose that in the program of Fig. 11.1, all the variables of all the blocks are scalars. Then the address of each variable is known at compile time: we are essentially in the static storage allocation situation of Section 11.2. The code compiled for the first **begin** can move SF to reserve space for all the variables; that is, by the larger of:

(i) size of variables of block 1 + size of variables of block 2

and

(ii) size of variables of block 1 + size of variables of block 3 + size of variables of block 4.

At the corresponding **end**, the whole space is recovered. No code then need be planted for the **begin**s and **end**s of block 2, 3 and 4. Consequently, there is no need for the stack base directory entries 2 and 3: all variables are accessed relative to the first entry. When we consider the effect of introducing procedures (as we do in the next chapter) we find that this coalescence is restricted to the blocks of a procedure (and of the main part of the program) rather than operating over the whole program. Consequently, it is often termed *procedure-level addressing* (see ref 11.1) in contrast to the simple *block-level addressing* discussed initially.

The cost of obtaining the advantages of this technique is clear: within a procedure (or the main program) the maximum amount of storage required by the procedure is allocated on entry and remains allocated throughout. [The effect of this will be seen in the next chapter, when a procedure calls another which calls another. . . .] Since the number of scalars in any program is small, the cost is often thought acceptable. [The technique is, however, open to the objection that it deliberately overides the programmer's attempt to dynamically allocate storage by the mechanism which is expressly provided to do it: it essentially converts blocks into compound statements.] When the blocks contain arrays, however, the cost of the technique is quite unacceptable since arrays are often much larger; and if the arrays are dynamic then the technique is inadequate. Consequently, the technique is modified.

Suppose now that blocks 1, 2 and 4 of the program of Fig. 11.1 have array declarations, and that the static variables are allocated at the **begin** of block 1. Then at the array declaration of block 2, for example, code must be compiled to reserve space for the array and advance SF: at the **end**, code must be compiled to recover the space of the array by retarding SF. The other blocks are similar. The situation is illustrated in Fig. 11.4.

In this situation the speed gained by not compiling orders for the **begin**s and some of the **end**s is negligible when compared with orders involved in allocating the store for the arrays (and, presumably, in orders involved in setting and subsequently processing the arrays). The gain though lies in that only one stack base directory entry is required, since access to the array elements is via the descriptor which is held as one of the static variables. However, reference back to the orders compiled using the block-level addressing technique (Section 11.3) shows that the stack base directory entries (and SB) were used not only for accessing during the block but also for re-setting SF at the end of the block. Consequently, with procedure-level addressing, the corresponding values must be held as static variables to allow SF to be reset correctly. This *stack front directory* is quite small, of course, the same size as the stack base directory that this technique eliminates.

11.6 Separating static from dynamic variables

The time required to modify the relative address of each static variable by SB has also worried compiler writers. This is especially true when SB, itself, has been held in the store. (In large pipe-lined machines such as the ICL 1906A and MU5 the problem is not

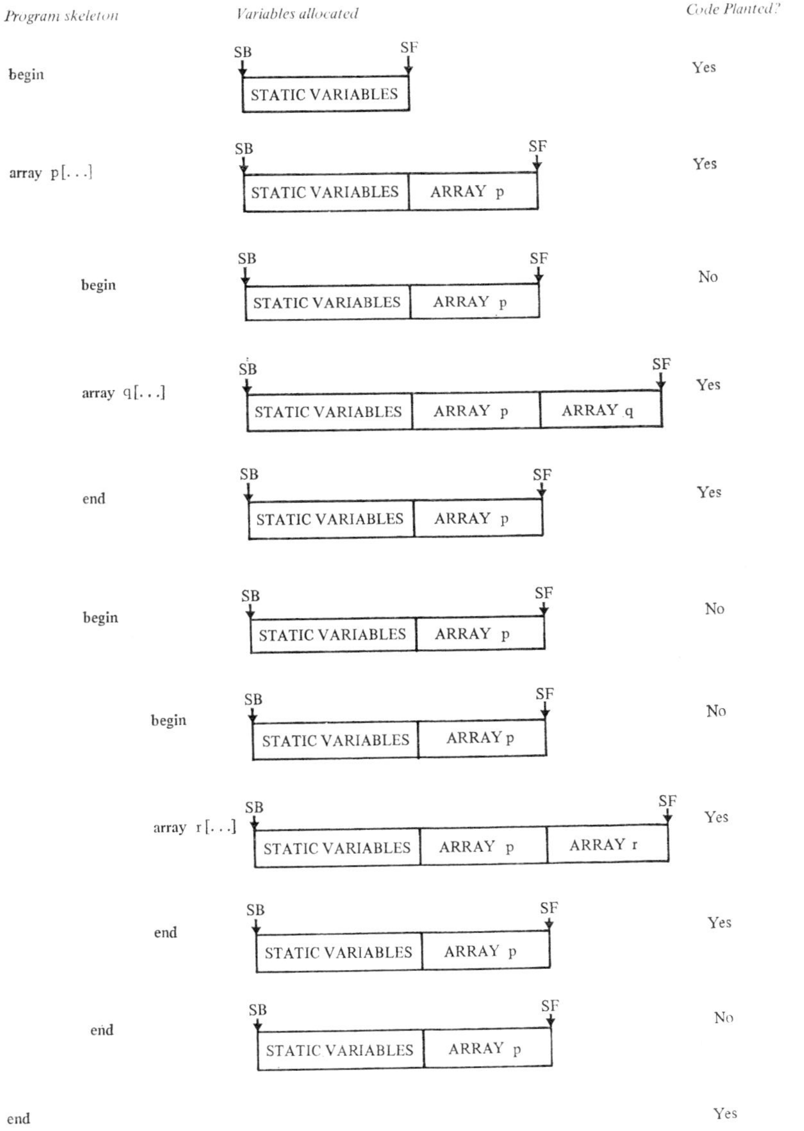

Fig. 11.4. The allocated variables of the program of Fig. 11.1 assuming certain array declarations

relevant since the speed of orders is the same whether or not such modification takes place.)

The solution is to separate out completely the static variables, allocating them fixed locations at the front of the stack so that they can be accessed by means of their absolute addresses. The dynamic variables are then allocated at run time on the end of the *static variables area*. The size of this area is known right at the end of compile time, so the compiled code for the initial **begin** can include an order to set SB appropriately on entry.

This solution will require rather more store than the orthodox method since storage for the maximum number of accessible static variables is always allocated. Its greatest weakness, however, lies in the fact that it is inapplicable when recursive procedures are allowed (see section 12.14).

11.7 Compile time considerations

Blocks have one characteristic that we have not yet discussed. Within a given block we may not always be able to access all the variables of an enclosing block: in particular, if an identifier is declared in both blocks, then only the variable (or other quantity such as a label) of the given block is accessible. We talk of the *scope* of a variable, which is the area of the program over which the variable is accessible. This is a very important facility since it contributes towards the independence of a block from its enclosed and enclosing blocks. Loop counters, such as i and j, temporary variables, such as x and temp, and so on, are often used in every block of a program.

Thus, within a block, when we require the properties of a variable we need to search through the properties of the current block first; followed by those of the enclosing block; and so on. Thus, at compile time we need to maintain a structure of properties lists which varies as the compilation progresses in exactly the same way that the structure of run time variables varies as the running of the program progresses. Fig. 11.5 illustrates this with respect to the skeletal program of Fig. 11.1.

This compile time structure is necessary even when the variations in run time structure described in Sections 11.5 and 11.6 are used.

If we use the simplest technique for storing the properties (no hash

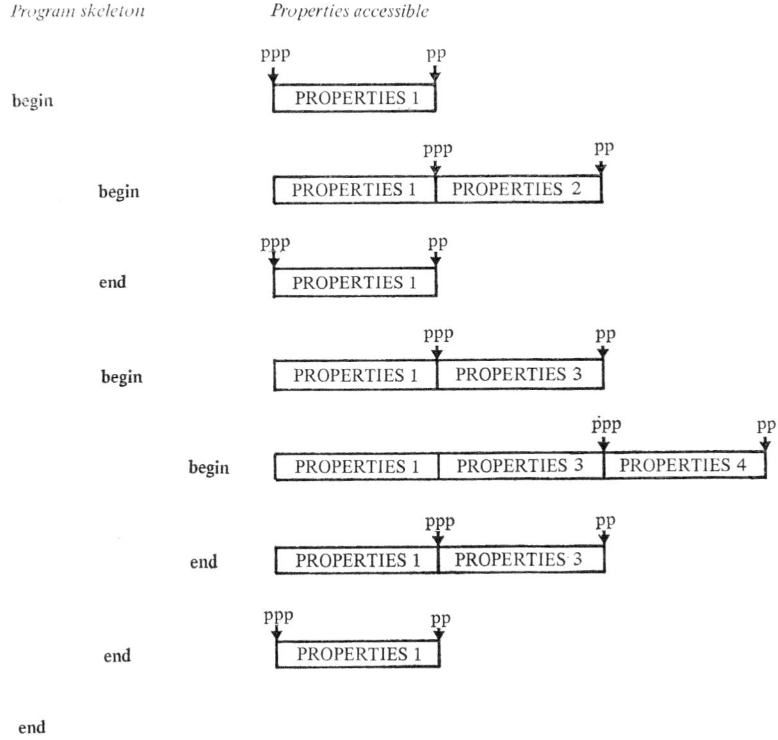

Fig. 11.5. The accessible properties of the program of Fig. 11.1

addressing and no separation of identifier from other properties) then this structure is very easy to use and maintain. Identifiers are looked up, simply by scanning the properties backwards from pp. At each **end** the properties of all the quantities of the block are deleted by moving pp back to the end of the properties of the enclosing block. It is convenient to use another pointer *ppp* (*previous properties pointer*) to point to this position. As we reset pp (to ppp), so too we must reset ppp. One technique is to give each block some extra properties (as well as those of the quantities declared within it), which are stored first. One such property might be the value of ppp for the enclosing block. Another might be the value of the begin pointer, bp, of the enclosing block.

We rejected this simple form of properties list structure in Chapter 3 as being too inefficient. We mention it here only because it illustrates the problem quite well and because it serves as a basis for

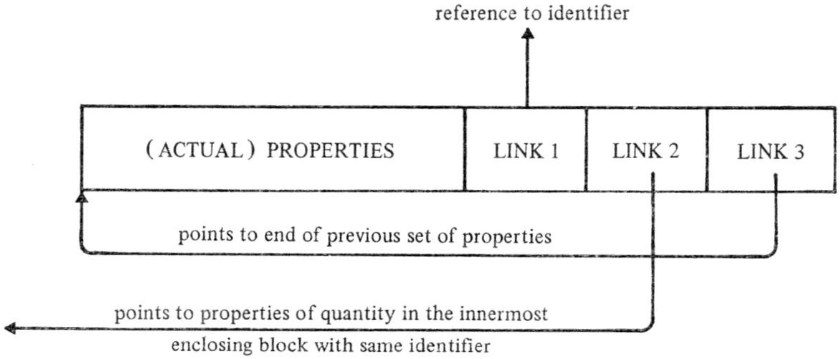

Fig. 11.6. Structure of a set of properties in a block structure context

comparison. Suppose we now return to our favoured structure, which separates the identifiers from the other properties, and which groups the identifiers by some hashing algorithm.

Each identifier refers to the other properties associated with the quantity. In a block structure context, we must ensure that, when an identifier is redeclared, it is made to refer to the new set of properties, in such a way that, at the end of the block, it can be made to refer back to the previous set of properties. This implies that we need to extend the properties of each quantity. Three extra properties are required:

(i) A link which refers to the identifier (LINK 1).
(ii) A link which refers to the properties of the quantity in the innermost enclosing block with the same identifier (LINK 2).
(iii) A link which points to the start of the set of properties (LINK 3). This is required to take account of the fact (previously mentioned but since ignored) that different quantities have a different number of properties. The structure is illustrated in Fig. 11.6.

At an **end**, the compiler works its way backwards through the sets of properties from pp (using LINK 3). Each identifier (LINK 1) is uncoupled from these properties and reset to those relevant outside the block (LINK 2).

12 Procedures

In this chapter we will discuss the last of the extensions to our basic language—the procedure. This gives it almost the full power of Algol and Fortran. True, there are a few concepts not covered—such as switches and own arrays; these are, however, fairly simple to deal with.

12.1 Procedure or subroutine structure

Algol and Fortran unfortunately use different terms, *procedure* and *subroutine* for what is essentially the same concept (though they do have their differences). In what follows we shall use the term procedure in an inclusive sense.

There are essentially two forms of procedure structure, the disjoint (as in Fortran) and the nested (as in Algol). Fig. 12.1 illustrates this by outlines of two programs.

Note that the form here is deliberately different from that of Algol. We shall find it more expedient, for the moment, to consider a procedure as a piece of code delimited by **procedure** and **end procedure** than to dwell on the implications of an Algol procedure's being a declaration. We will, return to it in section 12.15.

Now, in practice, most languages with a disjoint procedure structure, actually embed the discrete procedures (and main program) within an implicit surrounding program. This also contains further implicitly defined procedures such as sine and cosine, and often a set of global variables. Thus, we can, and will, regard the discrete procedure structure embedded in this outer level as a special case of the general nested structure.

It is, perhaps, pertinent to note that the choice of procedure structure is quite independent of the choice of dynamic or static allocation. Languages can, and do, have a disjoint structure together with dynamic allocation.

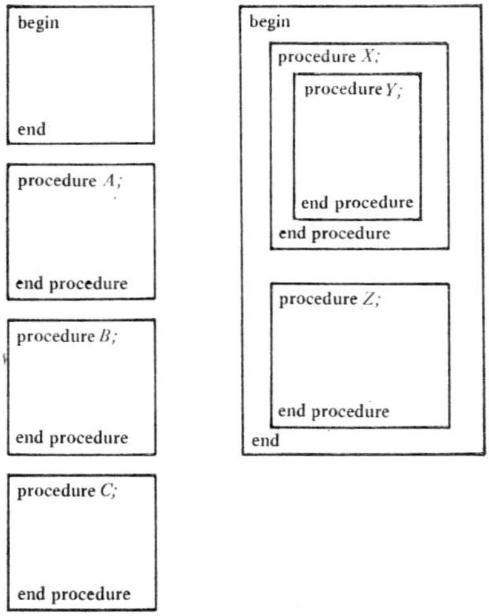

Fig. 12.1. Procedure structure: (i) disjoint (Fortran); (ii) nested (Algol)

12.2 Compile time considerations

At compile time, a procedure in this structure behaves in exactly the same way as a block with respect to the scope of its variables (see section 11.7).

Of course, procedures may contain blocks, and blocks may contain procedures. In this chapter we will generally ignore blocks and concentrate on the procedure aspect, since procedures can exist, and often do (as in Fortran), in the absence of blocks.

Note that we have introduced a new quantity—the procedure itself. This is regarded as being local to the enclosing block, and its properties are stored with those of the quantities of the enclosing block. Its local quantities and (see later) its parameters, belong to itself.

It is because a procedure belongs to its enclosing block that one procedure may call another procedure embedded within that block. Of course, a procedure may also call another procedure embedded within itself since that second procedure belongs to the first. Thus, in Fig. 12.1 (ii):

Main program can call *X*, *Z*
Procedure *X* can call *Y*, *Z* (and *X*)
Procedure *Y* can call *X*, *Z* (and *Y*)
Procedure *Z* can call *X* (and *Z*)

Note that procedure *Y* is quite inaccessible to *Z* and to the main program. Indeed, this is the attraction of a nested structure: procedure *X* behaves as an independent entity regardless of its own internal structure.

Note, too, that since a procedure belongs to its enclosing block it can call itself—unless the definition of the language specifically excludes it.

12.3 Run time considerations

The significant difference between blocks and procedures, is that blocks are entered in the natural sequence of events from the top and are left at the bottom. It is this regular pattern that enables blocks to share space. Procedures, on the other hand, are entered as the result of a call, which may occur in a number of different places, a much more irregular pattern. This is the problem.

12.4 Procedures in a language with static storage allocation

Languages which have a static storage allocation scheme, have it so that all accesses to variables are to a fixed (unmodified) address. The concern is to avoid the time required for modification. When extended to procedures this means that their variables, too, must be allocated a fixed address. We will use the example of Fig. 12.1 (i) as an illustration. Note that static allocation of variables automatically excludes recursion. In theory, procedures may share space. For example, if in Fig. 12.1 (i) each of the procedures *A*, *B* and *C* were called only by the main program, then *A*, *B*, and *C* could clearly share the same space. However, because *A*, *B* and *C* may also call each other and because a sophisticated analysis needs to be performed to detect the simple case, the procedures are generally allocated separate (exclusive) areas of store. For example, the program of Fig. 12.1 (i) would have a storage allocation as shown in Fig. 12.2.

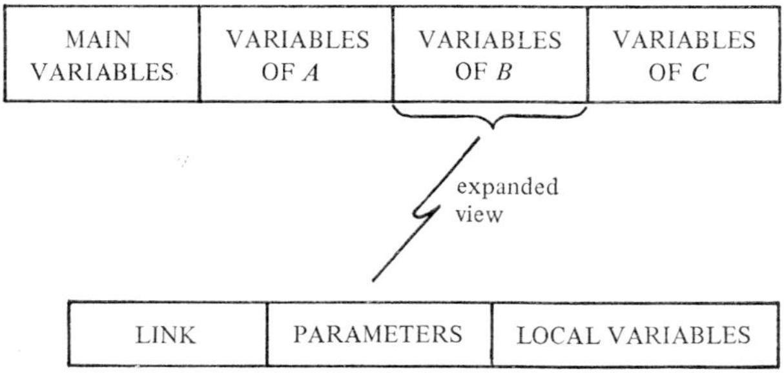

Fig. 12.2. Storage allocation for the static procedure structure of Fig. 12.1 (i)

As we have indicated, this can be expensive of space and so other means are adopted of sharing storage, such as Fortran's common blocks.

The variables of a procedure consist of:

(i) The link.
(ii) The parameters.
(iii) The local variables.

The *link* is the address in the calling block to which control is to be returned at the completion of the procedure. It is the address of the instruction immediately after the call. We will discuss the *parameters* in section 12.6.

Static procedures are implemented as follows:

A *procedure call* is compiled into orders which:

(i) Evaluate and assign the parameters.
(ii) Store the link.
(iii) Jump into the procedure.

The *procedure heading* (like the block heading in a similar situation) produces no code.

The *procedure end* is compiled simply into one order to:

(i) Jump back to the calling procedure at address stored in the link.

12.5 Procedures in a language with dynamic storage allocation

In a language with dynamic storage allocation, store is allocated on the stack for the variables of a procedure immediately upon entry to the procedure—just as for a block.

Consider the program of Fig. 12.3, which contains a call for *X*

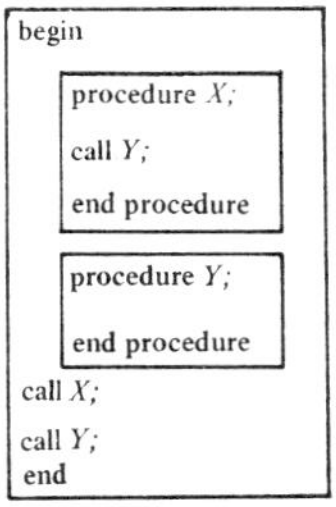

Fig. 12.3. A skeleton of a program with procedures and their calls

from the main program, and two calls for *Y*, one from the main program and one from *X*.

Fig. 12.4 shows the state of the stack at key points during the execution of this program. Ignore for the moment the stack base directory.

As in the static situation the variables of a procedure consist of three distinct groups:

(i) The links.
(ii) The parameters.
(iii) The local variables.

But consider the situation just after procedure *X* has called procedure *Y*, Fig. 12.4 (iii). *X* and *Y* are at the same level and the variables of X are inaccessible to Y. [During compilation the properties of X would have been deleted before Y had been processed.] The second element of the stack base directory must point to the variables of Y as shown and so there is nothing pointing to the start of the variables of X and so no way of returning to the state of Fig. 12.4 (ii) on exit from Y as shown in Fig. 12.4 (iv). Two solutions are possible:

(i) Associate stack base directory entries with procedures and blocks rather than textual levels. This leads to a large stack base directory especially when the run time package is at all large. It also, as we shall see in section 12.14, inhibits recursion.
(ii) Include with each procedure, an extra link which is, for any procedure at level n, the value of the nth element of the stack base directory immediately prior to entry. As this solution allows recursion we choose it as shown in Fig. 12.4.
The links then are:

(i) The *return address link*, i.e. the address of the instruction immediately after the call.
(ii) The *stack base link*, i.e. the entry of the stack base directory which was over-written by the stack base of the procedure.

For a call at level m for a procedure at level n this is implemented as follows:

The *procedure call* is compiled into orders to:

(i) Evaluate and assign the parameters.
(ii) Store return address link.
(iii) Jump into the procedure.
(iv) (Re)set SB from entry m in the stack base directory.

The *procedure heading* is compiled into orders to:

(i) Store stack base directory n as the stack base link.
(ii) Set SB to SF.
(iii) Store SB as entry n in the stack base directory.
(iv) Advance SF over the static variables of the procedure.

The *procedure end* is compiled into orders to:

(i) Reset SF to SB.

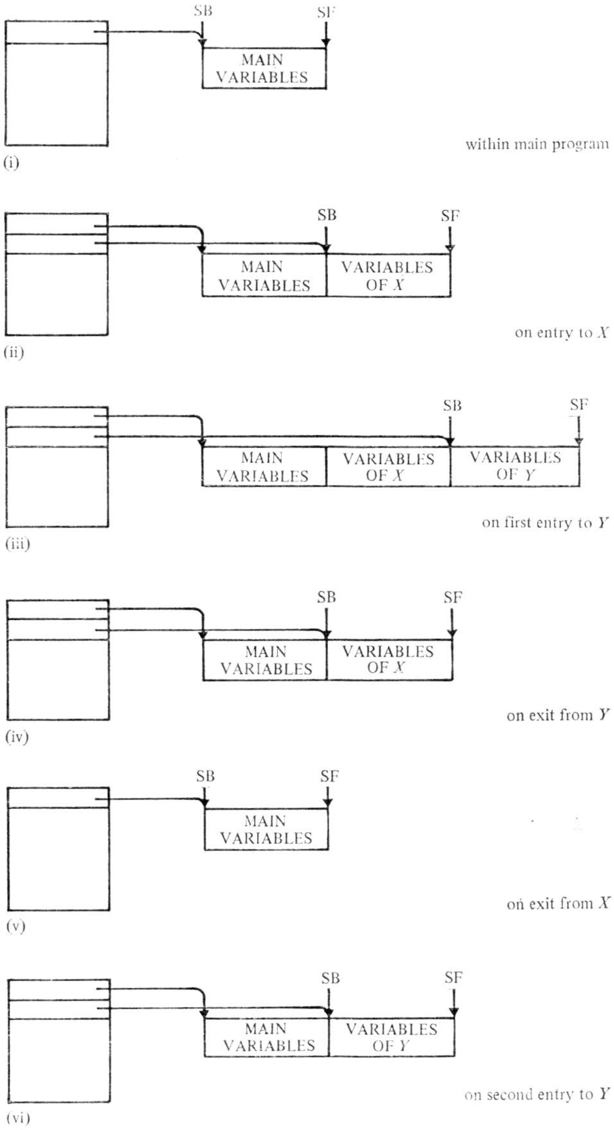

Fig. 12.4. The stack during the execution of the program of Fig. 12.3

(ii) Reset entry n in the stack base directory to stack base link.
(iii) Jump back to the calling procedure at the return address link.

These overheads are not insignificant (ignoring parameters, 13 for a simple order code) and hardware is often provided to help.

If the body of a procedure is small then it may be worthwhile treating the procedure as a macro. (See section 9.2.)

12.6 Parameters

Procedures are not just named blocks; they have parameters. Similar problems occur within both dynamic and static storage allocation schemes. We will use the dynamic model in our discussion: the solution in the static case generally follows closely. We will concentrate on variable parameters though in section 12.12 we will briefly discuss arrays and procedures. Parameters may be called in one of at least three ways: by *value*, by *reference* (or simple name), or by *substitution* (or name). We assume a basic understanding of these notions, describing only those characteristics which are significant to the compiler writer.

12.7 Parameters called by value

The simplest way is *call by value*. Consider the following procedure skeleton (in which we have departed from Algol's method of specifying the way a parameter is called):

```
procedure value (integer value m, n);
integer p, q;
      .
      .
      .
n  := m + p;
      .
      .
      .
end procedure
```

Within the procedure the *formal parameters* m and n behave just like local variables (such as p and q), and all references to them are compiled that way. So that:

$$\begin{array}{rl} & \text{AFX} = m \\ n := m + p \Rightarrow & \text{AFX} + p \\ & \text{AFX} \Rightarrow n \end{array}$$

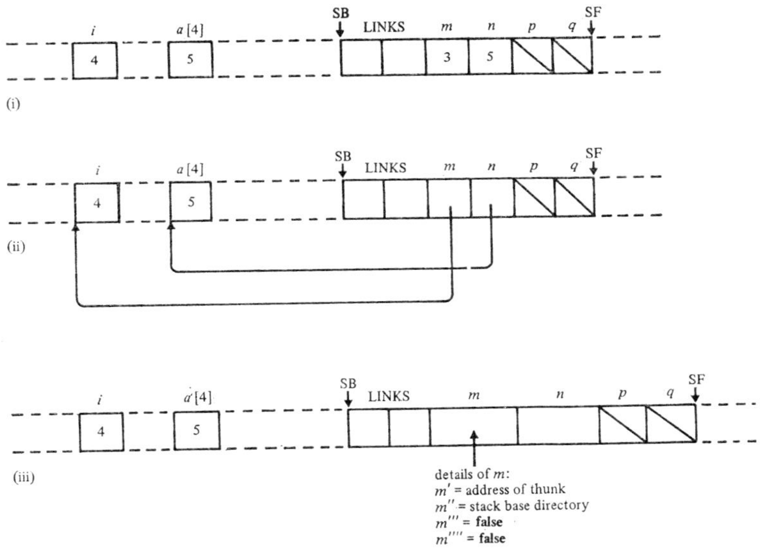

Fig. 12.5. Parameters: (i) called by value; (ii) called by reference; (iii) called by substitution

The distinction between a formal parameter and a local variable is just that the parameter is initialised to the value of the *actual parameter* at the call. For example, after the sequence in the calling procedure:

$i := 4$; $a[i] := 5$;
value $(i - 1, a[i])$

m would have the value 3 and n the value 5. The situation is as shown in Fig. 12.5 (i).

The call:

$$\text{value } (i - 1, a[i]) \Rightarrow \begin{array}{l} m := i - 1; \\ n := a[i]; \\ \text{value} \end{array}$$

where by 'value' we mean call the procedure as if it has no parameters (storing the links and jumping to the procedure). At this point, *m* and *n* have not had store allocated to them: this is done on entry to the procedure. However, SF points to the start of the store which will be allocated, and so the values are stored at locations relative to SF. Using a hybrid notation, the parameter evaluation is performed (leaving two locations for the links):

$$\{2/\text{SF}\} := i - 1; \{3/\text{SF}\} := a[i]$$

To reasons of clarity, we will, in future, revert to using the identifiers of the formal parameters rather than the addresses relative to the stack front.

12.8 Parameters called by reference

Parameters called by value cannot be used for transmitting values back from a procedure; parameters *called by reference* can. Consider the following skeleton of a procedure in which the parameters are called by reference:

```
procedure reference (integer ref m, n);
integer p, q;
        .
        .
        .
n   := m + p;
        .
        .
        .
end procedure
```

Within the procedure all references to m and n are interpreted as indirect references to the actual parameters, so that after the sequence:

$i := 4; a[i] := 5;$
reference $(i, a[i])$

the stack would appear as shown in Fig. 12.5 (ii). We can think of m and n as being descriptors of arrays of one element so that:

$$n := m + p \equiv n[0] := m[0] + p$$

which, in terms of our order-code is compiled into:

DR $= m$
AFX $=$ DR[0]
AFX $+ p$
DR $= n$
AFX $\Rightarrow$ DR[0]

where, rather than load BM with zero, we have an address part which explicitly says there is no modification. At the call these descriptors must be assigned to m and n, so that:

$m :=$ **descriptor**(i);
reference $(i, a[i]) \Rightarrow n :=$ **descriptor** $(a[i])$;
reference

12.9 Optimisation of parameters called by reference

In a language which allows calls both by value and reference, programmers usually use value parameters for values given to the procedure, and reference parameters for values returned by the procedure. However, reference parameters are self-sufficient (given that procedures may also be parameters, see section 12.12). Fortran allows only one type of parameter, which is a variant of the reference parameter. Access to reference parameters is slower than access to value parameters because of the indirection involved, and it is tempting to consider whether a compiler could treat reference parameters as value parameters.

There is only one problem. Consider Fig. 12.5 (ii) again. If the procedure reference were embedded in the same procedure as the call, then the variable whose value is 4 can be referred to within reference in two ways: non-locally as i, and indirectly through m. A procedure which utilised this fact would be an inelegant one indeed, and some languages, including Fortran, forbid any access by its non-local identifier to any parameter called by reference. With this restriction it is possible to convert a reference parameter, say m, to a value one as follows:

(i) Within the procedure an extra local variable (m') is created.
(ii) The call is unchanged.
(iii) Extra orders are compiled for the procedure heading so that on entry the *value* of the actual parameter is calculated and placed in the extra variable (m'):

$$m' := m[0]$$

(iv) Throughout the body this variable (m') is used directly in place of the parameter ($m[0]$).
(v) If the parameter is altered within the procedure (for example, by an assignment statement) then at the end of the procedure, orders are planted to store the value of m' in the actual parameter:

$$m[0] := m'$$

Note that this optimisation may make the program run slower, in the case where the procedure makes only one reference to the parameter to set it before exit.

12.10 Parameters called by substitution

When a parameter is called by value, a *value* is transmitted to the procedure (and so the actual parameter may be an expression); when a parameter is called by reference, a *descriptor* is transmitted (and so the actual parameter must be a variable). There is more general form, *call by substitution*, in which the actual parameter itself, is transmitted. The procedure behaves as if the actual parameter is substituted for all appearances of the formal parameter. This form of parameter association is the same as that normally produced by macros (see section 9.2). The result of this substitution must be a valid statement, so that provided the formal parameter is never assigned a value within the procedure, the actual parameter may be an expression. If all three forms of calling a parameter are provided, then call by substitution is used only where the evaluation of the procedure causes the quantity referred to by the actual parameter, to change. The classical case is Jensen's Device. Consider the following procedure (which would be more usefully recast as a function):

```
procedure sigma (integer ref y, i, integer value n, integer subst x);
y := 0;
for i := 1 step 1 until n do y := y + x
end procedure
```

The call:

sigma (sum, *j*, 10, *a*)

would merely set:

sum = 10**a*

However, the call:

sigma (sum, *j*, 10, *v*[*j*])

would set:

$$\text{sum} = \sum_{j=1}^{10} v_j$$

This implies that within the procedure, each access to the formal parameter *x* must cause the actual parameter *v*[*j*] to be (re)evaluated. This is done in what Ingerman (see ref. 12.1) has called a *thunk*. Consider a similar procedure to those used earlier for the other parameters:

```
procedure substitution (integer subst m, n);
integer p, q;
    .
    .
    .
n := m + p;
    .
    .
    .
end procedure
```

The thunk (which we describe below) places in DR a descriptor of the appropriate quantity and returns, so that:

$$n := m + p \;\Rightarrow\; \begin{array}{l} \text{call thunk for } m \\ \text{AFX} = \text{DR[0]} \\ \text{AFX} + p \\ \text{call thunk for } n \\ \text{AFX} \Rightarrow \text{DR[0]} \end{array}$$

For consistency, we store the address of the thunks (and other information to be described shortly) in the stack as m and n, so that after the sequence:

$i := 4;\ a[i] := 5$
substitution $(i - 1, a[i])$

the stack would appear as shown in Fig. 12.5 (iii).

The thunk itself, is compiled at the call so that in outline the call:

$$\text{substitution } (i - 1, a[i]) \;\Rightarrow\; \begin{array}{rl} & \textbf{go to } \lambda 0; \\ \lambda 1: & \text{thunk for } i - 1; \\ \lambda 2: & \text{thunk for } a[i]; \\ \lambda 0: & m := \text{details of the thunk at } \lambda 1; \\ & n := \text{details of the thunk at } \lambda 2; \\ & \text{substitution} \end{array}$$

So far, we have specified only one of the details of a thunk, its address. There are others, and so m and n actually occupy a number of locations. First, we note that the environment of the actual parameter (i.e. all the quantities accessible at that point) is different from the environment of the formal parameter. In the simplest case where the procedure containing the call and the called procedure are at level n, then different sets of variables at level n are accessible in each case. More complicated situations do arise. Consequently, the environment at the call must be temporarily created while evaluating the thunk, and the environment of the called procedure recreated before returning. The details of a thunk (created at the call) must, therefore, include a copy of the stack base directory. In practice, we need store only part of the stack base directory, but for simplicity this description assumes that we store it completely. The third of the details arises from the fact that the formal parameter may be assigned a value within the procedure, in which case the actual parameter must be a variable. It is difficult to decide at compile time (even in a multi-pass compiler) whether this situation arises, and so it is often done at run time. We use a Boolean which is set to **true** if the actual parameter is a variable. So the compiled sequence given earlier is more precisely as follows, where n''' refers to this Boolean quantity:

		call thunk from m'
		AFX = DR[0]
		AFX + p
$n := m + p$	$\Rightarrow$	BN = n'''
		IF NOT BN JUMP fault monitor
		call thunk from n'
		AFX $\Rightarrow$ DR[0]

We can now describe the thunk for $i - 1$:

store stack base directory
set it to the environment of the call (from m'')
AFX = i
AFX − 1
AFX $\Rightarrow$ $\gamma 0$
DR = **descriptor** $\gamma 0$
re-set the stack base directory
return

and the thunk for $a[i]$:

store stack base directory
set it to the environment of the call (from n'')
DR = **descriptor** $a[i]$
re-set the stack base directory
return

The assigning to m of the details of the thunk for $i - 1$ is, more fully:

m' := address of the thunk
m'' := stack base directory
m''' := **false**

Essentially, the thunk is a procedure (with a rather curious entry and exit), so that it should reserve space on the stack for storing the stack base directory and any values it calculates.

12.11 Optimisation of parameters called by substitution

The accessing of a parameter called by substitution is clearly quite expensive and should be used only in those situations (e.g. Jensen's Device) in which its effects cannot be achieved by using value or reference parameters. In Algol 60, however, the reference concept is missing and the programmer has to use substitution parameters instead; in particular, for those parameters which simply return values to the calling procedure. Unfortunately, a compiler cannot easily recognise those formal parameters which are used purely as reference parameters. What it can do easily is recognise those actual parameters which will always refer to the same quantity: scalars and array elements with constant subscripts. The details of the formal parameter is expanded to include a fourth quantity, a Boolean, m'''' say, which is **true** if the actual parameter is a scalar or an array element with constant subscripts. In this case, no thunk is required and m' is replaced by the descriptor of the actual parameter. The sequence within the procedure for accessing a parameter has to include a sequence for testing m'''' and deciding whether to access directly when m′ is a descriptor or to call the thunk. To return to the earlier example:

```
                        BN = m''''
                        IF NOT BN JUMP λ0
                        DR = m'
                        JUMP λ1
                    λ0: call thunk from m'
                    λ1: AFX = DR[0]
n := m + p  ⇒           AFX + p
                        BN = n'''
                        IF NOT BN JUMP fault monitor
                        BN = n''''
                        IF NOT BN JUMP λ2
                        DR = n'
                        JUMP λ3
                    λ2: call thunk from n'
                    λ3: AFX ⇒ DR[0]
```

Note that this technique speeds up access to those parameters it recognises as reference parameters, at the expense of slowing down all other accesses.

12.12 Other types of parameter

We have considered, so far, only variables as parameters. There are, of course, others: the two most important are arrays and procedures. We consider these in turn.

(i) *Arrays*. In general, few languages allow operations on arrays as such: the operations are generally on array elements. Consequently, when we are considering array parameters, the actual parameter will always be the explicit name of an array. This implies that call by substitution merely gives the same facility as call by reference, and so we need consider only call by value and call by reference.

First, call by reference. To fix ideas consider the following procedure for copying a matrix:

> **procedure** matrix copy (**array ref** *m*, *n*, **integer value** *p*, *q*);
> **integer** *i*, *j*;
> **for** *i* := 1 **step** 1 **until** *p* **do**
>   **for** *j* := 1 **step** 1 **until** *q* **do**
>   *m*[*i*, *j*] := *n*[*i*, *j*]
> **end procedure**

and the call:

> matrix copy (*a*, *b*, size, size)

If the Iliffe vector scheme is being used for accessing arrays, then the descriptor of *a* is assigned to *m*, and the descriptor of *b* is assigned to *n*, as shown in Fig. 12.6.

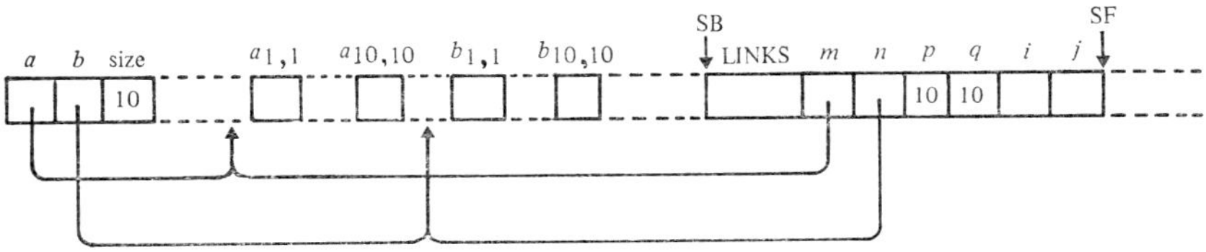

Fig. 12.6. Stack after the call: matrix copy (*a*, *b*, size, size)

If the multiplication scheme is being used, then *m* and *n* are allocated two descriptors each, one for the actual array and one for its dope vector. The two descriptors of *a* are assigned to *m* and the two descriptors for *b* assigned to *n*. This is the reason for modifying the multiplication method: with the simple scheme the whole dope vector would have had to be assigned.

Note the symmetry: we can access an element of the array with exactly the same orders, in exactly the same time, regardless of whether it is a parameter or a local array.

Now call by value. Variable parameters are called by value when their function is to provide a value for the procedure to work on. Efficiency ensues on two counts. First, the actual parameter may be an expression and calling by value ensures that it is evaluated once only (at the call where it is assigned to a local variable). Second, all subsequent accesses are to a local variable which is faster than accessing indirectly. With array parameters, indeed any form of structure parameters, neither of these are relevant. Because, in most languages, there are no facilities for operating on the complete structure, the procedure is generally concerned with operating on its elements and so there is no question of evaluating the actual parameter within the procedure. Consequently, even one evaluation (at the call) can be expensive. For an array the evaluation means making a copy of the whole array in the local workspace. In practice then, arrays are called by value only when a local copy is required, because the procedure intends to alter it and because the original value needs to be retained.

To implement call by value, we make no changes to the sequence compiled at the call (it still assigns the descriptor); we expand the sequence at the heading to reserve space for a local array and to copy the actual array to it, modifying the descriptor to point to this local version.

(ii) *Procedures*. In most languages, (Algol 68 is an exception) there is no concept of the value of a procedure or a reference to it and so we have to consider only call by substitution. This is just the problem that we discussed with respect to thunks, earlier. At a call, we assign to the formal parameter the address of the procedure and the stack base directory. Calling this parametric procedure involves the same interchanging of stack base directory.

2.13 Functions

A function is merely a procedure which has one implicit parameter (the value of the function) and is accessed as an operand of an expression rather than by a formal call statement. For example, the procedure sigma of section 12.10 would be better recast as an integer function.

integer procedure sigma (**integer ref** *i*, **integer value** *n*, **integer subst** *x*);
integer *y*;
y := 0;
for *i* := 1 **step** 1 **until** *n* **do** *y* := *y* + *x*;
sigma := y
end procedure

where the assignment:

sigma := *y*

specifies the value of the function sigma to be y. We compile such a statement into a sequence which leaves the value in the appropriate register, here AFX.
To set:

$$\text{sum} = \sum_{j=1}^{10} v_j$$

we write:

sum := sigma (j, 10, v[j])

Note that it is because of this general definition of a function that the side effects problem arises. The function may not only provide a value, it may alter any of its parameters, or indeed, any of the variables that are accessible non-locally.

The introduction of the function produces only one minor compiling problem. If the temporary variables are stored beyond SF (that is, if $\delta 0$ is at SF, $\delta 1$ at SF + 1 and so on), then SF must be advanced over these variables before calling the function to avoid their being over-written, and retarded on exit. If, however, they have been stacked, then they are already protected.

12.14 Recursion

We have suggested that languages can be categorised as having either static storage allocation or dynamic storage allocation. This is a simplification. The storage allocation scheme is essentially an implementation feature not a language feature. If a language designer wishes to have his language implemented with static storage allocation (for run time speed or simplicity of compiler) then he must choose language features which are consistent with static allocation: constant array bounds, no recursion and so on. It is possible to define a language so that either static or dynamic allocation is possible. Standard Fortran does. It is even possible to define a language with features that make either scheme inadequate. For example, requiring that the values of the local variables of a procedure be preserved after exit so that they are available on a subsequent call, cannot sensibly be combined with requiring dynamic arrays. [This is part of the problem of Algol's **own arrays**.]

Even when a dynamic scheme is indicated (because of the specification of dynamic arrays), there are two alternatives depending on whether or not recursion is allowed. The traditional example of a recursive procedure is that of factorial:

> **integer procedure** fact (**integer value** *n*);
> fact := **if** *n* = 0 **then** 1 **else** *n**fact (*n* − 1)
> **end procedure**

The characteristic of a *recursively defined procedure* like this is that during its evaluation, a call must be made on itself to evaluate some part of it. We talk of an *activation* of a procedure in this context. Thus, if we call this procedure:

> *f*1 := fact (4)

then at some point there will be five activations of the fact procedure. Each activation has its own set of variables (sometimes called an *activation record*) on the stack, so that one physical procedure corresponds to five sets of variables on the stack. It is this which causes us to store the stack base link on entry to a procedure and is part of the price to be paid for recursion. That is, recursion requires an extra link to be set on entry to all procedures and reset on exit.

The other part of the price, we have already alluded to in section 11.6. Because a recursive procedure may have a number of activations at any one time, requiring a number of activation records, it is impossible to separate out the static variables from the dynamic to avoid the modification time required to access all quantities relative to SB.

This cost of recursion has sometimes been thought excessive. An early suggestion by Strachey and Wilkes (see ref. 12.2) which was concerned specifically with Algol, was to distinguish in the language, non-recursive and recursive procedures, preceding recursive procedures by the symbol **rec**. The compiler then could use the appropriate techniques. More recently this has been thought to be of less significance, especially with changes in hardware, and nowadays, all dynamic storage schemes allow recursion.

It is worth noticing that recursion may occur in a different way. Consider again the function sigma:

integer procedure sigma (**integer ref** *i*, **integer value** *n*, **integer subst** *x*);
integer *y*;
$y := 0$;
for $i := 1$ **step** 1 **until** *n* **do** $y := y + x$;
sigma $:= y$
end procedure

There is clearly nothing recursive about this procedure. But x is called by substitution and so the actual parameter may be any expression; in particular, this expression may include a further call for sigma:

$$\text{sum} := \text{sigma}\ (i, p, \text{sigma}\ (j, q, m[i, j]))$$

This sets:

$$\text{sum} = \sum_{i=1}^{p} \sum_{j=1}^{q} m_{ij}$$

This is called a *recursive call.* The procedure sigma is called initially and on each traverse of the loop a further call to sigma to evaluate the parameter x is made.

This form of recursion is automatically allowed with the techniques of run time storage allocation we have described.

12.15 Some further compile time considerations

We noted earlier in this chapter that a procedure belongs to the procedure (or block or main program) in which it is embedded. Thus, its properties must be held with those of the other quantities of the enclosing procedure. The properties of a procedure are:

(i) Mode.
(ii) Address of the compiled code.
(iii) Number of parameters.
(iv) Mode of the first parameter.
(v) Mode of the second parameter.
etc.

In our basic language, and all extensions to it, we have specified that quantities must be defined before they are referred to. It is this that makes one-pass compiling possible. This implies that procedures (or at least their heading) must appear before any calls, and this leads to the concept of the whole procedure's being a declaration as in Algol. [Algol does not insist on a quantity's being declared before it is accessed which compounds the problem described below.] This concept is adequate in the absence of recursion and when dealing with the recursive situation that we have seen so far. But consider the case where procedure A calls procedure B and procedure B calls procedure A, *indirect recursion.* This is clearly allowable given our concept of scope; it also happens to be useful. The problem is that we cannot put each procedure before its call. Consequently, we *have* to use at least a two-pass compiler. This is the second reason we have found for a multi-pass compiler. (The first was concerned with optimisation over larger loops.) We will return to multi-pass compilers in Chapter 15.

It is interesting to note that we can define a language which allows indirect recursion in such a way that one-pass compilation is possible. To do this we separate out the declarative part of a procedure from its body. For example, we may specify the properties of sigma:

integer procedure spec sigma (**integer ref** *i*, **integer value** *n*, **integer subst** *x*) or even, since the parameters are local to the procedure:

integer procedure spec sigma (**integer ref, integer value, integer subst)**

These specifications are placed with the other declarations and then the procedure, itself, (quite unchanged) may be placed anywhere.

12.16 An alternative strategy

When considering how to implement the accessing of variables in a language with procedures, there are three aspects to be considered:

(i) The entry and exit sequences.
(ii) Accessing non-local variables.
(iii) Accessing parameters called by substitution.

Accessing local variables and parameters called by value and by reference is generally invariant to the method chosen.

So far we have nothing to compare our technique with. [The reader might care to produce the relevant details for the case where the stack base directory is held in registers, and effect a comparison.] However, it is clear that accessing parameters called by substitution is expensive. [One "solution" is to abolish substitution parameters. It is interesting that no language since Algol 60 has included the feature. Even so a similar problem remains with procedure-type parameters.]

An alternative solution (see ref 12.3) overcomes this by eliminating the stack base directory and distributing the information it would have contained through the stack.

Each procedure contains two stack base links:

(i) *The dynamic stack base link*. This points to the start of the variables of the procedure which called the given procedure. At the end of the procedure, SB is reset from this value.

(ii) *The static stack base link*. This points to the start of the variables of the procedure in which the given procedure is directly embedded. This is used for accessing non-local variables. If the variable is local to this enclosing procedure, XSB is set from the static base link before access. The static base link of the enclosing procedure points to the start of the variables of the procedure which encloses it and so on. Thus, to access a variable from a procedure embedded n levels within the procedure in which it is declared, requires n orders to set XSB before access. It is important then that the compiler does not reload XSB unnecessarily.

Both links are set at the call. The dynamic stack base link is easy: it is the current value of SB. The static stack base link is more complicated. There are two cases:

(i) If the called procedure is (directly) embedded within the calling procedure, SB is the static stack base too.

(ii) Alternatively, the calling procedure will be embedded (not necessarily directly) within a procedure in which the called procedure will be directly nested. The static link of the called procedure then points to the start of the variables of this enclosing procedure. This can be found by moving back through the chain of static links starting with that of the calling procedure.

Thus a call at level m for a procedure at level n is implemented as follows:

The *procedure call* is compiled into orders to:

(i) Evaluate and assign the parameters.
(ii) Store return address link.
(iii) Store dynamic link (current value of SB).
(iv) Reset SB $m - n + 1$ times from the chain of static links.
(v) Store static link (this new value of SB).
(vi) Jump into the procedure.

The *procedure heading* is compiled into orders to:

(i) Set SB to SF.
(ii) Advance SF over the static variables of the procedure.

The *procedure end* is compiled into orders to:

(i) Reset SF to SB.
(ii) Reset SB from dynamic link.
(iii) Jump back to the calling procedure at the return address link.

We can now compare with dynamic and static link technique with the stack base directory technique according to the criteria specified earlier.

(i) Entry and exit sequences. For a call at level m of a procedure at level n, (ignoring parameters and assuming a simple order code), the new technique is slightly better: $11 + m - n$ orders as against 13.

(ii) Accessing non-level variables. The difference in the techniques lies in the operations to access a random non-local variable. For an access at level m of a variable declared at level n, the directory technique requires a single order to load XSB; the dynamic and static link technique requires m — n orders. The significance of this depends on the pattern of access to variables in a program and on the ability to avoid reloading XSB.

(iii) Accessing parameters called by substitution. When using the dynamic and static link technique, the environment of any procedure is precisely specified by the value of SB, because from it all non-local variables can be accessed using the static link chain. Consequently, when entering thunks only SB is involved in the setting and resetting sequence, rather than the stack base directory in the directory technique. Whether this is significant depends on the frequency of parameters called by substitution.

[The reader may care to consider a solution in which the stack base directory is held locally for each procedure.]

13 Full syntax analysis

We have stressed the importance of the syntactical analysis phase of a compiler but so far we have considered only one technique, precedence, in one situation, expressions. In this chapter we will go to the other extreme and consider a very general procedure which will perform a syntactical analysis of all statements and, indeed, on a whole program. We will use the term *syntax analysis* for this specific technique (others use the term *syntax-directed analysis*), retaining the term syntactical analysis to describe all techniques which establish syntactical structure.

13.1 Backus Naur Form

Backus Naur Form (BNF) is a simple language for describing the form or *syntax* of a language. This is done by a series of *meta-linguistic formulae*, or to use a more manageable term, *phrase definitions* such as:

<digit> :: = 0|1|2|3|4|5|6|7|8|9

Here, we are defining a class of things called, for mnemonic reasons, digit. The names of classes, or *phrases*, are surrounded by the pointed brackets, < and >. The :: = is the 'defined to be' symbol and |, separating *alternatives*, means 'or'. Thus, this definition can be read: a digit is defined to be a zero or a one, or a two, ...

We can define phrases in terms of previously defined phrases, as well as in terms of basic symbols:

<pence> ::= <digit>|<digit><digit>

This defines the phrase pence to be a one- or two-digit number and illustrates that the juxtaposition of two phrases or symbols means 'followed by'.

The power of BNF derives from the fact that the definitions can be recursive:

<integer> ::= <digit>|<integer><digit>

This defines an integer of arbitrary length, which is either a digit, or else some other integer followed by a digit. This definition is said to be *left-recursive* because <integer> appears as the left-most element in one of the alternatives.

With BNF we can build up the definition of a complete language. (Appendix 1 gives the definition of the basic language.) A set of phrase definitions for a language is called a *grammar* for the language. Let us concentrate on the definition of an expression of a little less power than that of Chapter 4 in that we do not allow unary operators or exponentiation. We do, however, allow brackets. To keep the description within bounds, we restrict an operand to be a single, lower-case letter:

<expr> ::= <term>|<expr><plus or minus><term>
<plus or minus> ::= + | −
<term> ::= <factor>|<term><mult or div><factor>
<mult or div> ::= * | /
<factor> ::= <operand>|(<expr>)
<operand> ::= *a*|*b*|*c*|*d*|*e*|*f*|*g*|*h*|*i*|*j*|*k*|*l*|*m*|
n|*o*|*p*|*q*|*r*|*s*|*t*|*u*|*v*|*w*|*x*|*y*|*z*

3.2 Syntax trees

It is the purpose of syntactical analysis to produce the structure of a statement or program as we have noted before. The structure of a statement with respect to its grammar can be described by means of a *syntax tree*. Fig. 13.1 gives the syntax tree for:

$$u + f * t$$

with respect to the definitions of an expression just given.

The tree says that $u + f * t$ is an <expr> because it consists of an <expr> (u) followed by a <plus or minus> (+) followed by a <term> ($f*t$). Now u is an <expr> because it is a <term>; it is a <term> because it is a <factor>; it is a <factor> because it is an <operand>; and it is an <operand> because it is a u. And so on.

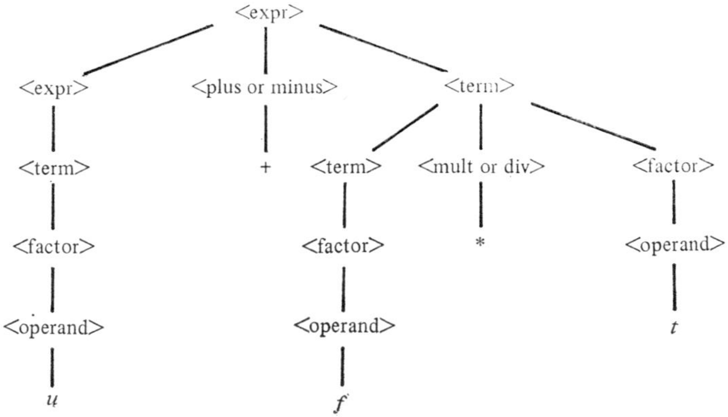

*Fig. 13.1. Syntax tree for u + f*t using the definition for* <expr>

13.3 A modified set of definitions

In this chapter we are going to describe an algorithm which, given a grammar for a language, will take a string of source characters which purports to be a statement of the language and will determine whether it is or not; if it is, it will also produce the syntax tree. Before we do this we must first modify the form of the phrase definitions.

The definitions as usually given (and as we have given them) are *generative*: they describe how to generate a legitimate form. For example:

<integer> ::= <digit>|<integer><digit>

says that to generate an <integer> we generate a <digit>, or that having generated an <integer> we can generate another by following it by a <digit>.

For syntax analysis it is convenient to have the definitions in an *analytic* form, so that we can *analyse* or *parse* a string of characters to see whether they conform to the grammar. For example, the modified definition:

<integer> ::= <digit><integer>|<digit>

says that to recognise an <integer> we must look for a <digit> and then look for another <integer> and if that fails we just look for a <digit>. We will shortly consider a procedure which works in this way. Note that if this procedure were to be applied using the original definition:

<integer> ::= <digit>|<integer><digit>

it would recognise the first <digit> only; and using this definition:

<integer> ::= <integer><digit>|<digit>

it would go into an infinite recursive loop looking for an <integer>. The rules to which an analytic grammar must conform in order to be used along the lines above are:

(i) There must be no left recursion.
(ii) Any alternative which is a *stem* of another alternative must not precede that alternative.
(iii) A more specific alternative must precede a less specific one.

[Rule (ii) can be regarded as a special case of rule (iii) if we regard <*A*><*B*> as more specific than <*A*> in the sense that <*A*> means that we are not concerned with what follows <*A*> whereas <*A*><*B*> means <*A*> followed specifically by <*B*>.]

It is possible to define algorithms for which restrictions (ii) and (iii) above are unnecessary. These are, however, quite slow, and, as the restrictions are not particularly onerous, they are almost universally applied. Our algorithm is described as *fast-back*, the more general one as *slow-back*. For example, one form of modified grammar for our expression is:

<expr> ::= <term><plus or minus><expr>|<term>
<plus or minus> ::= + | −
<term> ::= <factor><mult or div><term>|<factor>
<mult or div> ::= * | /
<factor> ::= <operand>|(<expr>)
<operand> ::= *a*|*b*|*c*|*d*|*e*|*f*|*g*|*h*|*i*|*j*|*k*|*l*|*m*|
n|*o*|*p*|*q*|*r*|*s*|*t*|*u*|*v*|*w*|*x*|*y*|*z*

and the syntax tree for:

$u + f * t$

with respect to this modified definition, is given in Fig. 13.2.

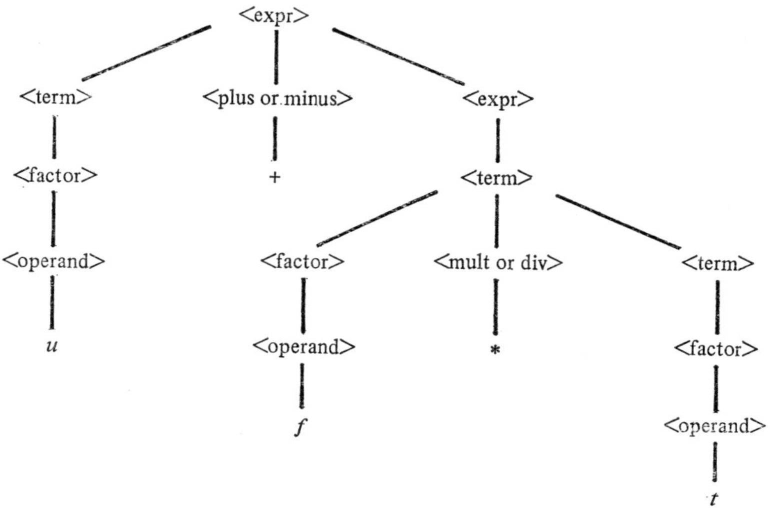

*Fig. 13.2. Syntax tree for u + f*t using the modified definition for* <expr>

As we have mentioned, there are always a number of possible grammars for any language, each with its own particular advantages. We have chosen this purely because of its close similarity to the initial generative grammar. It has one disadvantage, though. The phrase definition:

<expr> ::= <term><plus or minus><expr>|<term>

suggests that the <plus or minus> is associated with the following <expr> instead of just the first term of it. This causes no practical problem since the <plus or minus> can be associated with its <term> when processing the tree. Alternative grammars such as one starting:

<expr> ::= <term><rest of expr>|<term>
<rest of expr> ::= <plus or minus><term><rest of expr>
|<plus or minus><term>

resolve the problem.

3.4 Processing syntax trees

Processing the syntax tree is quite simple since it contains at each node a complete description of the structure of the statement. We merely work down the tree, taking the appropriate action at each node.

3.5 An analysis or parsing algorithm

An algorithm which performs an analysis of a source string with respect to a grammar modified as described in section 13.3, to produce a syntax tree, is given as Fig. 13.3.

It is quite straightforward and is perhaps best understood by following through a few examples.

(i) Consider the case of a trivial phrase:

<go to> ::= go to

and a source string:

go to

The algorithm stores the state of the analysis (the extent of the source string so far recognised and the extent of the syntax tree generated) in case the analysis fails but only after some partial, but premature recognition. It then proceeds along the first (here the only) alternative of the definition. The first component of the alternative is a symbol, which is the same as the source character and so the procedure creates a sub-tree for 'g' and a reference to it at the top node. It then moves to the next component and the next source character. The symbol 'g' is thus recognised. The next three traverses of the loop recognise and create sub-trees for 'o', 't', and 'o'. Finally, the end of the alternative causes the top node which now contains four references to sub-trees to be designated a <go to>.

(ii) Consider a slightly more useful phrase definition:

<go to> ::= go to|go via

and the source string:

go via

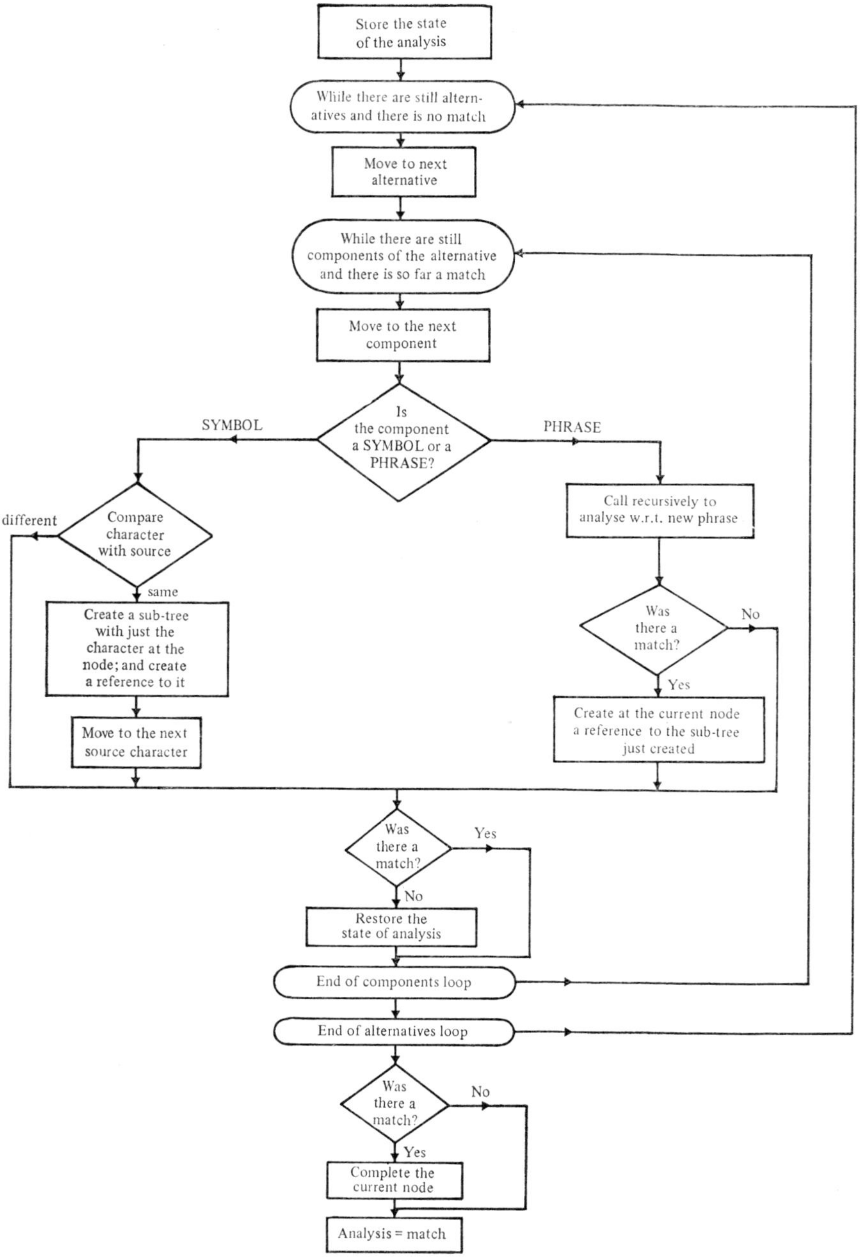

Fig. 13.3 An analysis algorithm

The algorithm proceeds as before until 'go' has been recognised. Then the symbol 't' of the definition differs from the source character 'v' and so that alternative is abandoned. The state of the analysis as it existed on entry is restored. To coin an ungainly phrase for the next few paragraphs, 'go' is 'unrecognised'. The algorithm moves to the next alternative and continues from there. The characters 'go' are recognised again, followed by the characters 'via' and the syntax tree is completed by designating it a <go to>.

(iii) Consider the same phrase definition:

<go to> ::= go to|go via

and the source string:

go sub

The characters 'go' are prematurely recognised twice, once in each alternative and then unrecognised. The procedure then exits with nothing recognised and no syntax tree formed.

(iv) Finally, consider the phrase definition:

<go statement> ::= <go to><label>

without considering the definitions either of <go to> or <label> or any specific source string. After storing the state of the analysis, the algorithm finds that the first component of the first alternative is a phrase. This means that it must look for the phrase <go to> in the source string so far unrecognised (all of it in this case). The procedure calls itself recursively to do so. If it finds it, then on exit the appropriate characters will have been recognised and the appropriate sub-tree created. A reference to this sub-tree is then created in the upper-level node, and the algorithm continues through the definition. If at the lower-level nothing is recognised, then on return to the upper-level the alternative is abandoned and the next one tried, if there is one.

The reader is encouraged to follow through a more extensive example, say, for an <expr>.

13.6 Representation of phase definitions

So far, we have been talking in abstract data structure terms. It is interesting to see how we might implement this scheme. We consider, in turn, the representation of the phrase definitions and the syntax tree, and then give an Algol procedure to perform the analysis.

The simplest internal representation of phrase definitions corresponds closely to their written form. We will discuss this with reference to Fig. 13.4 which shows the definitions of <expr> and <plus or minus>.

There are five different elements which we will discuss in turn. Each has two parts, the element itself, and a marker showing its type. For convenience we assume that they occupy a word each. The elements are:

(i) A basic symbol. The element is the symbol, itself, its marker being SYMBOL.

(ii) A phrase. The element is a reference to the definition of the phrase, its marker being PHRASE.

(iii) A category. Each alternative is associated with a cardinal number 1, 2, . . ., called its *category number*. It is used to mark the end of an alternative, the element being the category number, its marker being CATEGORY.

(iv) A size. We are going to store the syntax tree in a vector in such a way that we need to know the amount of space required for each node. A node's size we define to be one more than the maximum number of phrases in the alternative. In <expr> the first alternative contains three phrases so this size is 4. The element's value is an integer equal to this number, its marker being SIZE.

(v) An alternative. We need to be able to try all alternatives in turn. Our simple representation is to precede all alternatives except the last by an element whose marker is ALT, and whose value is a reference to the start of the next alternative.

13.7 Representation of the syntax tree

We will represent the syntax tree as a general tree along the following lines. If all the references at a node are to sub-trees then it is represented by a node consisting of the category number of the alternative and references to the representations of the sub-trees. For example:

<expr> is represented as 1 | | |
/ | \

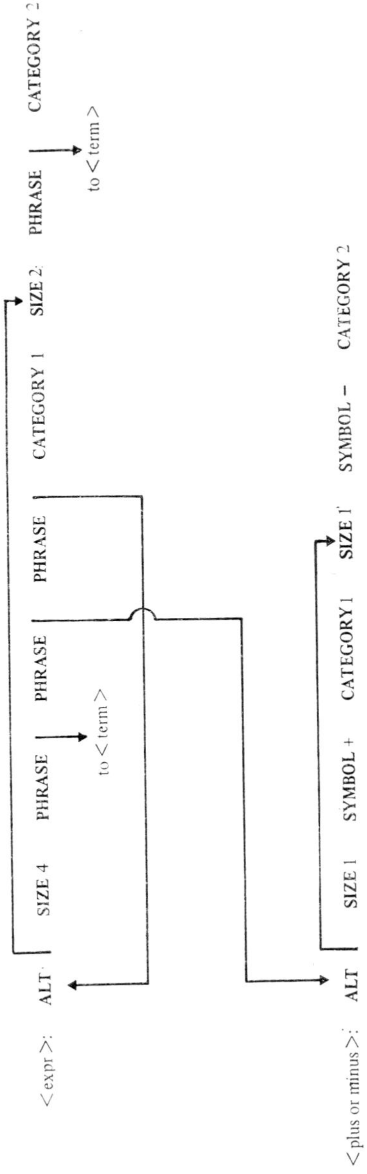

Fig. 13.4. Representation of phrase definitions

Any node which contains references to leaves is represented by a node which consists just of the category number of the alternative:

<operand> is represented as 21

The extension to the case where a node has references both to sub-trees and leaves is obvious. Fig. 13.5 (i) shows the representation of the syntax tree of Fig. 13.2.

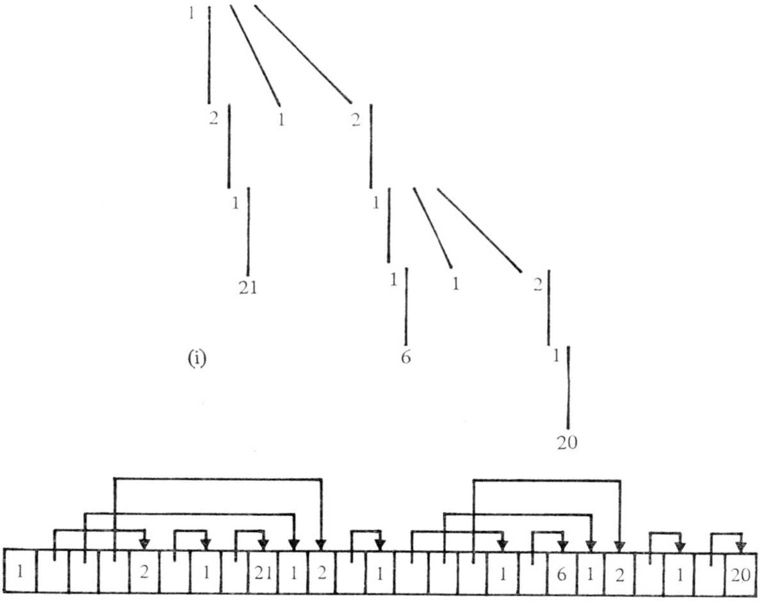

(ii)

Fig. 13.5. Representation of the syntax tree of Fig. 13.2. (i) As a structure; (ii) As a vector in the form produced by the analysis procedure

Note that there is nothing in the representation to indicate that the tree is that of an <expr>. It is implicit: the tree will have been produced as a result of the analysis procedure's being asked whether or not the string is an <expr>.

The analysis procedure will store this tree in a vector, in the order: the top-most node followed by its sub-trees from left to right, where the sub-trees are also held in this order. One problem is to decide how much store a node will require, since different alternatives may need different amounts of space. The simple solution, which we have chosen, is to reserve the correct amount of store by reference to the SIZE element, already mentioned, which precedes each alternative in the definition. However, more elegant solutions exist, which do not require a SIZE element, and which, therefore, reduce the size of the stored form of phrase definitions and make syntax tree generation more flexible. [These methods require the use of two stacks.] Fig. 13.5 (ii) shows a more detailed linear representation of the syntax tree of Fig. 13.2.

13.8 An analysis procedure

We now give an Algol procedure which will analyse a source string in an **integer array** source, starting at source [sp], with respect to a set of phrase definitions stored, as described in section 13.6, in an **integer array** phrases, starting at phrases [pp], producing a syntax tree of the form described in section 13.7, in an **integer array** syntax tree starting at syntax tree [stp].

For convenience, each element of the phrase definition occupies two words, one used to mark the type of an element, the other for its value. In practice the element's value and a tag marking its type could be combined into one word, saving space for large definitions.

```
Boolean procedure analysis (source, sp, phrases, pp, syntax tree, stp);
value pp; integer array source, phrases, syntax tree; integer sp,
                                                              pp, stp;
    begin
    integer i, j, sp initial, stp initial, pp next alt, stp next ref,
                                                    stp lower node;
    Boolean alternatives, components, match;
    sp initial := sp; stp initial := stp next ref := stp;
    pp next alt := pp;
    for i := 0, 1 while alternatives ∧ ¬ match do
```

```
        begin
        pp := pp next alt;
        alternatives := phrases [pp] = ALT;
        if alternatives then
              begin
              pp next alt := phrases [pp + 1];
              pp := pp + 2
              end;
        stp := stp initial + phrases [pp + 1];
        pp := pp + 2;
        for j := 0, 1 while components ∧ match do
              begin
              if phrases [pp] = SYMBOL then
                  begin
                  match := phrases [pp + 1] = source [sp];
                  if match then sp := sp + 1
                  end
              else begin
                  stp lower node := stp;
                  match := analysis (source, sp, phrases,
                              phrases [pp + 1], syntax tree, stp);
                  if match then
                     begin
                     stp next ref := stp next ref + 1;
                     syntax tree [stp next ref] := stp lower node
                     end
                  end;
              if ¬ match then
                  begin
                  sp := sp initial; stp next ref: = stp initial
                  end;
              pp := pp + 2;
              components := phrases [pp] ≠ CAT
              end of components loop
        end of alternatives loop;
   if match then syntax tree [stp initial] := phrases [pp + 1];
   analysis := match
   end
```

13.9 Merging alternatives

The simple analysis procedure as it stands, contains a number of weaknesses which we consider in this and the next section. Consider an expression as defined earlier:

<expr> ::= <term><plus or minus><expr>|<term>
<plus or minus> ::= + | −
<term> ::= <factor><mult or div><term>|<factor>
<mult or div> ::= * | /
<factor> ::= <operand>|(<expr>)
<operand> ::= *a*|*b*|*c*|*d*|*e*|*f*|*g*|*h*|*i*|*j*|*k*|*l*|*m*|
n|*o*|*p*|*q*|*r*|*s*|*t*|*u*|*v*|*w*|*x*|*y*|*z*

and the simple expression:

x

In the course of analysis <term> will be recognised twice, once prematurely while investigating the first alternative, and once successfully. This clearly is inefficient. The inefficiency multiplies since each recognition of <term> involves two recognitions of <factor> and, thus, <operand>; and if we had allowed exponentiation each recognition of <factor> would have involved two recognitions of <operand>, a grand total of eight. Clearly, then, we seek to eliminate the situation in which a phrase is recognised, unrecognised and then re-recognised. There are three solutions:

(i) Re-arrange the definitions. For example, <expr> could be re-defined:

<expr> ::= <term><rest of expr>
<rest of expr> ::= <plus or minus><expr>|<nil>

where <nil> is a special phrase which is always found. Similarly, <term> could be re-defined. This leads to a different, but equally valid, tree with extra levels in it corresponding to the extra definitions.

(ii) Add facilities to BNF to allow the merging of alternatives with a common stem.

For example:

<expr> ::= <term>{<plus or minus><expr>|<nil>}

where the common stem <term> is separated out, the remainder of the alternatives being enclosed in the braces. [Facilities along these lines have often been suggested as an extension to BNF in their own right.] This may be implemented more conveniently with the methods of analysis involving two stacks mentioned in 13.7. The structure within the braces is the same as that of the right-hand side of the original definition and is represented internally in exactly the same way. A new type of element must be introduced to mark the end of the common stem so that the analysis procedure can remember the state of the analysis in case partial, premature recognition occurs within the braces. The analysis procedure requires an extension to deal with this element and it will then produce a tree exactly the same as that produced from the original definition:

<expr> ::= <term><plus or minus><expr>|<term>

Indeed, the new form is merely a short-hand for this original definition.

(iii) Modify the procedure which reads definitions and forms their internal representation so that it looks for alternatives with a common stem and merges them to produce the same internal form as that of (ii). The original Compiler Compiler (see ref. 13.3) worked in this way, and does have the advantage of accepting pure BNF definitions (provided they are written in an analytic form). However, pure BNF is now being used rather less and the modified forms rather more and, consequently, the second solution now finds greater favour.

13.10 Phrase routines

Even when we have merged alternatives, and, for the expression:

x

we have looked for an <operand> only one, we still have the problem of finding the operand. Given the definition:

<operand> ::= $a|b|c|d|e|f|g|h|i|j|k|l|m|$
$n|o|p|q|r|s|t|u|v|w|x|y|z$

the algorithm goes round the outer loop twenty-four times, looking at symbols which, on the first twenty-three occasions do not match and on the twenty-fourth do. In almost any machine the letters are mapped onto the bit-patterns of consecutive integers and so it is far more efficient to test for the source symbol being within the range of the letters.

The *phrase routine* is a device for replacing the interpretive operation of the analysis procedure using a phrase definition, with a special-purpose procedure which can take advantage of relationships like that between letters described above. The phrase routine is constrained by the conventions of the analysis procedure and must be written in conjunction with it. A phrase routine for <operand> might be:

```
Boolean procedure operand;
    if source [sp] ≥ code ('a') ∧ source [sp] ≤ code ('z') then
        begin
        syntax tree [stp] := source [sp]−code ('a') + 1;
        sp := sp + 1;
        stp := stp + 1;
        operand := true
        end
    else operand := false
```

Here, 'code' is a transfer function which converts a symbol into an integer.

The representation of the definitions must be modified to cater for this. For example, in the definition of:

<factor> ::= <operand>|(<expr>)

<operand> is represented not as a phrase but as a sixth alternative, tagged PHRASE ROUTINE, whose element refers to the phrase routine for operand. It is impossible to describe this in Algol since there is no notion of a procedure variable: in machine code terms the analysis procedure must call the procedure whose address is held in the definition.

So long as a phrase routine moves over the source symbols it recognises and creates a sub-tree, it is free to do whatever it likes. The phrase routine we have considered was at the bottom-most level where all the alternatives were symbols. It need not be. Suppose the definition of <expr> were expanded to allow a multi-character identifier as an <operand>:

<operand> ::= <identifier>

<identifier> ::= <letter>{<letters or digits>|<nil>}

<letters or digits> ::= <letter or digit>{<letters or digits>|<nil>}

<letter or digit> ::= <letter>|<digit>

Analysis of, say:

compiler

with respect to this definition would produce a long tree, which, during semantic processing, would merely be scanned to collect together the letters to re-form the identifier 'compiler'. The phrase routine may, instead, recognise the whole identifier and create a sub-tree consisting only of a pseudo-category number, that is directly related to the identifier, perhaps the identifier, itself, perhaps its address in an identifiers list.

13.11 Syntax analysis and lexical analysis

In this chapter, so far, we have assumed that the input to the analysis procedure is the source string. The arguments for a standard form and for lexical analysis still hold, and in practice, the input is the lexically analysed string. This implies the use of the phrase routines to recognise pseudo-identifiers, pseudo-constants and pseudo-strings since there is no way of writing a formal phrase definition for them. The phrase routines are quite simple, of course, merely looking for whatever distinguishes say, a pseudo-identifier. Phrase routines, used in this capacity, are often referred to as *recognisers*.

13.12 Syntax analysis and precedence

The tree produced by the syntax analysis algorithm and by the precedence algorithm are clearly closely related. If the vertical branches of the syntax tree Fig. 13.1 are pruned and their leaves moved up, then exactly the binary tree of Fig. 4.3 (ii) results.

There are interesting differences, through. We note three:

(i) Syntax checking is automatic with syntax analysis. Unless the source string is syntactically perfect, the algorithm fails to recognise it. As it stands, it merely finds that the string is invalid without isolating the error. [But see section 14.4.] With the precedence technique, the fault can often be pinpointed. The precedence table contains entries corresponding to certain erroneous combinations of operators. The algorithm, though, must contain explicitly programmed sequences to check for other syntactical errors, such as two successive binary operators and so on.

(ii) When applied to complete programs the precedence technique requires a large matrix, since each new 'operator' expands the matrix by a row and a column. The store required by the phrase definitions expands much more slowly.

(iii) The syntax analysis procedures even when alternatives can be merged is very slow. We can distinguish the two techniques on the basis of the way they attack the problem. Syntax analysis is said to be a *top-down* method, since it endeavours to build the syntax tree from the top down. For example, to find an <expr> in:

$$u + f * t$$

it seeks first a <term> and so on. The precedence technique on the other hand is said to be *bottom-up*. It operates by trying to construct a tree from the characters of the source string. In the case above it constructs a tree for $f*t$.

Because of the slowness of the syntax analysis method nobody has ever suggested using it in a pure form. What happens in practice is a compromise. Expressions are recognised by a precedence technique, by using a phrase routine, while the structure of the higher levels of a statement (or program) is dealt with by the syntax analysis procedure. The compilers produced this way by the Compiler Compiler (see ref. 13.1) have been demonstrated to be only marginally slower than those produced by pure bottom-up techniques.

3.13 The theory of grammars

Although we have described the precedence technique as an independent algorithm (and, indeed, it was initially developed in that way) the relationship between it and syntax analysis is now clearly understood. The *theory of grammars* has been developed to describe the characteristics of grammars, to divide them into classes, and to specify parsers appropriate to their characteristics. More fundamental questions, such as whether a grammar is ambiguous, and whether two grammars generate the same language are also considered. Clearly, this has wider application than the syntactical analysis phase of a compiler, and is now a subject in its own right. The serious compiler writer will make himself well versed in the theory, though it is outside the scope of this book. Gries (see ref. 13.2) gives a thorough account of those aspects relevant to compiler writing.

14 Fault monitoring

If all programs that were written were perfect, then compiler writing would be quite easy. Of course, they are not, and the problem of detecting and monitoring the faults is fairly important as we have already seen. In this chapter we are going to consider different classes of fault, and how the need to detect them alters the structure of the compiler. There are, however, two general points which must be made:

(i) There is very little to be said for a monitor which merely prints a number when it detects a fault, forcing the programmer to look up the number in a table in a manual, especially as this process, looking up entries in a table, is one that a computer is very good at. Indeed, it is ironic that compiler writers, who should know the capabilities of the computer better than most, have been so slow to harness its power in fault monitoring.

(ii) The compiler can detect only the symptoms of the fault; it cannot diagnose the fault itself. [The term '*fault diagnosis*' is a misnomer when used instead of '*fault monitoring*'.] There is a strong temptation to make a compiler 'diagnose' a fault and 'correct' the program. This must be done with extreme caution and in the knowledge that the diagnosis may well be wrong.

As every programmer knows, a fault can manifest itself in one of three different ways:

(i) The compiler may detect syntactical or semantic errors, the so-called *compile time errors.*

(ii) The running of the object program may be terminated due to errors detected in a number of ways, the so-called *run time errors.*

(iii) The program may run to completion but give the wrong results. We discuss these in turn.

14.1 Compile time errors

There are an infinity of ways in which a program may be written incorrectly. The objective of the compiler is two-fold: it must monitor

```
'BEGIN'
'INTEGER' I,SIZE;
SIZE:=READ;
   'BEGIN'
   'ARRAY' A[1:SIZE];
   'PROCEDURE' SORT(A,SIZE);
      'ARRAY' A; 'INTEGER' SIZE;
      'VALUE' SIZE;
      'BEGIN'
      'INTEGER' START,SUB;
      'FOR' START:=1 'STEP' 1 'UNTIL' SIZE 'DO'
         'BEGIN
         SUB:=MINSUB(A,START,SIZE);
         SWOP:=A[SUB]; A[SUB]:=A[START]; A[START]:=SWOP
         'END'
      'END';
   'INTEGER''PROCEDURE' MINSUB(A,START,SIZE);
      'VALUE' START,SIZE;
      'ARRAY' A; 'INTEGER' START,SIZE;
      'BEGIN'
      'INTEGER' I,SUB;
      SUB:=START;
      'FOR' I:=START+1 'STEP' 1 'UNTIL' SIZE 'DO'
         'IF' A[I] 'LT' A[SUB] 'THEN' SUB:=I;
      MINSUB:=SUB
      'END'
   'FOR' I:= 1 'STEP' 1 'UNTIL' SIZE 'DO' A[I]:=READ;
   SORT(A,SIZE);
   'FOR' I:=1 'STEP' 1 'UNTIL' SIZE 'DO' PRINT(A[I],4,2)
   'END'
'END'
```

Fig. 14.1. An Algol program for reading and sorting a list of numbers. Faults have been deliberately induced

the fault, and it must carry on compiling, in order to detect (the symptoms of) as many faults as possible.

Fig. 14.2 shows the fault monitoring for the Algol program of Fig. 14.1 in which faults have purposefully been induced.

Faults can be classified in a number of ways. In Fig. 14.2 they are classified according to their severity. We will classify them according to the part of the compiler in which they are detected.

```
LINE    1      BEGIN PROGRAM
LINE    2        BEGIN BLOCK 1 AT ADDRESS 11445
LINE    5          BEGIN BLOCK 2 AT ADDRESS 11465
LINE    7            BEGIN BLOCK 3  'PROCEDURE'SORT(A,SIZE); AT ADDRESS 11494
LINE    8 !!           'ARRAY' USED AS SPECIFIER - INTERPRETED AS 'REAL''ARRAY'
LINE    9 !!           'VALUE' OUT OF POSITION
LINE   10              BEGIN BODY OF SORT
LINE   13 !!             CLOSING QUOTE INSERTED AFTER DELIMITER 'BEGIN'
LINE   13                BEGIN COMPOUND STATEMENT 'A'
LINE   15 **               UNDECLARED IDENTIFIERS SWOP, SWOP
LINE   16                END COMPOUND STATEMENT 'A'
LINE   17              END BODY OF SORT
LINE   17            END BLOCK 3 AT ADDRESS 11597
LINE   18            BEGIN BLOCK 4  'INTEGER''PROCEDURE'MINSUB(A,START,SIZE); AT ADDRESS 11598
LINE   20 !!           'ARRAY' USED AS SPECIFIER - INTERPRETED AS 'REAL''ARRAY'
LINE   21              BEGIN BODY OF MINSUB
LINE   26              END BODY OF MINSUB
LINE   28 ??           COMMENT (AFTER 'END') INCLUDES DELIMITERS 'FOR' := 'STEP' 'UNTIL' 'DO' :=
LINE   28            END BLOCK 4 AT ADDRESS 11683
LINE   31          END BLOCK 2 AT ADDRESS 11732
LINE   32        END BLOCK 1 AT ADDRESS 11738
LINE   33      END PROGRAM
```

Fig. 14.2. The compile-time fault monitor resulting from the program of Fig. 14.1

** indicates an error
?? queries some feature of the program which is valid but which could indicate an error
!! is a warning that the compiler has made an assumption

14.2 Faults detected while converting to a standard form

The procedure which processess a program to produce a standard form converts delimiter words and other symbols, punched in one of a series of punching conventions, to a single symbol. We will, here, consider only one such convention—the enclosing of delimiter words in quotes—using it as an example of the problems that arise.

We were, in Chapter 3, quite unspecific about how the procedure should effect the conversion apart from a cryptic note suggesting that an optimum hashing algorithm might exist. We now consider the problem in more detail. To use the hashing algorithm in the way we have suggested, we need to have all the letters of the delimiter word available. We might choose the obvious algorithm that the first appearance of a quote heralds the start of a delimiter word and the next its end, the third the start of the next delimiter word and so on. But consider the statement:

area := **if** $x \geqslant 0$ **then sqrt** x **else** 0

Suppose it is punched according to the above conventions with a single quote sign omitted:

AREA := 'IF *X* 'GE' 0 'THEN' 'SQRT' *X* 'ELSE' 0

The simple algorithm for conversion treats this as:

area := **ifx** ge **0** then sqrt **x** else **0** . . . . . .

which is, of course, gibberish and will result in the procedure printing out a monitor for four unknown delimiter words. Subsequent procedures will produce further monitors because of unknown operators (such as **ifx**) in the expression and because of undeclared identifiers (such as thensqrt). Conversely, if there had been a genuine error in that x had not been declared, this would not have been monitored.

Furthermore, the effect is to produce gibberish until a second quote sign is omitted. The effect can be limited to a single statement by slightly amending the algorithm, to reset the significance of a quote at the start of each statement. (In a multi-pass compiler the resetting could be done at some specific symbol such as a semicolon.)

Even so, the amount of useless fault monitor produced by such a simple error is quite unacceptable especially as this fault is a common one. To overcome this we must use a different strategy. We do not attempt to isolate a delimiter word by looking for its enclosing quote; instead, we merely look for the opening quote. More precisely we look for the first quote and assume for the moment that it is the opening quote. We then compare what follows character by character with the delimiters. The delimiters could be stored linearly; they could be indexed on their first letter; they could even be merged in the same way as a phrase definition. If a delimiter is found, and IF will be, we then check for a closing quote. If it is not there we assume that it should be and monitor a *warning* that the assumption has been made. The fault then gives rise to no further symptoms.

In practise it is quite likely that it is the closing quote that is omitted, and this technique is then particularly appropriate but consider:

> **begin**
> **real** *x*, *y*, *z*

when punched faultily as:

> 'BEGIN
> 'REAL' *X*, *Y*, *Z*

Then the opening quote of REAL appears as if it were the closing quote of BEGIN, and so, in practice, the procedure must be capable of dealing with missing opening quotes as well. Thus, after a delimiter word has been recognised, we look for the next quote, assuming that it is the opening quote of a subsequent delimiter word. In the example above there is no delimiter word starting with *X*, and so we now assume that it is a closing quote. We compare the string backwards from the point with a list of delimiter words stored backwards. In this case, REAL is recognised and its opening quote assumed to have been omitted by the programmer.

It is worth spending a few moments thinking about this algorithm. It is based on an assumption that a source string such as:

> 'IF

is synonomous with (as a mis-punching of):

> 'IF'

The assumption is quite a good one, but an assumption, nevertheless. The only reason this algorithm is used is that it is very successful, its assumption for the most part being correct. It can, however, produce some unexpected effects. Consider a program, which calculates currents within some electrical network. Its declarations might start:

real *if*, *ig*, *ia* . . . .

If the opening quote on **real** is omitted:

REAL' *IF*, *IG*, *IA*

the algorithm assumes that the existing quote is not the closing quote of REAL, but the opening one of IF. It monitors the 'fact' that the programmer has omitted the closing quote on IF (which can irritate the programmer especially when subsequent processing produces monitor messages based on this erroneous assumption).

This procedure (assuming the validity of its use) illustrates how the desire to produce meaningful messages can alter significantly the structure of the compiler. The alternative is a simple hashing algorithm as we have already seen.

The problem that this section has discussed is the result of a trivial mistake of language design—the use of a single symbol, the quote, rather than a pair of distinguishable symbols to enclose delimiters.

It is surprising to find it repeated in Algol 68, which has only one symbol, **comment** or **c**, to delimit comments.

14.3 Faults detected during lexical analysis

Lexical analysis is the procedure which replaces identifiers, constants and strings by pseudo-identifiers, pseudo-constants and pseudo-strings. We consider each in turn.

No faults can be detected when processing identifiers. An identifier is recognised by the appearance of a letter and is terminated by the appearance of any character other than a letter or a digit. Thus, the mis-punching of:

manchester

as, say:

man=hester

would be seen by the lexical analysis procedure as perfectly acceptable and 'man' and 'hester' regarded as identifiers (hopefully to be monitored as undeclared in subsequent processing).

The same is true of constants, the appearance of a digit constituting the start of a constant. Thus, the mis-punching of:

3·14159

as:

3·14·59

would also be seen as perfectly acceptable by the lexical analysis procedure, which would add '3·14' and '·59' to the constants list. During syntactical analysis the juxtaposition of these two constants would be monitored.

Note that if the constant were mis-punched:

3·14 + 59

the error would be quite undetectable. There is one fault that can be detected during lexical analysis. Each constant has to be evaluated and added to the constants list. A constant may exceed the capacity of the machine, and so overflow may occur during its evaluation.

Strings pose a difficult problem. The omission of a closing string quote causes everything up to the closing string quote of the next string to be regarded as a single string. This can have far-reaching consequences as the statements which are coalesced into the string may include declarations and the **begin**s of blocks. It is a similar problem to the one that arises with quoted delimiters. Some compiler writers have been tempted to restrict the consequences of a missing string quote by forbidding, say, a semicolon in any string, and terminating all strings, if necessary, at a semicolon. This is, of course, undesirable in that such a compiler is non-standard.

Let us assume, as is common, that the lexical analysis procedure eliminates comments. Algol has the curious comment convention that anything after an **end**, up ot the next **end**, **else** or semicolon is a comment. Consider, for example, a sequence for calculating and printing the HCF and LCM of two numbers p and q:

$p1 := p; q1 := q;$
for $i := 1$ **while** $q \neq 0$ **do**
begin
$r := p - p \div q * q;$
$p := q; q := r$
end
for $i := p1, q1, p, p1*q1 \div p$ **do** print (i, 6, 0);

The whole of the last line is a comment and the compiler must treat it as such. This comment convention is a ripe source of error, of course, as the above example shows. A compiler might usefully issue a *query* (rather than a fault monitor) if it finds a comment which contains one or more delimiter words. In practice, most compilers do this and as a consequence most programmers avoid delimiter words in their comments. This problem again arises from a weakness of the design of the language.

14.4 Faults detected during syntactical analysis

Syntactical analysis is the procedure which establishes the structure of the statements of the language. If a compiler writer follows strictly the dictum of monitoring out symptoms rather than attempting a diagnosis, it would merely print a message saying that it could not recognise the statement. Most compiler writers, though, succumb to the temptation of printing what seems to be a more specific message. For example, using the precedence algorithm of section 4.11, the compiler writer would print out at label ERROR that there is a missing right bracket. In a relatively well-structured language like Algol, this technique does work, but curious effects can occur. There is a compiler which monitors the fault in the Fortran statement:

1 DO I = 1, N

as:

INVALID RIGHT HAND SIDE OF ASSIGNMENT STATEMENT

This technique is sometimes extended to include some element of program correction. The common situation is typified by:

no of roots = **if** $b \uparrow 2 = 4*a*c$ **then** 1 **else** 2 which can be 'corrected' to:

no of roots := **if** $b \uparrow 2 = 4*a*c$ **then** 1 **else** 2

by a special entry in the precedence table corresponding to the (invalid) operator pair (=, **if**).

Precedence techniques are flexible as the preceding paragraphs show; syntax analysis is rather more rigid. In the pure form it can only detect a faulty statement, and neither pinpoint it accurately nor correct it. One technique which helps to locate the fault is to use a global pointer which the analysis procedure arranges to keep pointing to the furthest character recognised in the source string. This is a fairly accurate indication of the fault. Of course, if the mixed approach (syntax analysis for upper levels, precedence for expressions) is used, the power of the precedence technique isolates most of the faults.

If syntax analysis is used on a whole program, a further technique is relevant to enable a number of faults to be monitored. An extra statement is added to the language to describe all faulty statements. Clearly, this must be implemented by means of a phrase routine, which is entered only after all other statements have been tried, and which accepts everything up to the next statement terminator (in Algol, **end**, **else** or semicolon).

14.5 Faults detected during semantic processing

During semantic processing, the internal structures are processed, which causes the properties list to be updated or code to be compiled or both. The only faults detected in this procedure concern identifiers which have not been declared or have been declared twice. These give no problem.

The input to the semantic processing procedure has already been lexically analysed and so contains pseudo-identifiers rather than identifiers. A fault monitor which says that identifier #7 had not been declared is a little primitive; it would be better to say that identifier 'hester' had not been declared. This requires a change in the structure of the identifiers list. So far, we have been concerned only with the conversion from an identifier to a pseudo-identifier, and the structures of Fig. 3.1 reflect this. Now, purely for fault monitoring purposes, we need to go the other way, from pseudo-identifier to identifier. The identifiers list must be indexed to enable this to be done.

The information available during semantic processing is more extensive than that during syntactical analysis, and so the monitoring is generally more informative. Consequently, compiler writers often modify the syntax so that it defines a much larger language than that for which the compiler is being written, postponing the fault detection until the semantic processing phase. A simple example occurs in Algol. An Algol <program> is defined to be a <block> or a <compound statement> and a <block> is defined (making some simplifications):

<block> ::= **begin** <declarations>; <statements> **end**

where <declarations> is a string of <declaration>s separated by semicolons, and <statements> is a string of <statement>s similarly separated. Thus, any declaration appearing after a statement would result in the <block>'s not being recognised. An expanded grammar:

<block> ::= **begin** <declarations and/or statements>**end**

where <declarations and/or statements> is a string of <declaration>s and/or <statement>s separated by semicolons, will accept such a program as syntactically correct. During semantic processing the fact that a <declaration> is out of place will be monitored and all <declaration>s and <statement>s will be processed to detect the symptoms of any further fault. This technique is particularly relevant to Algol where all procedures are classed as declarations. Simple faults in the procedure heading may cause the compiler to ignore it; the procedure body (either a basic statement or a block) then appears to the compiler as a statement of the enclosing block, and so subsequent declarations (of other procedures, perhaps) seem out of place. The expansion of the grammar along the lines above resolves the problem.

14.6 Other information printed at compile time

High-level languages are very redundant and it is this that allows fault monitoring. (Not many faults can be detected in a binary program.) The compiler can use the redundancy to print out information that might be useful. For example, in Algol it might list all those identifiers which have been declared but not referenced. Such a declaration might be quite innocuous (where a programmer has modified his program but not bothered to delete the declaration of the quantity no longer used) or it may be a clue to a mis-punching. In Fortran, it might list all identifiers which are implicitly typed, again as an aid for detecting mis-punchings.

Fig. 14.2 illustrates another form of informative printing. The structure of the program is indicated showing the beginning and end of all blocks and procedures, indented to give it a two-dimensional aspect.

Information is often printed during compilation as a help in the interpretation of the run-time monitor. For example, since an Algol block has no name and yet needs to be referred to at run time (see section 14.8), the compiler allocates it a number which must be indicated to the programmer as shown in Fig. 14.2.

14.7 The layout of the compile time monitor

Most compilers provide a listing of the source program as they compile it. With programs punched on cards this is very useful, being much easier to read than the interpreted cards. With programs punched on tape it is less useful, since the programmer will have the listing produced on the editing device as the tape was produced; indeed, since lineprinters usually have a restricted character set, the program is listed on the lineprinter by what we might call *printing conventions* (delimiter words in quotes perhaps, and with upper and lower case letters indistinguishable). This is less readable than the original, though it has the advantage of being provided with the results of the compilation.

Given that it will produce a listing, the compiler may produce its monitor in one of two places:

(i) The information pertinent to a line may be printed immediately after the line. This is relevant to line-by-line compilers such as those for Fortran (or the language we used in earlier chapters). It has the advantage, from the compiler writer's point of view, that it is simple to implement. From the user's point of view, it has the advantage that the information about a fault is adjacent to the listing of the line where the symptoms of the fault have been detected. (The fault may be elsewhere, of course.)

(ii) The information may be collected together and printed after the program listing. This is appropriate to multi-pass compilers like those of Algol, where faults may be detected in each pass. They will, presumably, be held in some coded form internally (to save space) and converted to meaningful messages on output. As they are held internally the messages can be processed before printing. In Fig. 14.2 the messages are ordered according to their line number, and all query messages relating to delimiters within the same comment are condensed into one. Other techniques, such as merging into one statement all references to the same undeclared quantity, are applicable.

To be able to associate a line number with a fault, no matter in what pass it is detected requires that the line number be stored during all stages of processing; converting to a standard form, lexical analysis, syntactical analysis and semantic processing. It also implies that those procedures are modified to ignore this line number during their operation.

14.8 Run time monitoring

At run time faults can be detected in one of three ways:

(i) By the hardware. Diversion by zero and arithmetic overflow are the classical cases. Assuming the array-accessing hardware of Chapter 10 an array subscript out of range would be detected in this way.

(ii) By the operating system. Exceeding allowable resources, such as time, output volume and even money, are dealt with in this way.

(iii) By tests compiled into the object program by the compiler. In the absence of the array-accessing hardware of Chapter 10, an array subscript out of bounds would be detected in this way; with the looping statement of Chapter 9 (with integer parameters and so on), orders could be compiled to ensure that the parameters defined an arithmetic progression; and so on. These tests are time-consuming and it is one of the aims of modern language design to eliminate them, all testing being done at compile time. However, given existing languages (Fortran is especially bad here), the tests must be compiled to ensure that faulty programs are stopped as soon and as helpfully as possible. Compiler writers often provide an option by which the user can omit the tests if he is sure (or is prepared to take the risk) that his program is correct.

Sometimes the hardware provides only a partial solution and tests have to be compiled as well. For example, the ICL 1900 machines on detecting overflow merely set a register and carry on; the compiler must compile orders at carefully chosen points to test this register and enter the fault monitor if it is set.

However a fault is detected, it should give rise to the same fault monitoring, since to the user, the means of detection are irrelevant. This implies that there is an appropriate interface between the operating system and the compiler to deal with those faults found by the operating system and those faults found by the hardware which result in interrupts.

14.9 Post-mortem dumps and stack interpretation

When a program fails at run time the fault monitor procedure in the run-time package should print out all relevant information to help the programmer to detect the fault.

In the earliest compilers this meant a dump of the whole store of the machine, maybe in octal, maybe as machine instructions, maybe as floating point numbers. Apart from including the irrelevant with the relevant, this technique assumes that the programmer understands the order code of the machine and the details of the compiler, an assumption which was never more than partly true and which is now quite indefensible. That octal dumps are still provided even on the largest machines available today is a source of wonder.

A more satisfactory solution is to interpret the information in the core, restricting it to the variables and excluding the program. This technique originated in an Algol-like language, Atlas Autocode (see ref. 14.1), in 1963, which explains the term *stack interpretation*. The technique is applicable to languages with static storage allocation schemes, however, and Fig. 14.4 shows a fault monitor for the Fortran program of Fig. 14.3. In this example the values of the array elements have not been printed, though this is by no means fundamental.

To achieve this form of monitoring requires two things:

(i) The identifers and properties lists must be retained at run time (or at least the identifiers list and an abbreviated properties list). This

```
            REAL A(100)
            INTEGER SIZE,I
            READ(1,100) SIZE
      100   FORMAT(I5)
            READ(1,101)(A(I),I=1,SIZE)
      101   FORMAT(5F10.2)
            CALL SORT(A,SIZE)
            WRITE(2,200)(A(I),I=1,SIZE)
      200   FORMAT(1H ,F10.2)
            STOP
            END

            SUBROUTINE SORT(A,SIZE)
            REAL A(SIZE),SWOP
            INTEGER SIZE,START,SUB,MINSUB
            DO 1 START=1,SIZE
            SUB=MINSUB(A,START,SIZE)
            SWOP=A(SUB)
            A(SUB)=A(START)
            A(START)=SWOP
      1     CONTINUE
            RETURN
            END

            INTEGER FUNCTION MINSUB(A,START,SIZE)
            REAL A(SIZE)
            INTEGER SIZE,START,START1,I
            MINSUB=START
            START1=START+1
            DO 1 I=START1,SIZE
            IF(A(I).LT.A(MINSUB))MINSUB=I
      1     CONTINUE
            RETURN
            END

            FINISH
```

Fig. 14.3. A Fortran program for reading and sorting a list of numbers. A fault has been induced

has some marginal effects on the structure of the compiler. At run time, it can increase the amount of store required, unless it is held on backing store until a fault is detected.

(ii) Information must be held on the stack to associate the variables of the stack with the identifiers and properties. This implies an extra link and, hence, an extra order or two in the sequence compiled at the call. The effect on the speed of all programs, faulty or not, has been measured at less than 1 per cent.

Perusal of Fig. 14.4 shows three other points of interest:

```
A RUN-TIME FAULT HAS OCCURRED AT STATEMENT  29 IN FUNCTION MINSUB

DO VARIABLES NOT POSITIVE OR FINAL VALUE LESS THAN INITIAL


MINSUB =         5
START  =         5
SIZE   =         5
START1 =         6
I       IS UNDEFINED

THIS WAS CALLED FROM SUBROUTINE SORT    AT STATEMENT    17


SIZE   =         5
SWOP   =    5.0000000000
START  =         5
SUB    =         4

THIS WAS CALLED FROM THE MAIN PROGRAM BY STATEMENT     8


SIZE   =         5
I       IS UNDEFINED
```

Fig. 14.4. The run-time fault monitor resulting from the program of Fig. 14.3

(i) The line of the source program in which the error was detected is printed. This implies either:

(*a*) The compiler adds to the identifiers and properties list a list in which line numbers are associated with the machine address of the first order compiled for it; or

(*b*) The compiler uses a register to hold the current line number at all times, compiling orders to maintain it at its correct value, at the start of each line and after each procedure call.

In either case storage space is required, though in the first case it may be on backing storage. The second case has a time penalty, again about 1 per cent.

(ii) A *trace-back* is printed which shows for each procedure active, the line in which the procedure was called. This requires a link in the stack though it can be combined with the one introduced earlier.

(iii) Some variables are printed as being undefined. This depends on the machine having a special bit-pattern which can be recognised as different from a legitimate number and which will cause an interrupt if the machine tries to interpret it as a number. The compiler then sets the variables to this value on entry and, as in the case of the example of Fig. 14.4, when a variable becomes undefined.

Note that the stack interpretation procedure interprets the stack as it sees it, which is the stack as produced by the object program which has been running. If the compiler has made significant transformations during compilation then the interpretation of the stack might not easily be related to the source text. For example, some variables might not have their current values stored, this value being held in a register (the delaying-of-storage technique of section 9.14). The variable might even spend all its life in a register and have no storage allocated to it.

14.10 Fault recovery

In many situations where a program is dealing with a number of sets of data, any one of which may be faulty, it is unsatisfactory if the program terminates on the first error. The error may manifest itself in a number of places, and putting tests in all appropriate places (even assuming it possible) is not an attractive solution, especially as hardware is there to detect the faults. A better solution, called *fault-trapping*, gives the programmer the opportunity of intercepting a fault, so that instead of control passing to the fault monitoring procedure, it passes instead to a recovery sequence specified by the programmer. There is no problem of implementation (see the Atlas Autocode paper); the only problem is defining how the programmer should specify his intentions especially if he wishes to differentiate between types of fault.

14.11 Tracing

The stack interpretation technique is static in the sense that it considers the state of the computation only at its failure. An alternative technique, called *tracing*, provides the programmer with information about the dynamic behaviour of his program. In its simplest form, every procedure entry and exit, every jump, and every change to the value of selected variables is printed out. This is extraordinarily expensive, of course, slowing a program down by a factor of some hundreds and, because of its bulk, very difficult to interpret. Consequently, refinements are usually made. First, the user is given the option of specifying which of the three traces, *procedure trace*, *jump trace* and *variable trace*, he wants. Second, he is usually allowed to restrict the tracing to specific areas of his program. Third, he is often allowed within these areas to switch the tracing on and off dynamically. This allows him, for example, to trace the behaviour of the program during the first and last traverse of a loop, or during, say, every tenth traversal.

4.12 A comparison between stack interpretation and tracing

On the surface tracing seems the more powerful tool since it reflects the dynamic behaviour of a program. It is, however, very expensive, even if the programmer is judicious in exercising his options, and rather difficult to interpret because of the mass of detail. Consequently, most programmers use it only as a last resort, in which case, it means an extra run of the program.

The stack interpretation technique, on the other hand, adds so small a cost to the running of a correct program that the user is never given the option of running without it. Consequently, an extra run is never needed. The information provided, insofar as it consists of the currently active variables, is usually highly relevant.

In the only compiler known to the author in which both techniques were available, the Atlas Autocode system referred to earlier, the tracing facilities fell into disuse very soon after the stack interpretation was implemented.

4.13 When a program just gives the wrong results

When a program runs to completion but gives the wrong result, and the error cannot be found by the usual deductive debugging approach, another run of the program is required. Both run time techniques, stack interpretation and tracing, can be modified to this purpose.

With stack interpretation available, the standard technique is to precede the end of the program by a statement which will deliberately cause a run time fault. (Evaluating $\sqrt{-1}$ is often chosen.) This produces an interpretation at that point which can often be helpful. There is a certain lack of finesse in this technique, since it can only be used at the end of the computation, and compiler writers often make available to the programmer the procedure which interprets the stack. He may then call it as many times as he likes during the program.

Alternatively, the tracing facility can be modified so that instead of the information being printed as it is produced, it is stored in a buffer of, say, a hundred messages. On completion of the program these one hundred messages are printed. This technique is slow, since messages have to be added to the buffer, but not as slow as the pure tracing technique; and the last one hundred messages often turn out to be useless. [This abbreviated tracing technique is sometimes used as the run time fault monitoring technique.]

14.14 The user's options

Throughout this chapter we have mentioned the options that a compiler writer must allow the user. How does the user exercise these options?

If we ignore tracing for the moment, the information required can be provided once and once only for a program. There is further information that the compiler writer might require from the user, such as the amount of stack space required, the nature of the input-output peripherals and so on, and all this information can be collected together in a *program description* and placed in front of the program proper. For example, the program description might appear:

```
PROGRAM ROHL SYNTAX ANALYSIS
INPUT 1 = CRO
OUTPUT 1 = LPO
TIME 20 SECS
```

```
VOLUME 250
NO OVERFLOW CHECK
FULL ARRAY BOUND CHECK
UPPER CASE DELIMITERS
END
```

Alternatively, it may consist of a single line in which the user specifies his options by means of parameters.

When we consider tracing, and in particular in delimiting the areas over which it operates, it is more convenient to distribute the requests from the user throughout his program. The usual technique is to use the comment facility, so that if a comment starts with a special symbol, say, **trace**, then it is not ignored, but regarded as a special command.

15 Compiling systems

We chose to use a one-pass, compile-and-go compiler, Fig. 1.1, throughout this book for its simplicity. It is not the only form, nor even the most frequently occurring one. In this chapter we look at the other ways in which a compiler may operate. The basic techniques and structures are the same; all that differs is the way they are organised and the way they are integrated into the total computing system.

15.1 Semi-compiled format and relocatable binary

An early alternative to the compile-and-go system, and one which has dominated manufacturers' designs, is a system in which the compiler compiles not into binary code in core for immediate execution, but into a special format called *semi-compiled* or *relocatable binary* which is generally filed and later loaded for execution (Fig. 15.1).

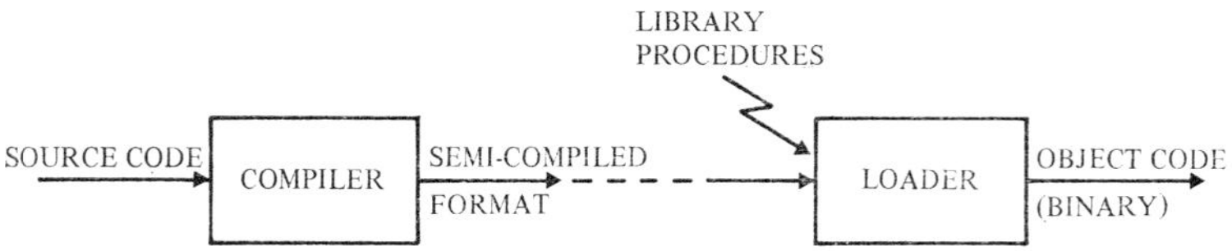

Fig. 15.1. A system using a semi-compiled format

As the names imply the compilation process performs most of the tasks of the compile-and-go system but not all.

The system is best understood by considering a language with a disjoint procedure structure such as Fortran and most assembly languages. The compiler (semi-) compiles a procedure at a time and files it. Since the place in which each procedure will subsequently be loaded is unknown (and may vary from job to job), the compiler cannot compile the address part of jump orders (unless the machine is provided with the appropriate relative jump orders). Neither can it compile the addresses in those orders concerned with procedure calls, since the address at which the called procedure will be loaded is unknown. Further, if the language has static storage allocation it may not be possible to compile the address parts of operand accessing orders either. [It is worth noting that because of this many Fortran compilers store the variables of each procedure adjacent to the code of the procedure, rather than in a separate area as we have done. As segmentation facilities are added to computer systems, providing, as they do, automatic protection against overwriting, the separation of variables and code will become the norm.]

Semi-compiled format then consists of the code which has been compiled without some address parts, together with information necessary for the loader to fill in the internal addresses and to link the procedure to other procedures and to any blocks of common data. There must be further information to enable the procedure to be linked to others. The action of the loader can be deduced from this description. For the full details the reader is referred to Barron (see ref. 15.1).

On the surface this system seems merely to complicate the problem by adding the extra stage and indeed, as compiling techniques have improved, so the overheads of this system have become more significant. For example, on the ICL 1900, the loader takes approximately the same time as the compiler. On the other hand, if the machine has only a small core, the size of the object program being compiled, which can fit in the space left by the compiler, may be minimal. Since the loader can be quite small, it is possible to compile and run much larger programs.

The other advantages of this system, advantages which cause it to be used on even the largest computers available today, stem from the nature of the semi-compiled format and the loader. If these are standardised for all languages on a machine, including its assembly language, then two advantages follow.

(i) It is possible to store within the machine a library of procedures in the semi-compiled format. The loader can be arranged to load automatically all library procedures referred to by the program (as shown in Fig. 15.1). There need be only one copy of the library procedure, too, which may be linked into programs in Algol and Fortran or whatever.

(ii) A program may be composed of procedures of different languages. This is called *mixed-language programming*. While the full generality of this concept is rarely required (few people wish to add sections of Cobol to, say, an Algol program) it is sometimes useful for adding assembly language procedures to programs in Fortran or Algol, either to access special peripherals, or to improve the speed of critical loops.

The use of this system places some constraints of the language being compiled. Each procedure must be capable of independent (semi-) compilation: hence, it must contain adequate information to enable all references to other procedures and to common blocks of storage to be compiled. Fortran was designed with this system specifically in mind, and the constraints are formalised as part of the language. The COMMON statement, for example, is used in all subprograms which refer to variables in a common block: if the program were compiled as a whole only one such specification would be necessary in, say, the block data subprogram. [Of course, the use of the COMMON statement in each subprogram allows the variables of the common block to be given different names in each subprogram.] The design of the subprogram facilities is less felicitous. Within a subprogram, no information is available about the subprograms it calls. All actual arguments (as Fortran calls its actual parameters) are addresses, so that there is no problem with compiling any call, but no means of checking the consistency of arguments either. In practice, most systems will accept almost any call as valid. In languages with a nested structure like Algol, the programmer is often required to insert special statements to enable this system to operate.

This system is only as comprehensive as the facilities provided in the loader. Loaders have generally been designed with Fortran and the assembly language in mind and so are often limited in their application. The facilities allowed in an Algol procedure to be linked into a Fortran program, for example, might be restricted and the checking of the validity of the call might be minimal.

15.2 Libraries with a compile-and-go compiler

In the last section we discussed libraries as they can be implemented in a system which produces a semi-compiled format. Libraries can be implemented with a compile-and-go system as well. In this case we often divide the procedures which are required at run time into two classes: those which will be required in every or almost every program (called the *permanent material* or just *perm*) and those which will be required only by a small proportion of programs (the library proper).

The perm, which includes procedures required to maintain the run time structures if necessary, procedures for fault monitoring, basic functions and input and output (and sometimes matrix and differential equation procedures) is kept in a fully compiled form and one of the functions of the initialisation procedure of the compiler is to transfer a copy of it to the start of the object program area. One of the consequences of this solution is that the object program requires more storage to run in because the perm procedures are included whether or not they are required. For example, on the ICL 1906A, the manufacturer's normal Fortran compiler, which uses a semi-compiled format, produces programs which require a minimum of 5K words, while the Manchester Fortran compiler, which is a compile-and-go system produces programs which require a minimum of 16K. In this case the perm includes all the procedures necessary to run a standard Fortran program. The gain, of course, is in the elimination of the time required for loading (and searching and incorporating library procedures) in the alternative system, and this, as we have noted, might be significant.

The library proper is held in source form and a procedure is compiled every time a program requires it. This is a slower process than that of loading and linking required with the system which produces a semi-compiled format, though perhaps not significantly so. A given procedure, though, must be stored in a number of libraries, one for each source language, and this leads to maintenance problems if more than two or three languages are involved. It is quite economical of space, however, the source form being much smaller than the corresponding semi-compiled form.

To deal with library procedures in machine code, the compiler must be expanded to provide it with facilities to assemble machine orders. This is fairly trivial since most of the mechanism already exists in a compiler. All that is necessary is a set of procedures to process the mnemonic function parts and sometimes octal or hexadecimal integers. There is an advantage with this technique that the machine orders can be provided with a special interface to the host language, so that, say, the Algol parameters and variables can be accessed symbolically.

15.3 In-core batching compilers

Within teaching establishments there is a great demand for processing large numbers of small teaching and development programs. In the University of Manchester, for example, there is a load of about 1200–1500 student jobs a day, generated mainly in a three-hour period during the afternoon. Clearly, in this situation the speed of compilation is important; the run time speed, however, while not completely irrelevant is rather less important since less than half the programs run and those that do are of short duration. Consequently, compilers processing these jobs are single-pass and do little optimisation. The best-known and one of the earliest such compilers is the University of Waterloo's WATFOR (see ref. 15.3).

The major problem lies in the overheads normally required to start any job. This problem has been overcome by arranging that the compiler processes a *batch* of jobs at a time, remaining in the core the whole time. A batch of jobs might be presented as shown in Fig. 15.2.

There are usually slight restrictions placed on the user. For example, as illustrated in Fig. 15.2, he may be restricted to one input channel, the data being placed immediately after the program.

Once the complete job has been initiated, control remains within the compiler and the object programs it compiles. Initially the compiler is entered and it compiles program 1 (using information in the program description to guide it). At the textual end of the program, control is transferred to the object program which processes data 1. At the dynamic end of the program, control passes to the compiler which compiles program 2, and so on.

Clearly, the store required is quite large since it must contain the

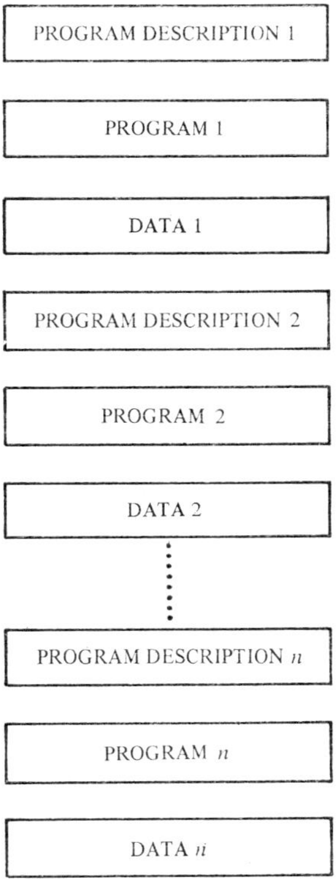

Fig. 15.2. A batch of jobs

compiler, its lists, the object programs in turn and their variables as sketched in Fig. 15.3.

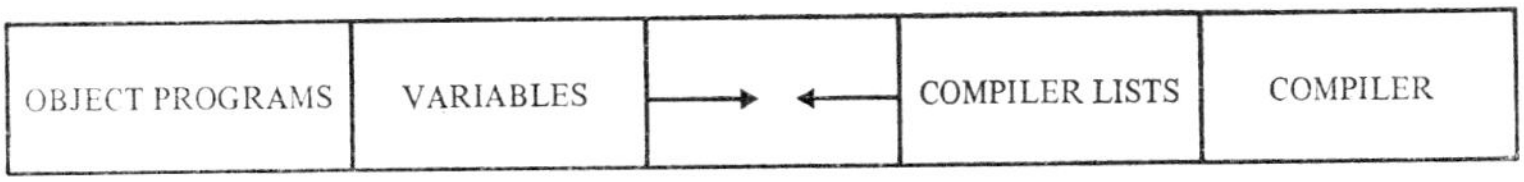

Fig. 15.3. An in-core batching compiler

For example, on an ICL 1900 machine, the Fortran and Algol compilers working in this mode require 45K words of core, which allows programs up to 1000 lines long.

Three problems can occur and the compiler must be modified to overcome them.

(i) Any of the source programs may contain compile time errors, so that the object program is not entered and the data not read; alternatively, a source program may contain a run time error which is detected before all the data has been read. Consequently, the compiler must be provided with a *monitor*, so that every time it is entered it first moves off to the start of the next program skipping over any unread data that precedes it. The start of the next program can be detected either by detecting the first card of the program description or by requiring the student to add a special card preceding the job description.

(ii) A source program may contain a run time error which causes it to read more data than is provided. Clearly, it must be prevented from reading subsequent programs as its data. Consequently, the run time input procedures must be modified so that they stop reading at the start of the following program. This can be detected using the two methods described above. Often the second method, detecting a special card, is used because it can be both short (minimising this overhead) and distinctive (minimising the restriction on the data a program can process).

(iii) The possibility that an object program might corrupt the compiler must be avoided. If the machine is provided with segmentation then the problem is catered for by the operating system; if the machine is not segmented then the compiler must provide the protection. In particular, it must ensure that the variables stack does not extend into the area of store holding the compiler and that, whenever an array element is altered, its subscripts are checked for being within range.

15.4 Cafeteria systems

A *cafeteria system*, as its name suggests, is one in which students queue at a card reader to present jobs, which are processed separately, and then join a queue at the line-printer to collect their output, which is produced separately. Such systems can be constructed in a number of ways. We mention here only one, a modification to the in-core batching system of the previous section.

The compiler is modified so that it starts processing, not when a complete batch has been submitted, but when any cards are placed in the reader. Whenever the reader becomes empty the compiler becomes dormant (and maybe swopped out of core by the operating system). When cards are placed in the reader (or within a very short time thereafter) the compiler is reactivated and continues processing. This system clearly requires a card reader and a line-printer dedicated to this task.

15.5 Multi-pass compilers

Although throughout this book we have used a single-pass compiler as our model, we have, on occasion, referred to multi-pass compilers and now we consider them in a little more depth. With a *multi-pass compiler* we process the complete program a number of times, each process (called a *pass*) performing some processing of the program, or collecting information for subsequent passes. Fig. 15.4 shows a possible structure where, in line with our previous practice, we have allocated each distinct action to a separate pass. In practice, of course, some of these actions are likely to be condensed into a single pass.

We have already seen two situations in which multi-pass compilers are of use. We now consider these, and one other, in more detail.

(i) A multi-pass compiler is indispensible when the speed of the object code is important. In this situation we might have three semantic processing passes. The first pass might establish the extent of loops, the dependencies of variables of the loops upon others, in particular upon the controlled variables of the loops and so on. The second pass might, in the light of this information, transform the internal structures so that invariant calculations are moved outside loops, strength reduction techniques are applied and so on. The third pass then would produce the object code. In practice, highly optimising compilers are designed round these optimisation passes and the earlier passes are often condensed into one; indeed, often into the first of the semantic passes.

(ii) A multi-pass compiler is often dictated by the nature of the language. If in the language it is not necessary to declare variables before they are referred to (the case with Algol), then there must be at least two semantic processing passes, one to process the declarations, the other to process the imperatives. This leads to some changes in the way the properties list is handled. As described in section 11.7, the properties list expands and contracts as compilation progresses, the properties of the quantities of a given block existing only during the compilation of that block, so that at the end of compilation the list is empty. Clearly, this system must be modified if the declarations are processed in a separate pass. The pass processing declarations must create and retain all the properties but add links so that the pass processing the imperatives may access the appropriate properties. The details are left to the reader. As we have noted, the use of two semantic processing passes is more or less obligatory in Algol: many Algol compilers are written with precisely two passes, the early passes of Fig. 15.4 up to and including syntactical analysis being merged with the first processing pass.

(iii) A multi-pass compiler might be dictated by the machine's having a restricted core, so that it is impossible to have the complete compiler in the core at once. [We have already alluded to this situation when discussing semi-compiled format in section 15.1.] With a multi-pass compiler we can arrange to store the passes of the compiler and the compiler lists on backing store, transferring into the core for each pass the appropriate procedures and lists.

The size of program that can be compiled is determined by the pass which requires the most space. If we are writing a compiler in this way then we must endeavour to minimise this space, if necessary, by splitting passes into two. Once we have done this we minimise the number of passes by grouping together actions into passes so that each pass uses, to the full, the space available to it.

15.6 Interaction: re-entrant (or pure) code

So far we have discussed compilers only in a *batch-processing* environment, that is, where programs are submitted to the machine by means of cards or paper tape, and some time later the results are returned from it. An alternative environment is the *interactive* one, in which the programmers submit the jobs from a keyboard at a console and to varying degrees interact with the system. Interaction can take place in a number of ways and we consider in this section and the next how these affect the structure of the compiler.

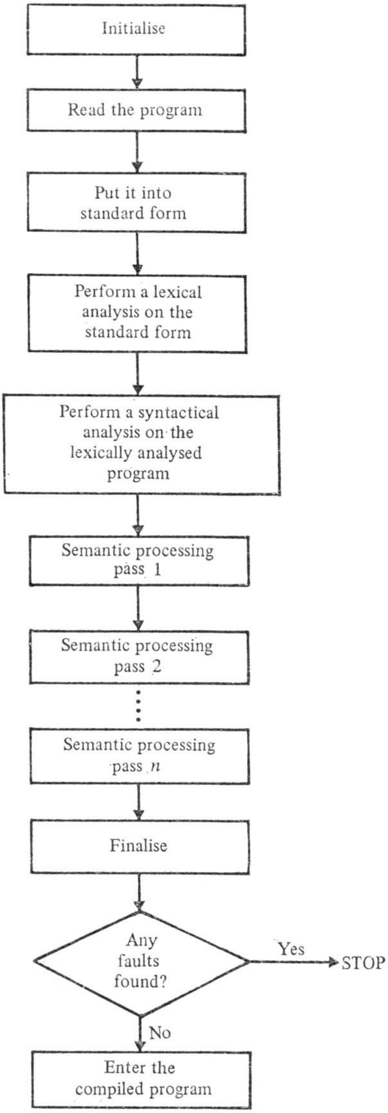

Fig. 15.4. A multi-pass compiler

19 24 pp.

The simplest form of interaction is that where a programm. allowed to compose and edit a program from a console, to subn. the completed program to be compiled and run, to interrogate the results, and finally to cause them to be printed, if necessary, on a central line-printer. This may be viewed as an alternative way of achieving a fast turn-round to the in-core batching compiler described in section 15.3. The interaction is provided by the operating system: the programmer interacts with an editor, a file-handling procedure and a part of the scheduler. No interaction takes place with the compiler. In many computer systems the ordinary batch-processing compiler is used, the job being submitted, maybe with high priority, to the batch-processing stream. An alternative approach, which is more often used in an interactive environment is to process the jobs in parallel rather than in series as is done in the batch-processing environment. That is, rather than run a job to completion, it is run for a predetermined slice of time and then suspended while the next and subsequent jobs are run for their time-slices. Clearly, with any significant number of consoles, not all the jobs will fit in the core and so they are held on backing store each being moved into core as it is about to be reactivated and moved out of core as it is suspended. If a job consists of the compiler and its lists then the time for moving the job in and out of core becomes significant. This time can be reduced by speeding up the channels between the core and backing stores but a more elegant solution is to use only one copy of the compiler, retaining it continuously in the core. Fig. 15.5 illustrates the scheme.

Here, the compiler and its lists are held in two quite distinct segments. Moving a job out of core implies merely moving its lists out of core and since these are much smaller, the time required is correspondingly reduced. Further, it is often possible to keep the lists for a number of programs in the core so that if only a few consoles are active no movement out of core is required; and if more core is added to the machine this number of consoles can be increased to any desired number. Clearly, for this system to work we require some extra hardware to effect this segmentation so that swopping control from one program to another merely means altering the appropriate registers so that subsequent references by the compiler causes it to access the correct lists.

Clearly, the use of this system implies that the compiler does not alter itself. A procedure which does not alter itself is said to be a *pure procedure* or a *re-entrant procedure*. [Almost all the high-level procedures that are written are pure; the existence of the terms reflects the fact that many assembly language programs are not.]

A completely different form of inter-action arises in the classical computer-aided design situation. Here the user (who is often not the writer of the program) interacts with the object program. He

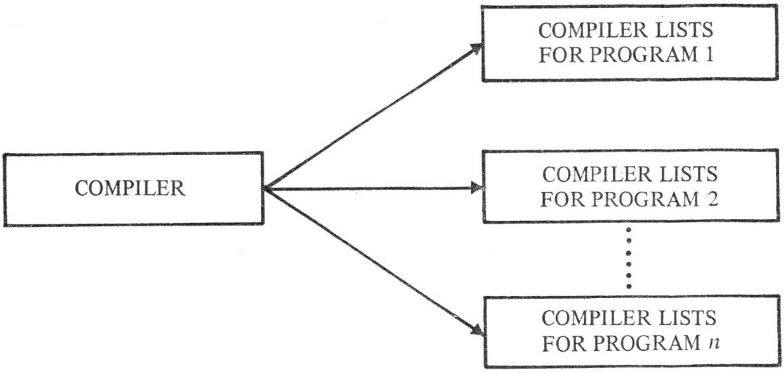

Fig. 15.5. A re-entrant compiler and its lists

provides data for the program at the console as requested and is allowed to ask for information from the program. Once again the interaction is provided by the operating system, which arranges for output to be sent to the console and for input to be accepted from the console. Clearly, the program must be written with this use in mind so that messages are sent to the console to ask for the information to be typed. Further, if the user is allowed to ask for information from the program, then the program must contain a nontrivial procedure for interpreting these requests. No changes are required to the compiler, however.

If we consider a large number of consoles all operating in this manner then savings can be made by using only one copy of the run time package, in particular the perm, which is retained permanently in the core. The program then is divided into two distinct sections, the re-entrant perm on the one hand, and the object code corresponding to the program plus the variables on the other. The problems are clearly similar to those discussed earlier with respect to Fig. 15.5.

15.7 Interaction: incremental compiling

Let us now return to the problem of composing and debugging a program from a console. [We ignore the important philosophical question of whether this is a valid approach to programming.] The simple technique of the last section, which allows the programmer to edit, submit the program for running and interrogate his output, is quite powerful. A more powerful system arises from allowing the programmer to interact with his program in a general way. The system we will describe is most often implemented by designing languages especially for the purpose such as the original JOSS and ICL's JEAN. We will, however, illustrate the basic ideas with respect to our original basic language. The programmer thinks exclusively in terms of the source language: as far as he is concerned the machine is a source language machine.

Statements are of two types: those which form part of the program and are to be stored and those which are commands to the system and are obeyed immediately. The classical means of distinguishing the two is to precede the first class by a line number. Thus, the program of section 3.1 would be typed:

```
 10       begin
 20       real h,f0,f1,f2, integral;
 30       integer j, no;
 40       j := 0;
 50       read no;
 60 loop: read h,f0,f1,f2;
 70       integral := 4·0 * f1;
 80       integral := f0 + integral;
 90       integral := integral + f2;
100       integral := h * integral;
110       integral := integral / 3·0;
120       print integral;
130       j := j + 1;
140       if j ≠ no then go to loop;
150       end
      run
```

Here the first fifteen lines are the program and the sixteenth, the statement 'run' causes the program to be run. Fig. 15.6 outlines the flow diagram for such a system.

The line numbering system allows of a simple editing technique. The program is assumed to be ordered in ascending sequence of line numbers, regardless of the order in which they were typed. (This is the reason for retaining the source text referred to in Fig. 15.6.) If two or more lines have the same line number then the last one typed is assumed to be correct and the others are ignored. Thus, a line may be altered by merely retyping it, preceding it by the same line number; a line may be deleted by typing just the line number; a line may be inserted between the two lines by giving it a number between those of the two lines.

Thus, the sequence:

```
 70  integral := h*(f0 + 4·0*f1 + f2)/3·0;
 80
 90
100
110
```

would convert the program given earlier to that of section 4.1.

The facilities described so far are very similar to those available in the simple system of the previous section. However, since the editing is done here by the compiler, rather than by an independent editor, some economies can be made. Rather than recompile the whole program afresh after each set of edits, we can, instead, merely compile the new lines and link them into the exisiting code. This is called *incremental compiling*. Fig. 15.7 shows the structure for the integration program after the edits given above.

Two things are clear. First, as the number of edits mounts so, too, does the space occupied by redundant code. Second, the system breaks down if an edit alters a declarative statement or one of the statements such as **begin** and **end** which give the program structure. Consequently, this system is more often used with languages specially designed to avoid this problem. Alternatively, the process of compiling is replaced by one of interpretation (see ref. 15.2), which we will describe in the next section.

So far in this section the statements for immediate execution ('run' is the only example given) are disjoint from those forming the

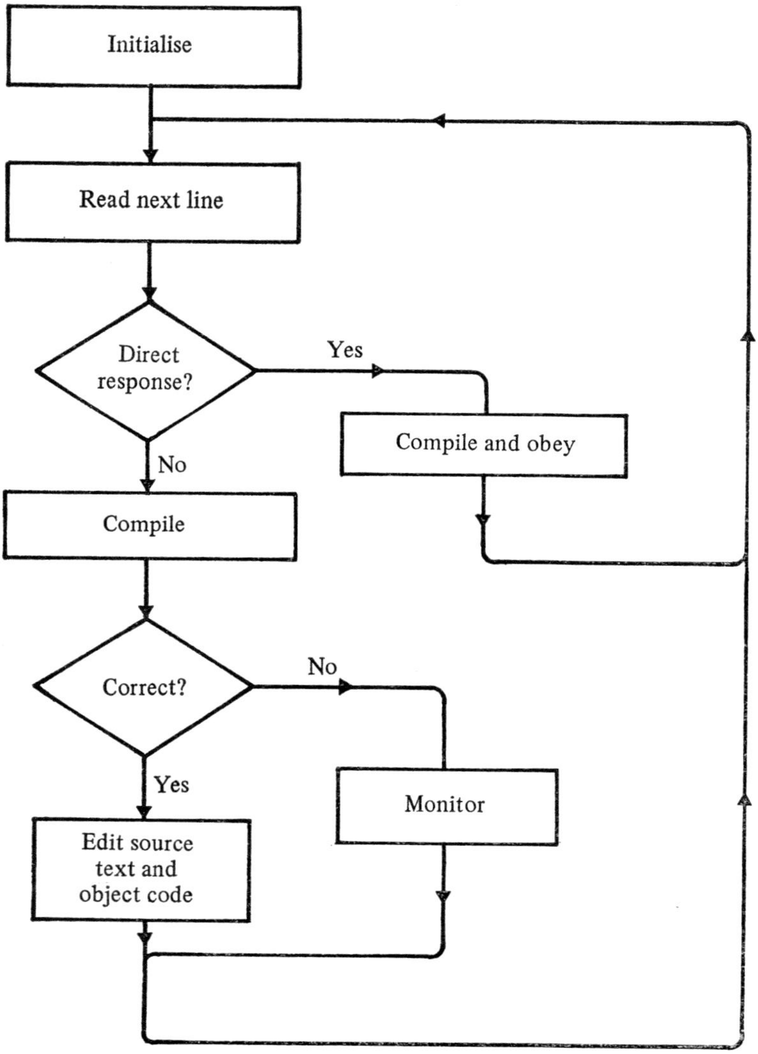

Fig. 15.6. Flow diagram for an incremental compiler

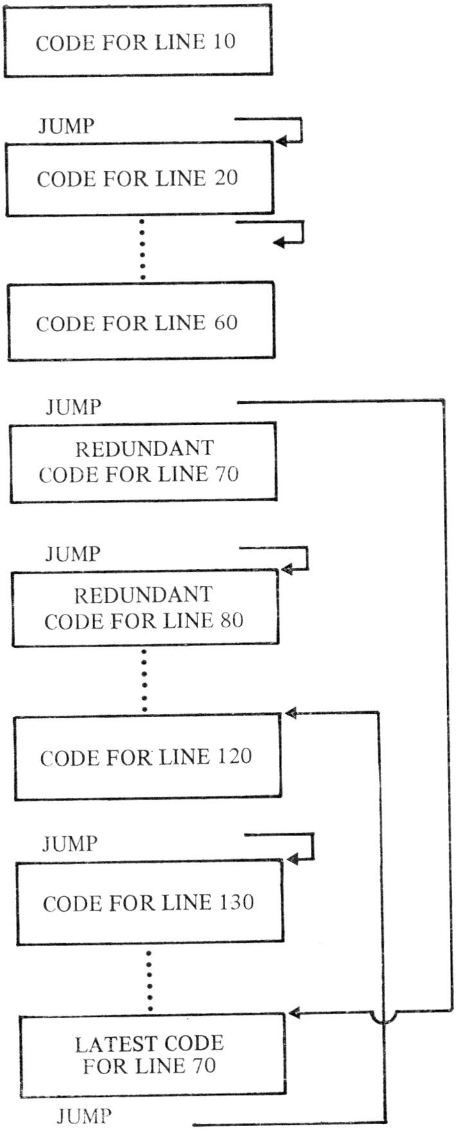

Fig. 15.7. The structure of the object code for the integration program after editing

program. Powerful advantages arise if we allow them to include the program statements. Suppose that, when a run time error is detected the object program merely prints out a message to that effect and waits for further input. The user may type a (direct response) print statement to access information which may lead him to the error; he may type a (direct response) assignment statement to alter information; he may type a (numbered) statement to alter the program; and he may type a run statement to restart or rerun his program. This clearly is full interaction in the sense that a programmer can dynamically modify both a program and its variables.

There are some formidable problems in this area and it is still the subject of much research.

15.8 Interpreters

The characteristic of a compiler is that it translates a statement once only into object program and during the running it is this object program that is obeyed. With an *interpreter* on the other hand, the translation takes place each time a statement is to be obeyed. Consequently, given the machine structure we have been considering, interpreters are much slower than compilers. They are very useful in a number of situations as we have already mentioned.

First, suppose, as in section 5.7, that the machine has no floating-point hardware, then the code compiled for a real expression is compiled as if it were a series of procedure calls. As indicated in section 5.7, the integration expression:

$$h*(f0 + 4{\cdot}0*f1 + f2)/3{\cdot}0$$

is compiled as:

```
fetch (h);
fetch (f0);
fetch (4·0);
fetch (f1);
mult;
```

```
add;
fetch (f2);
add;
mult;
fetch (3·0);
divide
```

The procedures, especially those for performing the operations, are quite long and dominate the calculation. In this context, the translation time is relatively small and so the difference in speed between an interpreter and a compiler becomes less significant. Further, the space required to hold to object code for these procedure calls is quite large when compared with the space required to hold the source program (or some more suitable transformation of it, see later) and if the machine has a small store the difference in space required between an interpreter and a compiler becomes more significant.

Second, consider, as in section 15.7 above, that the system being built is a fully interactive one in that the user may alter dynamically both his program and its variables. We have already noted that altering a declarative statement implies that the code compiled for some of the subsequent imperatives will change. With a compiler, this means a recompilation probably of the whole program, or at least of a whole procedure. With an interpreter the translation takes place each time the statement is obeyed and so the alteration of a declarative requires no immediate changes to the imperatives. A much simpler system ensues.

We have not yet considered how we should store the program in an interpretive system. The simplest would be to store the text as typed. This would, of course, be very slow because the interpretation of a statement would involve all the processes normally associated with compiling; it would be better to store the program in its standard form, or even in a lexically analysed form or even in a syntactically analysed form. The fastest interpreter results from an internal form which has had the maximum preprocessing applied to it. Clearly, though, none of this preprocessing must have a semantic processing character or else subsequent modifications to the program (to declarations, for example) may render it invalid. Reverse Polish is often the form chosen.

15.9 The future

All systems described here, and many more, have been used in practice. The broad characteristics are well understood but there has been, as yet, very little work done to measure the detailed characteristics, so that, at present, the choice between systems is often made intuitively. This is another aspect of the rapid expansion of computer science: ideas are being produced and their utility demonstrated far faster than they can be evaluated and compared.

16 Compiler writing aids

If this book were written five years ago this chapter would have been a large one and would have described *compiler writing languages*. In 1968, for example, Feldman and Gries (see ref. 16.2) gave a very fine description of *Translator Writing Systems*, describing the situation at that time. Since then, however, it has been realised that the characteristics required of a language for writing compilers are very similar to those required of a language for writing operating systems, editors and so on and hence there developed the notion of *systems programming languages*. Following on (though the more far-sighted were suggesting it earlier) it has been realised that these characteristics are similar to those required for most advanced programming and that the modern programming languages PL/1, Simula 67 and Algol 68 can be used for this purpose. The current situation is that the manufacturers are developing and using systems programming languages based on the general purpose languages (ICL's S3 based on Algol 68, Control Data's SYMPL based on Algol 60). Rather than describe these we will consider the characteristics that such languages must provide. We will follow this by a description of some techniques which have proved useful in the construction of compilers in practice.

16.1 Control structures in a compiler writing language

We noted very early on that a compiler has a hierarchical structure, and clearly any language used for writing compilers must have an adequate procedure structure. Whether the language has a disjoint procedure structure or a nested one is irrelevant: what is important is that the means of communication between the procedures be adequate and efficient. At the top level, the procedures are entered only once and sometimes have rather extensive interfaces. The procedures then should be able to communicate through common storage (in a disjoint structure) or through non-local variables (in a nested structure). At the lower levels, procedures are called a number of times from different places in the compiler. They should be able to communicate efficiently by parameters. Most languages are reasonably satisfactory from this point of view though Algol's lack of call-by-reference parameters is a weakness.

The ability of a procedure to call itself recursively is important, too. It would be relatively easy to rewrite the analysis procedure of section 13.8 to avoid its use, but it would be rather more difficult to recast the procedures for encoding and transforming binary trees. It is the lack of recursion which limits Fortran's use as a compiler writing language.

One facility that is very useful (but is not often provided) is the macro. Within a compiler we often have need to perform fairly simple operations: such as accessing the properties of a quantity (given its pseudo-identifier) or compiling an order which will stack the accumulator. Each of these requires two or three statements. Rather than write down these few statements every time the action is required, it is preferable to write down a single statement to minimise mistakes. Given the overheads that are normally associated the use of a procedure is obviously too expensive. It is, in fact, the classical case for the use of a macro.

Within procedures there is a need for an adequate control structure to deal with loops. Given that much of a compiler's time is spent in associatively searching lists, it must be possible to terminate the loop when a certain condition becomes true (or false). The while-clause of Algol and Pascal and the repeat-clause of Pascal are useful in this context; Fortran, though, is somewhat defective.

16.2 Data structures in a compiler writing language

As we have noted throughout the book, a compiler has to maintain structures. There are the well-defined structures such as the stack, that we have used in the precedence and Reverse Polish algorithms, and the binary tree, that we have used to represent expressions. There are also the more general structures such as the one we used to implement the hashing of identifiers. Very little help is given in the traditional languages with this problem: their data structures are usually confined to scalars, vectors and matrices. It is, however, no great problem to simulate a wide range of data structures with these basic ones, using integers to simulate references. If the components of an element of a structure are of different types, then these components must be separated out into separate vectors and this can be irritating. It is in this area of data structures that the modern programming languages such as PL/1 and Algol 68 have the most to offer.

With the traditional data structures, the list, the stack and the binary tree, where they have to be simulated with vectors it is generally convenient to define operators to add an element, delete an element and so on. These provide another example of the desirability of macros. It would probably be adequate to use a procedure for adding an element to a list if this procedure has always to test for an empty list and perform different actions depending on the result of the test. It would probably be too expensive, on the other hand, to use a procedure to stack an element since this requires only two orders (assuming that there is no possibility of exceeding the capacity of the stack).

The elementary data items that a compiler requires are rather more extensive than those required in normal computation. Floating-point numbers are required only during the evaluation of constants during lexical analysis, and during the folding of constants where that optimisation is performed. On the other hand a compiler requires bits for Boolean quantities, 6- or 8-bit bytes for holding characters, longer integers for holding addresses and references, and even some representation of the component parts of the machine orders it is compiling. It is in this area that the languages referred to in the introduction to this chapter, have often been extended.

Conversely, the operations required on these data items are quite simple: simple arithmetic, maybe logic, and loading and storing. Floating-point operations such as multiply and divide, and functions such as sine and cosine are never used (except if constants are folded). Consequently, floating-point features are missing entirely from many of the systems programming languages.

16.3 Fault monitoring in a compiler writing language

Compilers have to go through a debugging and development stage like any other program: and the compiler writer needs adequate debugging information like any other programmer. This is an area which has been sorely neglected. If the compiler is written in a standard language, then that monitor is available. Hopefully, it is at least as informative as that of Fig. 14.4. Even so, while this is adequate for the data structures relevant to numerical computation, it is quite inadequate for more general ones.

If these general data structures are simulated in arrays, then the printing of all the array values does at least provide the information, but in a most indigestible form. There is very little joy to be found in deciphering a tree, a circular list, or a more general linked structure from its linear representation in a vector. What is required is a monitoring procedure which will interpret the structure, and provide an output in which the structure is shown rather more diagrammatically. Unfortunately, these procedures are rarely (if ever) provided.

Neither are such facilities provided in languages specially designed for compiler writing.

It is a sobering thought that compiler writers have had so low an opinion of the computer's data processing ability.

16.4 Special procedures for compiler writing

If we are using a standard language, or a more general systems programming language, then it can be made more amenable to compiler writing by the provision of special procedures. We have already indicated a number of such procedures: procedures for maintaining special data structures such as lists, procedures for displaying fault monitors. These are applicable, too, to say, operating systems. There are procedures which are more specific to compiler writing such as the analysis procedure of section 13.8, or, more likely, a modified analysis procedure written along the lines suggested in section 13.9.

16.5 Compiler target languages

The compiler we have developed through this book compiled directly into binary, and in Section 15.1 we considered a system in which the compiler produced a semi-compiled form. It is attractive to consider what advantages might ensue if we could raise the level of this *compiler target language* (CTL) especially if we are considering a machine with a number of compilers available. The basic idea is quite simple as can be seen from Fig. 16.1.

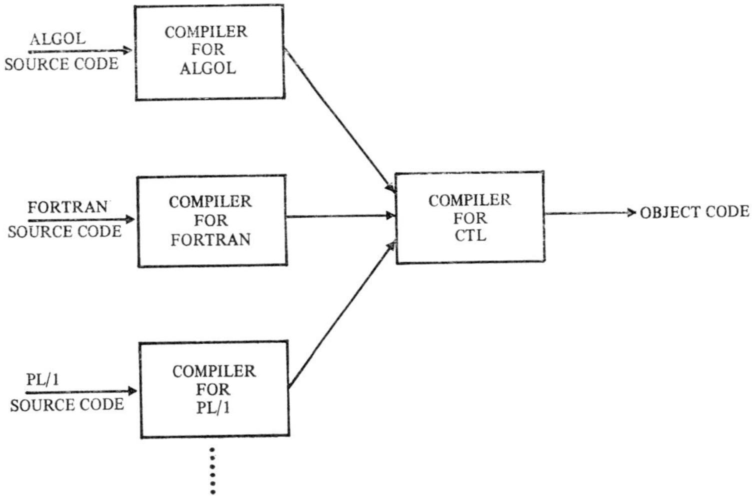

Fig. 16.1. A compiler system based on a CTL

The higher the level of the CTL (that is, the more high-level concepts such as declaratives, expressions, control structures and so on that it has), the more code of the individual compilers can be transferred to the CTL compiler. Thus, the code for all the compilers can be reduced, though maybe the code required for each individual compilation (say, the Algol compiler + the CTL compiler) may be increased due to the separation. The most attractive characteristic of this system is that if the CTL is correctly chosen then the compilers can be moved to another machine merely by writing the appropriate CTL compiler, all other compilers being invariant to the machine used. These systems have had a long history. The earliest attempt, in which the CTL was called UNCOL (see ref. 16.3), failed because the CTL was a real language and the compilers did produce as output a valid text in UNCOL. This was then compiled by the UNCOL compiler, maybe on another machine. In practice this meant that in order to ensure a correct translation from the source text to UNCOL, the Algol compiler, for example, had to maintain identifiers and properties lists and so on; and to ensure a correct translation from UNCOL to binary, the UNCOL compiler had also to maintain identifiers and properties lists and so on. Thus, the system resulted in duplication: the precise opposite of its design objective.

A more recent attempt, on MU5 (see ref. 16.1), is based on the notion that the CTL be a conceptual rather than a written language. With UNCOL, the communication between the Algol compiler, say, and the UNCOL compiler is purely one-way: it is the UNCOL text

In the MU5 scheme, the communication is two-way. The CTL compiler is a collection of procedures to which the Algol and other compilers have access. Many of these procedures set up lists and store information (corresponding to CTL declaratives); others compile code (corresponding to CTL imperatives); the remainder are used by the Algol and other compilers for accessing information stored by other CTL procedures. It is this latter class which gives the CTL its two-way communication and which prevents the CTL from being a written language.

This is an exciting idea and all the MU5 compilers are being written in this way. The system has been demonstrated, though at the time of writing no quantitative results are available.

16.6 Generators

In section 16.4 we discussed procedures which would be desirable in a compiler writing language and which, therefore, were useable by a number of compilers. These included procedures for maintaining data structures, procedures for adequate fault monitoring and an analysis procedure. There are a number of other situations in which the compilers require procedures which are substantially, though not completely, the same. For example, a procedure for converting to a standard form might be required for a number of languages, though each language might have differing requirements: the delimiter words might be different; the symbol used to surround them might be different; in some languages the same symbol might be used as the opening and closing symbol (leading to the problem discussed in section 14.2), in others different symbols might be used; and so on.

Because these variations of the procedure have much in common, it is advantageous to consider whether a master procedure can be written, and the variations produced automatically. Further, since the necessary data structures are often quite complicated, this automatic process might create them too.

This leads to the idea of a *generator*. We consider still the case of converting to a standard form. A generator for this might require the compiler writer to specify the delimiter words, the symbols they are to be converted to, and the symbol (or symbols) used to surround the delimiter words. From this the generator could tailor-make a procedure for performing the conversion, printing it out in the required (compiler writing) language. Such a generator can be extended: to deal with the compile-time errors in a way specified by the compiler writer, for example.

The notion of a generator can be used in a number of areas, such as lexical analysis (where the compiler writer would be required to specify the structure of identifiers and literals) and (partially at least) to syntax analysis. This technique points to the possibility of engineering a compiler by selecting generators, producing the appropriate specifications and knitting together the resulting modules. Unfortunately, not much progress has been made along these lines as yet.

16.7 Boot-strapping

Perhaps the most elegant technique devised for writing compilers is the *boot-strap*. A compiler is written in the language that it is a compiler for (an Algol compiler is written in Algol), and provided one binary compiler already exists for the language on any machine whatsoever, this compiler can be compiled into binary to run on a chosen machine. Consider Fig. 16.2 which illustrates the writing of an Algol compiler for machine *M*, given the one already existing in binary form on machine *X*.

The process is a two-stage one, both stages running on machine *X*. First, the compiler is compiled using the existing (machine *X*) compiler. The result is an Algol compiler which produces code for machine *M* but which itself is in machine *X*'s code. If the compiler in Algol is now compiled by this compiler running on machine *X*,

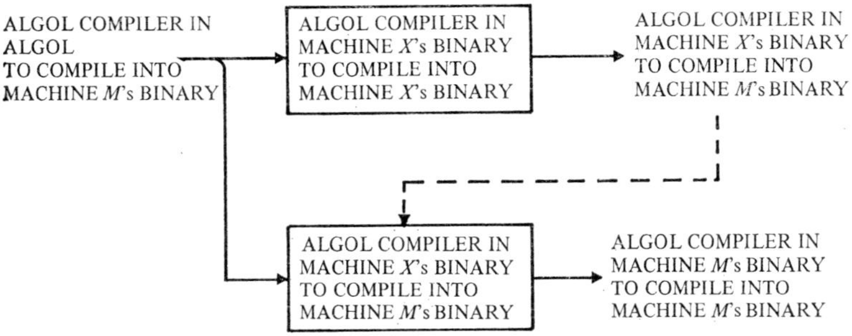

Fig. 16.2. Boot-strapping an Algol compiler

the result is an Algol compiler which produces code for machine *M* and runs on machine *M*.

The compiler can now be taken away to run on machine *M*. Furthermore, the Algol version of the compiler can be modified or refined, and a new binary version can be created using the existing binary compiler on *M*. It is even possible to correct the Algol version provided that the errors in the binary version do not affect the constructs used in the Algol version.

17 Designing compilers

We have chosen in this book to start with a very simple language and write a compiler for it; and then expand the language in a series of stages, each time considering how these expansions might affect the compiler and the structures it maintains at both compile and run time. In practice, of course, we are presented with a complete language initially and we have to consider how to *design* a compiler for the language. As with all design exercises, this is an iterative process, the effects of a bad decision at one stage becoming obvious only at some later stage. Nevertheless, there are some clear stages in the process and we consider them in turn.

17.1 Choice of compiling system

The first decision to be made is which compiling system to use. In many cases the choice will have been made already, and will be presented as a design criterion rather than a design choice. For example, if we are asked to write a compiler for a new range of machines, then clearly we will be expected to conform to the standard system for all compilers on the machine. (This probably means producing a semi-compiled format.) If the compiler is to be highly optimised, then a multi-pass compiler is almost inevitable. In other cases a real choice might have to be made. For example, if we are asked to produce a compiler for large numbers of small teaching and development jobs then we have the choice between a batching compiler (see section 15.3) and a cafeteria type of system (see section 15.4). Since the choice has implications on the use of peripherals it may have to be made in conjunction with others. There are some areas where the choice is completely that of the compiler writer. A relevant example at the time of writing can be found in the increasing use of mini-computers as remote job entry (RJE) devices for a large central machine. Generally, we find the mill of the mini under-utilised when performing the RJE function. One solution is to use the mini for processing small student jobs as well. The choice of system, single or multi-pass, compiler or interpreter, and so on is the priviledge of the compiler writer.

17.2 Choice of compiler writing aids

The second decision is to decide upon and possibly make the appropriate compiler writing aids. As with the compiler writing system this may be a design criterion. If we are to write a compiler for a new range of machines, then almost certainly we will be required to use the standard systems programming language that will have been developed for the range. Hopefully, the appropriate special procedures or generators have been provided as well; but if not, this second stage will involve their design and implementation. In many situations, no aids are provided at all. In the example of a compiler for running student jobs on a mini used above, it is likely that the only available language is the mini's assembly language (and possibly a primitive one, at that).

The compiler writer then must make a choice: whether to use a boot-strap procedure if he has access to some large machine (which he will do if the mini is acting as an RJE); whether, if the assembly language has a sufficiently powerful macro facility, to write macros to give the language some reasonably adequate facilities; or whether to design and implement a special compiler writing language. Regrettably, the choice made is often not one of these (or perhaps the question is never even considered). Instead, the compiler is written in the bare assembly language, this decision being justified on the grounds that 'assembly language programs are more efficient than high-level language programs'. There is, however, a trend towards regarding programming as an engineering discipline, which carries with it the realisation that, in all engineering projects, the choice and design of the tools is an important consideration.

17.3 Choice of mapping between source language and object machine

The choice of compiler writing aids discussed above is the crucial one when we are considering the speed of implementation of a compiler, or the ease of debugging it, or the facility with which it might be modified to improve, say, the diagnostics or the run time speed. When we consider the compile time or run time speed, then the important decision is how the source language is to be mapped onto the object machine. There have been a number of places throughout this book where we have discussed alternative solutions to a problem: the Boolean approach as against the conditional approach when compiling Boolean expressions and conditional statements; the use of Iliffe vectors as against the multiplication method of storing and accessing arrays, and so on. The book, however, has been concerned almost exclusively with an object machine whose order code has been tailored to the needs of the compiler writers. In practice, the problems are rather more difficult. Each computer, indeed, presents its own. By way of illustration we will briefly consider two problems presented by commercially available machines.

First, let us consider the CDC 7600. Its store is in two parts: a small (32K or 64K words) core memory (SCM) which is fast and which can be accessed for both operands and instructions; and a large (256K or 512K words) core memory (LCM) which is slower and can be accessed only for operands. However, the LCM is so arranged that its read-write cycle causes a number (4 or 8) of words to be read into a buffer, and all accesses to the store access the buffer. If the operand is not in the buffer then a read-write cycle is initiated, at the end of which, of course, it will be. Since the buffer is very fast flip-flop storage, some accesses are even faster than those to SCM. Clearly, the LCM is sympathetic to accessing matrices by row. The compiler writer's problem then is how to use these stores. Clearly, the program must go into SCM, but the operands may go in either. Should he arrange for arrays to go into LCM and scalars in SCM and (for a dynamic allocation system) arrange for two stacks to be maintained? Should he put all the operands in the LCM? Should he provide a number of options (including putting everything in

SCM) and allow the programmer to choose, providing a default option if necessary? And how does he reconcile his choice with the problems of providing a library?

Second, let us consider the ICL 1900. Here there is only one level of storage which may be quite a large size (typically 256K words in machines at the top of the range). The problem is that the address part of the instruction is short (12 bits) allowing direct access to only 4K words. All other words are accessed by modification, the modifier registers being long enough to hold the addresses of the whole store. How does the compiler writer allocate this storage? Does he regard the directly addressable part as the key, storing as many operands as possible in it; or does he, instead, ignore it completely accessing each operand by a relative address (relative, that is, to some modifier register)? Is one solution possible in a range of machines in which, at the lower end, modification takes a significant time, and, at the upper end, takes no time at all; or does he design a series of different compilers for different parts of the range?

The problems sketched in the two illustrations above are problems of addressing. There are many others: in Chapter 9 we mentioned the probem of register allocation and use of special orders for looping. In most machines there are many of these problems to be solved.

The result of this stage of the design should be a description of the mappings chosen. This often consists of a description of the basic strategy (illustrated by diagrams). This is amplified by diagrams of all the data structures and their representation, together with a list of typical examples of all the statements and their translations. This list should include examples of all the cases to be optimised.

17.4 Choice of algorithms and data structures

The next stage is to choose the algorithms to effect the translation and the data structures required by the algorithms. One fairly obvious choice lies in the syntactical analysis algorithm: should it be a precedence algorithm, or a top-down syntax analysis algorithm, or a mixture of the two, or should the theory of grammars be invoked to find a more suitable algorithm?

The problem of choice is more pervasive than this; at almost all levels there are alternatives to be considered. This is true of all programming: it is especially true where data structures are relevant, as here, because a different choice of data structure generally means a different strategy for the procedure. We give one example: the procedure to convert a program into a standard form. Suppose as suggested in section 14.2 we wish to insert any quote, leading or trailing, that has been omitted in the punching of delimiter words. This implies that we must be able to scan a table of delimiters both backwards and forwards. How do we store the delimiters: in one table or two (forwards in one, backwards in the other)? Is it adequate to scan all the delimiters until we find the one on hand (if it is there) or do we add some further structures to limit the amount of scanning? If we choose to limit the scanning and have only one list can we make the procedure scan equally fast in both directions? If not, is a difference in speed acceptable? And so on. This is, of course, the key to all program design and there is no need to dwell on it except to make the obvious comment that the more effort that can be devoted to this stage the better the compiler.

During this stage we might well find that some of the decisions made in the previous stage (the choice of mapping) ought to be revised. We might, for example, find that changes to a mapping would remove special cases from an algorithm. And so the iterative process commences. It is important, of course, that all the effects of the changes to the mappings be investigated and that the documentation previously produced be modified to conform.

At the end of this stage of the design there should exist a hierarchical set of flow diagrams and a description of the important procedures. This description will include a specification of the procedure and its interfaces with other procedures, some examples of its function and some representation (usually pictorial) of the data structures used.

17.5 Encoding and testing the algorithms

This is, by far, the easiest part of the writing of a compiler—especially with the correct choice of compiler writing aids. It is even easier if the flow diagrams have been constructed in a structured fashion. It is merely a question of encoding the flow diagrams into the chosen compiler writing language and testing them.

We may well find during this stage that some of the decisions made earlier need revising though this is less likely. Nevertheless, if it is so, we must make the changes with care, ensuring that we understand the consequences of the changes.

The testing of the procedures is extremely important. We must be sure that all possible facilities have been tested; that all possible optimisations have been checked; that situations which are not amenable to optimisation do produce the normal code; that all fault conditions (both at compile and run time) do result in the correct monitoring; and so on. [We must not take consolation from the fact that most existing compilers were incorrect when released and many still are years after.] The problem of program testing and program verification is a formidable one and one that is receiving a lot of attention. All we can say here is that the more structured a program the easier it is to test.

It is perhaps worthwhile pausing here for a moment to reflect on the design process we have described. Producing and testing the actual code is the last stage in the process and comes at the end of a long design process. There is always the temptation in programming to use the computer at all times. This must be resisted (though too often it is not) because of the iterative nature of the design process: decisions made at one stage might have to be modified at a later stage and code produced after the earlier stage would have to be abandoned or (perhaps worse) modified in the light of the changes.

17.6 The future

We are now entering into a most interesting phase of compiler writing. Most of the techniques that we need (and only a selection of them have been described here) have been developed and have been demonstrated to work. We know very little of their characteristics, however, and so we are in no position to compare them. Neither do we know much about the characteristics of the programs people write; nor, even less, the characteristics of the programs they would like to write. In the future these characteristics will become clearer and we will then design compilers by choosing modules according to the criteria the compiler must satisfy and linking them together.

A1 The basic language used in Chapter 2

We defined the basic language in Chapter 2 in an informal way by specifying how it may be derived from Algol. We now define the language formally (except, for simplicity, for <constant>). We give two definitions: one for a line-by-line compiler like that used in Chapter 2 and one for a multi-pass compiler which compiles the program as a whole. In the latter case we class the newline symbol as a noise symbol (which we assume to have been deleted).

A1.1 A line-by-line definition

<line> ::= **begin**|<declarative>;|<possibly labelled imperative>;|**end**

<declarative> ::= <scalar declaration>|<array declaration>

<scalar declaration> ::= <type><list of identifiers>

<type> ::= **integer**|**real**

<list of identifiers> ::= <identifier>|<list of identifiers>, <identifier>

<identifier> ::= *a*|*b*|*c*|*d*|*e*|*f*|*g*|*h*|*i*|*j*|*k*|*l*|*m*|*n*|*o*|*p*|*q*|*r*|*s*|*t*|*u*|*v*|*w*|*x*|*y*|*z*| *A*|*B*|*C*|*D*|*E*|*F*|*G*|*H*|*I*|*J*|*K*|*L*|*M*|*N*|*O*|*P*|*Q*|*R*|*S*| *T*|*U*|*V*|*W*|*X*|*Y*|*Z*

<array declaration> ::= **array** <list of array specifications>

<list of array specifications> ::= <identifier>[0:<constant>]| <list of array specifications>, <identifier>[0:<constant>]

<possibly labelled imperative> ::= <label>:<imperative>| <imperative>

<label> ::= <identifier>

<imperative> ::= <assignment statement>| <go to statement>| <conditional statement>| <print statement>| <read statement>

<assignment statement> ::= <variable> := <expression>

<variable> ::= <identifier>|<identifier>[<subscript>]

<subscript> ::= <identifier>|<constant>

<expression> ::= <operand>|<operand><operator><operand>

<operand> ::= <variable>|<constant>

<operator> ::= +|−|*| /

<go to statement> ::= **go to** <label>

<conditional statement> ::= **if** <condition> **then go to** <label>

<condition> ::= <operand><comparator><operand>

<comparator> ::= =| ≠|>|≥|<|≤

<print statement> ::= **print** <operand>

<read statement> ::= **read** <list of variables>

<list of variables> ::= <variable>|<list of variables>, <variable>

A1.2 A definition of a complete program

We replace the definition of <line> in Section A1.1 by the three definitions following:

<program> ::= **begin** <list of declaratives>;<list of possibly labelled imperatives> **end**

<list of declaratives> ::= <declarative>|<list of declaratives>;<declarative>

<list of possibly labelled imperatives> ::= <imperative>| <list of possibly labelled imperatives>;<imperative>

Note that this definition is stronger than that in section A1.1. The line-by-line definition allows programs with more than one **begin** or **end** and this situation must be detected by the appropriate processing procedures.

A2 The order code of the object machine

Since none of the definitions are recursive we will not use BNF to describe the order code. Instead, we use a displayed format in which alternatives are written in a vertical list surrounded by braces. The address parts are symbolic and we have left undefined some quantities such as 'arithmetic variable' and 'constant' (written in lower-case) where their definitions are fairly obvious. Further, in the interests of simplicity we have used definitions which are loose in that they allow a class of orders (those which *store into a constant*) which clearly are not sensible.

A2.1 The arithmetic orders

$$\left\{\begin{array}{l} \text{AFL} \\ \text{AFX} \\ \text{BM} \end{array}\right\} \left\{\begin{array}{c} = \\ \Rightarrow \\ + \\ - \\ \theta \\ * \\ / \\ \phi \end{array}\right\} \left\{\begin{array}{l} \text{arithmetic variable} \\ \text{arithmetic constant} \\ \text{arithmetic array [BM]} \\ \text{DR[BM]} \\ \text{DR[0]} \end{array}\right\}$$

FIX
FLOAT

A2.2 The Boolean orders

$$\text{BN} \quad \left\{\begin{array}{c} = \\ \Rightarrow \\ \wedge \\ \vee \end{array}\right\} \quad \left\{\begin{array}{l} \text{Boolean variable} \\ \text{Boolean constant} \\ \text{Boolean array [BM]} \\ \text{DR[BM]} \\ \text{DR[0]} \\ \text{IF} = \\ \text{IF} \neq \\ \text{IF} > \\ \text{IF} \geqslant \\ \text{IF} < \\ \text{IF} \leqslant \end{array}\right\}$$

BN NOT

A2.3 The comparison orders

$$\left\{\begin{array}{l} \text{AFL} \\ \text{AFX} \\ \text{BM} \end{array}\right\} \left\{\begin{array}{l} \text{COMPARE} \\ \text{REV COMPARE} \end{array}\right\} \left\{\begin{array}{l} \text{arithmetic variable} \\ \text{arithmetic constant} \\ \text{arithmetic array [BM]} \\ \text{DR[BM]} \\ \text{DR[0]} \end{array}\right\}$$

A2.4 The control orders

$$\text{IF} \left\{\begin{array}{l} \text{BN} \\ \text{NOT BN} \end{array}\right\} \text{JUMP label}$$

$$\text{IF} \left\{\begin{array}{c} = \\ \neq \\ > \\ \geqslant \\ < \\ \leqslant \end{array}\right\} \qquad \text{JUMP label}$$

JUMP label

A2.5 The descriptor operations

$$\text{DR} \left\{ \begin{matrix} = \\ \Rightarrow \end{matrix} \right\} \left\{ \begin{matrix} \text{descriptor variable} \\ \text{array name [BM]} \\ \text{DR[BM]} \\ \text{DR[0]} \end{matrix} \right\}$$

A2.6 The orders concerned with SB and SF

We did not detail the orders associated with the SB and SF registers in the text and so we will not do so here, but clearly we need orders to load, store and increment these registers and we need to be able to use each as an operand in the orders associated with the other.

A3 Line reconstruction

Line reconstruction is the process of reading in a paper tape and producing internally a representation of it which corresponds to the printed form of the tape. Essentially it simulates the flexowriter or whatever device it was produced on. Some of the characteristics to be considered are:

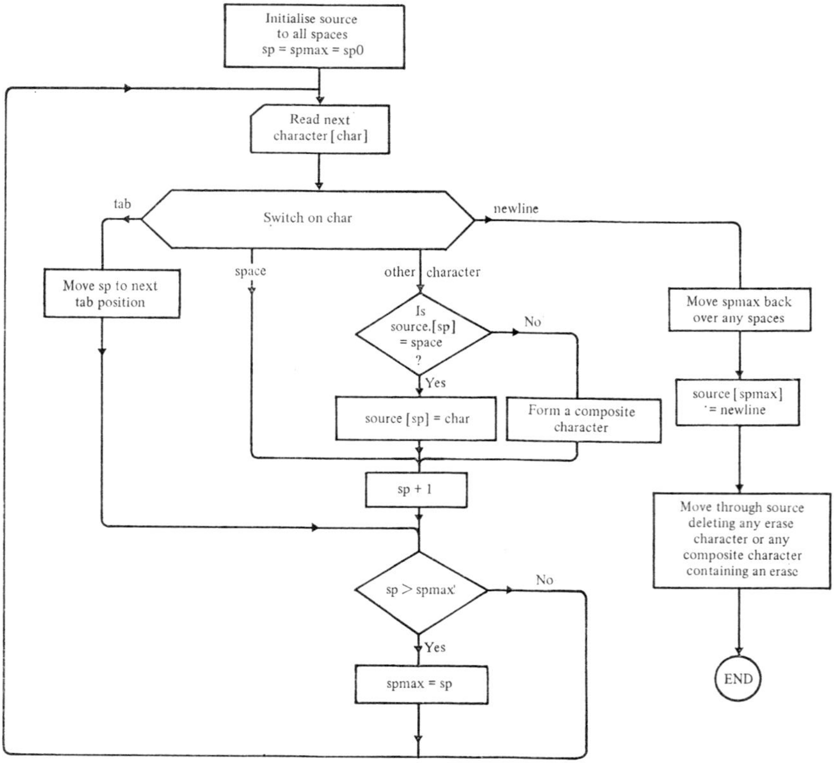

Fig. A3.1. Line reconstruction

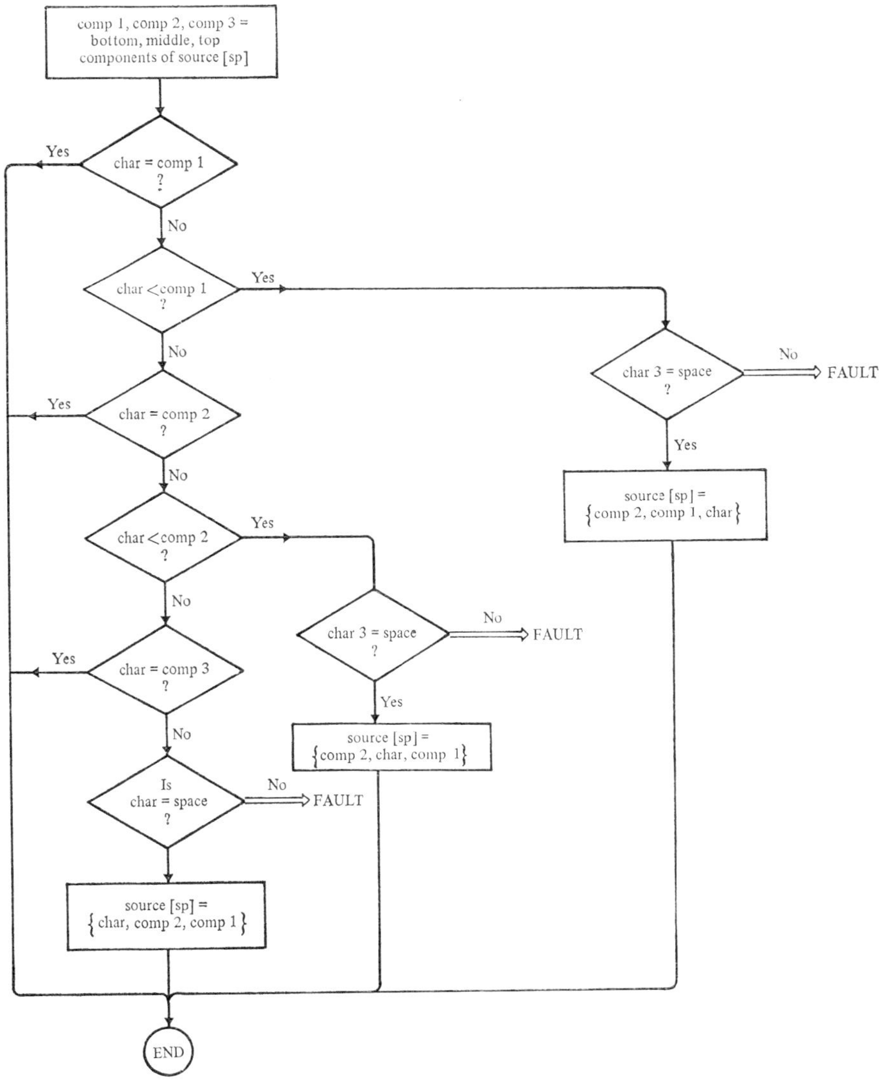

Fig. A3.2. Creating a composite character

(i) There is a tabulation key which causes the carriage to move to the next tab position.

(ii) There is a backspace key which moves the carriage one space backwards, except that, if the carriage is already at the left-hand margin, it has no effect.

(iii) Composite characters such as θ and $\neq$ can be produced by overprinting 0 with $-$, and $=$ with _ and /. We will restrict such overprinting to two or three basic characters. Further, we allow any character to be punched on top of itself. The criterion is: if two composite characters look the same on the printed form they should appear the same internally.

(iv) Any single erase character and any composite character containing an erase is deleted.

(v) Since it is impossible to tell from the printed form how many, if any, spaces are punched after the last printing character, these spaces are deleted.

Figs. A3.1 and A3.2 outline a line reconstruction procedure.

References

0.1 Kilburn, T., Morris, D., Rohl, J. S. and Sumner, F. H. 'A System Design Proposal', Proc. IFIP 68, North-Holland (1968).

3.1 Hopgood, F. R. A., *Compiling Techniques* (Macdonald, 1969).

3.2 Sale, A. H. J., 'The Classification of Fortran Statements', *Computer Journal*, Vol. 14, No.1, p. 10 (1971).

4.1 Graham, R. M., 'Bounded Context Translation', *Proc. E.J.C.C.*, Vol. 25, p. 17 (1964).

4.2 Gries, D., *Compiler Construction for Digital Computers* (Wiley, 1971).

4.3 Hopgood, F. R. A., *Compiling Techniques* (Macdonald, 1969).

5.1 Colin, A. J. T., 'Note on Coding Reverse Polish Expressions for Single-Address Computers with One Accumulator', *Computer Journal*, Vol. 6, No. 1, p. 67 (1963).

5.2 Dijkstra, E. W., 'Recursive Programming', *Numerische Mathematik*, Vol. 2, p. 312 (1960).

6.1 Knuth, D. E., 'An Empirical Study of Fortran Programs'. *Software: Practice and Experience*, Vol. 1, No. 2 (1971).

9.1 Allen, F. E. 'Programming Optimization', *Annual Review in Automatic Programming*, Vol. 5 (Pergamon Press, 1969).

9.2 Allen, F. E., and Cocke, J., 'A Catalogue of Optimizing Transformations' in *Design and Optimization of Compilers*, ed. R. Rustin (Prentice Hall, 1972).

9.3 Hopgood, F. R. A., *Compiling Techniques* (Macdonald, 1969).

9.4 Knuth, D. E., 'An Empirical Study of Fortran Programs', *Software: Practice and Experience*, Vol. 1, No. 2 (1971).

10.1 Iliffe, J. K., *Basic Machine Principles* (Macdonald, 1968).

11.1 Wichmann, B. A., *Algol 60 Compilation and Assessment*, (Academic Press, 1973).

12.1 Ingerman, P. Z., 'Thunks', *Comm. A. C. M.*, Vol. 4, No. 1, p. 55 (1961).

12.2 Strachey, C., and Wilkes, M. V., 'Some Proposals for Improving the Efficiency of Algol 60', *Comm. A. C. M.*, Vol. 4, No. 11, p. 488 (1961).

12.3 Wegner, P., *Programming Languages, Information Structures and Machine Organisation*, (McGraw-Hill, 1968).

13.1 Brooker, R. A., Morris, D., and Rohl, J. S., 'Experience with the Compiler Compiler', *Computer Journal*, Vol. 9, No. 4, p. 345 (1967).

13.2 Gries, D., *Compiler Construction for Digital Computers* (Wiley, 1971).

13.3 Rosen, S., 'A Compiler-Building System Developed by Brooker and Morris', *Comm. A.C.M.*, Vol. 7, p. 403 (1964).

14.1 Brooker, R. A., Rohl, J. S., and Clark, S. R., 'The Main Features of Atlas Autocode', *Computer Journal*, Vol. 8, No. 4, p. 303 (1966).

15.1 Barron, D. W., *Assemblers and Loaders* (Macdonald, 1969).

15.2 Berthand, M., and Griffiths, M., 'Incremental Compilation and Conversational Interpretation', *Annual Review in Automatic Programming*, Vol. 7, Part 2, p. 95 (1973).

15.3 Shanty, P. W., German, R. A., Mitchell, J. G., Shirley, R. S. K., and Zaruke, C. R., 'WATFOR—the University of Waterloo Fortran IV Compiler', *Comm. A.C.M.*, Vol. 10, No. 1, p. 41 (1967).

16.1 Capon, P. C., Morris, D., Rohl, J. S., and Wilson, I. R., 'The MU5 Compiler Target Language and Autocode', *Computer Journal*, Vol. 15, No. 2, p. 109 (1972).

16.2 Feldman, J., and Gries, D., 'Translator Writing Systems', *Comm. A.C.M.*, Vol. 11, No. 2, p. 77 (1968).

16.3 Strong, J., Wegstein, J., Tritter, A., Olsztyn, J., Mock, O., and Steel, T., 'The Problem of Programming Communication with Changing Machines', *Comm. A.C.M.*, Vol. 1, No. 8, p. 12 (1958).

Index